Power and Politics

For Pui —
thanks for your
interest. I look
forward to a growing
friendship.

Jerry

May 1994

Power and Politics

*The Psychology of
Soviet-American Partnership*

Jerome S. Bernstein

A C.G. Jung Foundation Book

Shambhala
Boston & Shaftesbury
1989

Shambhala Publications, Inc.

Horticultural Hall
300 Massachusetts Avenue
Boston, Massachusetts 02115

The Old School House
The Courtyard, Bell Street
Shaftesbury, Dorset SP7 8BP

The C. G. Jung Foundation for Analytical Psychology, founded in 1962 as a
nonprofit educational institution, is dedicated to helping men and women
grow in conscious awareness of the psychological realities in themselves and
society, find healing and meaning in their lives and greater depth in their
relationships, and live in response to their discovered sense of purpose. It
welcomes the public to attend its extensive program of lectures, seminars,
films, symposia, and workshops and offers a wide selection of books on Analytical Psychology for sale through its bookstore. The Foundation provides
space for the C. G. Jung Institute, which trains Jungian analysts; the Kristine
Mann Library of the Analytical Psychology Club of New York; and the Ar-
chive for Research in Archetypal Symbolism. It also publishes *Quadrant*, a
semiannual journal of distinguished articles on Analytical Psychology and related subjects. For information about Foundation programs or membership,
please address inquiries to the C. G. Jung Foundation, 28 East 39th Street,
New York, NY 10016.

9 8 7 6 5 4 3 2 1

First Edition

Printed in the United States of America on acid-free paper
Distributed in the United States by Random House and in Canada by
Random House of Canada Ltd.
Distributed in the United Kingdom by Element Books, Ltd.

Library of Congress Cataloging-in-Publication Data

Bernstein, Jerome S., 1936–
  Power and politics: the psychology of Soviet-American partnership
  Jerome S. Bernstein. p. cm. Bibliography: p.
  Includes index.
  ISBN 0-87773-471-2
  1. United States—Foreign relations—Soviet Union—Psychological aspects. 2.
Soviet Union—Foreign relations—United States—Psychological aspects. I. Title.
E183.8.S65B468   1989   88-34336
327.73047—dc19   CIP

This book is dedicated to the
present and future children of the
United States and the Soviet Union
and to my parents

Contents

Foreword by Edward C. Whitmont, M.D.   ix

Foreword by Senator Claiborne Pell   xiii

Preface   xv

Acknowledgments   xxi

1. Introduction   1
2. Jung's Theory of the Collective Unconscious and Archetypes   5
3. The Archetype of the Shadow   15
4. The Hero Dynamic   44
5. Power   58
6. War   62
7. Primary Cooperation   93
8. Paranoia between Groups and Nations   125
9. Conclusion: The Entelechy of Transformation   162

Appendix 1: Case History of the United States Institute of Peace   197

Appendix 2: A Hypothetical Structure for a Soviet-American Institute for War-Peace Research and Technology Development   201

Notes   205

Bibliography   211

Index   227

Foreword by
Edward C. Whitmont, M.D.

Jerome Bernstein's book is historically significant in more than one way. It addresses itself to a momentous historical problem of our particular time, the problem of collective survival, which never in human history has assumed the threatening importance it has for us now. And secondly, it is the first systematic attempt to apply the insights of Jungian depth psychology to transpersonal collective political dynamics. By and large, Jungians have been reluctant to concern themselves with problems of collective politics, feeling that only the orientation of the individual and individual answers were to be of value in bringing about changes. Classical psychoanalysis and psychiatry, on the other hand, attempted to achieve a psychological understanding of historical events exclusively through studying the personal psychology and psychopathology of leader personalities.

To be sure, the personal psychology of leaders is important. But the relative weight of this importance may be compared to the psychology of the captain or pilot of a ship that is exposed to the impersonal forces of weather and tides. A hurricane may defy the most able steersman unless, taking its possible effect into consideration, he set his course accordingly or had the foresight to seek or remain in harbor. Should he be unaware of or deny the hurricane's destructive potential, he as well as his ship is likely to fall victim sooner or later to the onslaught of those impersonal natural forces that are beyond his capacity to control.

Such impersonal or transpersonal forces, Jung has demonstrated, we meet in the archetypal predispositions common to all of mankind and the personal complexes which they determine. Archetypes can simply be defined as a priori predispositions of perceptions, emotions and ways of behaving typical for a given species, in our instance of the genus *Homo sapiens*. On the human level they are analogous to the instinctual patternings of animals. They underlie normal as well as pathological functioning, depending upon the degree of their integration into the conscious functioning of the ego personality.

What we consider psychopathology is based upon the unconscious presence of such archetypally determined complexes, the power complex being one example. Owing to their unconsciousness, they are likely to interfere with rational functioning. This state of affairs is not limited to patients of state hospitals or mental clinics, however.

Irrational complexes, hero obsession, shadow denial, and projection, with their ensuing paranoia, are basic ingredients of the "normal" psyche. Without any exception, they affect every single person and hence, in thousandfold amplification, the total body social.

The power urge which moves us to having to subdue others in order to prove our heroic superiority to ourselves and the world, the need for enemies and scapegoats who carry for us those undesirable qualities that we are loath to admit in ourselves and, hence, rather paranoically, fight in others, are examples of such "pathology in everyday life" that constitute grave dangers for interpersonal and international relationships.

Yet public opinion still indulges in an outdated idea of "psychic normalcy," which assumes that in the average "normal" person—and that includes oneself, of course—those complexes are supposed to be absent. Any public leader who is or has been seeking psychological counselling or psychoanalytic treatment is thus considered "sick" and disqualified for public service, rather than seen as one who has at least attempted to come to grips in him- or herself with a universal problem.

On the other hand, unconscious and unattended, the inevitable presence of such psychopathological factors affects, indeed infects, the collective atmosphere and tends to breed mass hysteria and paranoic obsession.

While Mr. Bernstein's approach may strike many a reader as highly unusual, it is based upon sound theoretical insights as well as the practical psychological and political experience of the author. In the working of science we test the validity of theoretical assumptions by how well they help explain observed phenomena and by their capacity to predict coming developments correctly. On both of these criteria Mr. Bernstein scores high. His application of Jung's theories to political life helps to elucidate dynamics hard to understand because of their obvious irrationality, such as the persistence of destructive warfare through the ages, in the very face of the fact that ethically, philosophically, and in most religious faiths peace, love, compassion, and mutual cooperation have persistently been taught and extolled.

The predictive value of his theories are shown by the fact that years before the present transformation taking place in Russia the author, then working on the book, had already insisted in conversations with his skeptical friends (myself included) that, since the Soviet "shadow" was democratic and capitalistic, it would be inevitable that sooner or later the Soviet Union would have to take the very turn in its political and economic evolution which we are now witnessing.

It is beyond my scope, indeed anybody's scope, to foresee whether and to what extent the remedies that Mr. Bernstein proposes will prove adequate. Perfect therapies are rarely if ever at our disposal at the beginning. The history of medicine and of psychoanalysis stands as eloquent witness to this fact. Neither were the Wright brothers able to invent the jet plane.

The merit of this book lies rather in its diagnosing and bringing to our attention some hitherto overlooked or disregarded psychological factors of crucial importance and in pointing in the direction in which remedies can be reasonably sought. The art of living no less than of politics lies in attempting the possible rather than merely the desirable. In attempting the impossible we merely waste our efforts and energies and may fail to apply ourselves where we might be effective. Hence, our greatest danger comes from lack of adequate awareness and discrimination.

Aggressive hostility and warfare of one kind or another are with us to stay. They are parts of the human condition, parts of our "weather and tides." With adequate insight and understanding we might—hopefully— be able to steer our course in such a way that instead of destroying the planet and ourselves, the explosive forces inherent in the atom as well as in our deepest nature may be turned into helpful and culture-enhancing factors.

Foreword by
Senator Claiborne Pell

This is an important book, written at an important time. Mr. Bernstein argues very persuadably that there is a psychological factor in the United States–Soviet relationship that is as powerful as the political ideologies and military alignments that have been the focus to date of most of the literature on the superpower rivalry.

I am not an expert in Jungian psychology, but Mr. Bernstein makes a compelling case that the deep psychological outgrowths of conflict must be addressed along with the more familiar political and military issues if a stable and peaceful world order is to be achieved.

Mr. Bernstein broadens the base for discussion in an area I have been unsuccessfully pursuing with different secretaries of state for many years. It has been my view that the conduct of U.S. foreign policy would be improved if professionals trained in psychology were part of the planning and negotiating process. Mr. Bernstein is much bolder than I in this area. As the reader will discover, what I think would be helpful, he asserts is imperative. He may be correct and I hope that his analysis will provoke a spirited debate on the subject.

There are several theses in this book that deserve special attention. While the book focuses primarily on the fearful apocalypse that a general nuclear war would fulfill, it also acknowledges that the world faces other, concurrent threats to the basic survival of humankind. Chief among these other threats is the global·ecological crisis the nations of the world have collectively created, and must collectively solve. The point is that the process Mr. Bernstein describes and the dynamics of its interaction are not problem-dependent. They are the stuff that explains why nations behave the way they do and hence give some hope that, where necessary, behavioral modification can be achieved, or at least overreaction to another nation's behavior can be avoided or reduced.

I am most intrigued by the author's ideas of peace technologies. He may be too optimistic to suggest that any time soon, if ever, we will have large-scale field war games with the Soviet Union. However, an alternative suggestion, which may assist in accomplishing the same goal of displacing the powerful aggressive instincts that can lead to war, would be to establish joint quick deployment task forces that are trained and rehearsed to engage in warfare against the effects of natural catastrophes and destruction of the planet. Given the will to make the ecological crisis the enemy of humankind, there are a host of joint activities that could be undertaken. These might include irrigation projects, port clearing, reforestation, toxic clean-up, and other activities that can be helpful in bringing the two superpowers into a constructive partnership to save the globe and to enhance moral consciousness in the international community. These and other activities could aid in shifting energy and resources from national defense to inter-natural defense as we struggle to nurture a battered earth.

This book challenges much conventional thinking on issues of aggression and possible paths to peace. It could not be more timely, as there is a sense of opportunity in U.S.-U.S.S.R. relations that could not have been predicted a decade ago—but which Mr. Bernstein's theoretical approach did anticipate prior to the Gorbachev era in Soviet politics.

Preface

This book intruded into my life unwanted. At the time I began to write it, I was engaged in writing another book—still to be completed—on the subject of masculine development and psychology. I came to write this book as a result of an evening in 1982 when I was putting my four-year-old son to bed. I had, of course, *thought* about the nuclear threat for quite some time—for years. But the problem had always seemed too awesome and frightening to touch.

My child was afraid of the dark then. It was a time when the magical realm of the collective unconscious would open in his psyche and all manner of wonders—and monsters—would come forth. It was a tender nightly ritual for me (or my wife) to sit with our son and read to him, and then to remain in the rocking chair in his room in the semidark until he fell asleep. Parental presence meant safety from everything threatening. The monsters knew better than to come when I was there. (I had been known to stand in the middle of his room and to bellow at those nasty monsters that if any of them dared try to scare my Matthew I would punch them in the nose and knock every single one of their teeth out!)

However, that particular night I became aware of a feeling of dread as I rocked in the chair. It was murky and threatening. There was a different monster present—one I didn't know or understand. I was frightened. Eventually I was able to let the feelings come into me. After a few minutes a question crept into my awareness: Would my son live to be as old as my other son, then twenty-three? Would I ever get to know my son Matthew in the way I knew my son Eric—as a healthy, vibrant, exciting young man? In crossing the threshold of my consciousness, that question brought with it some of the most profound grief I have ever known—grief for my children and the future they faced, grief for my wife and myself, grief for life itself and for the struggle I felt within God.

I lived (as I do now) in Washington, D.C., and was particularly aware at that moment of the new Reagan administration; it promised to change a lot in our lives. There was much talk about winnable nuclear wars, about most people surviving if there were "enough shovels" to go around, about evacuating whole cities in the event of threatened nuclear attack. There were assurances that even though a nuclear war would indeed be destructive—twenty to sixty million casualties—the nation would recover economically as well as physically.

I was frightened, and by the time I left my son's room that night, I promised myself that I would do something about the calamity I feared. But what could I do?

The next day—daytime does make a difference—I thought perhaps it wasn't so threatening after all. That night I called someone I happened to meet a year or so before. He was a highly placed professional in the intelligence community and was an expert on Soviet-American affairs. When I got him on the phone I told him straightaway that I was calling to allay intense inner anxiety about the state of relations between the United States and the Soviet Union. I said that I was more afraid of our government's actions at that point in time than of the Soviet's and what appeared to be our government's irrational policies, which I thought involved planning for a winnable nuclear war. I said that I feared that our policies would trip us into nuclear war.

To my surprise and disappointment, he said that he had the same fears. I was looking for reassurance from someone who I thought would "know." Out of that telephone conversation and our respective anxieties came a decision to meet twice a month for an hour or two, to share feelings and thoughts and to explore—from his vantage point as a professional "insider" and mine as a Jungian analyst—why the situation had so deteriorated and what might be done to influence it positively. We met for a year or so. It was in the context of those discussions that some of the ideas set down in this book began to jell. Soon after our meetings began, I found myself writing what was to become this book.

There are many things that come to mind to say about the book. One of the most difficult aspects of writing this work has been to link the "old" world view and superpower relationship with the "new"—the one that has emerged since General Secretary Gorbachev came to power (although it began well before his ascension to power).

Many in this country despaired of an administration they "knew" was so intransigent in its anticommunism—so much so that we would have to await the next administration before "real" changes could take place between the two superpowers. The archenemy of the "evil empire" was a hopeless ideologue and they despaired of any real positive change in a recalcitrant president. They were wrong. I was among this group up until late 1982. Then I began to see a different picture emerging—the one I have put forth in this book.

One of the reasons we were wrong is our tendency to accept a rationalist view of global politics. The reign of the patriarchal ego is still quite entrenched in the Western psyche and it leaves little room for "causes" of human behavior that do not emanate from itself. But, as I have presented in the second chapter and throughout the book, there are powerful collective forces at work in producing a scenario virtually no one would have imagined in 1982. In the words of former President Reagan himself, in his speech of June 3, 1988, in the wake of the Moscow Summit, "To those of us familiar with the postwar era, all of this is cause for shaking the head in wonder. Imagine the president of the United States and the general secretary of the Soviet Union walking together in Red Square, talking about a growing personal friendship. . . ."

It has become easy and gratifying for everyone to rush in to take advantage of the new and emerging relationship between the superpowers. And we should. However, it would behoove us at the same time to pursue *why* we find ourselves in a scenario that no one on either side would have imagined just six or seven years ago. Because if we cannot grasp the dynamics of the collective unconscious that have played a prominent role in producing such profound change and to learn from them and to *consciously* employ them (to the extent possible), they can slip between our fingers and we *could* find ourselves shaking our heads in wonderment once again, this time over how the superpower relationship could have regressed to its former hostile and primitive state.

It is undoubtedly true, as asserted by President Bush and former President Reagan, that the unprecedented military buildup in the Reagan administration and the ensuing military, technological, and economic pressures it put on the Soviet Union were significant factors in bringing about some of the dramatic changes in Soviet policies. However, there is a danger in going too fast and too far with conventional political wisdom in this regard. While the latter dynamics could be seen as putting unprecedented pressure on the Soviet economy, it is not conclusive that they are the primary factors. Nor does it follow that Mr. Gorbachev's broad policy of *perestroika* and especially his policy of *glasnost*—calling for sweeping democratization, the freeing of Soviet dissidents and other political prisoners, his elevation of Mr. Sakharov to the *de facto* equivalent of "minister of moral consciousness without portfolio," and other radical policy shifts away from traditional totalitarian behavior—were indispensable to bringing about a reduction of the military establishment and a restructuring of the economy. (And, if we were so certain of the efficacy of our policies, why has virtually *everyone*, including Mr. Reagan, himself the chief architect of his administration's policy, been surprised at the radical nature of Soviet reforms?)

Likewise, Soviet pressure on its client states in Eastern Europe to democratize their societies and political structures is not indispensable for reducing the size of the Soviet military and shoring up its own economy and those of its satellite states. On the contrary, a considerable argument could be marshaled to support the idea that these policies run against the short-term political interests of the Soviet Union and the Gorbachev administration in particular—witness the internal strife between the Soviet states of Armenia and Azerbaijan. So what is going on here?

At the present time there is considerable debate in American political circles as to whether the most efficacious policy for the United States is to continue (if not increase) military, political, and economic pressures on the Soviet Union to bring about more radical reforms (or, as believed in more right-wing circles, to bring about the full collapse of the Soviet Union as a viable economic and thus military power) or to cooperate with the Soviet Union in more direct ways (for example, by increasing trade and loosening restrictions on the transfer of some American technologies).

However, there really is no viable choice for the United States out of what increasingly appears to be its political dilemma. If the United States pursues the more radical policy of attempting to bring the Soviet Union to its knees politically and militarily, it runs the risk of bankrupting itself and imperiling its own economic and political viability as a superpower, as well as risking nuclear holocaust. On the other hand, as the argument goes, if the United States cooperates with the present policies and trends of the Gorbachev administration, then it runs the risk of helping the Soviet Union save itself from itself, ultimately becoming a more powerful economic and political power in the world. Is this in the long-term interests of the United States or counter to its interests? Could cooperation at this juncture mean an investment in a new era of confrontation with a stronger Soviet Union somewhere down the road? At present, the American policy debate is between the two horns of this dilemma.

This is where the primary thesis of this book enters in—namely, that there are powerful forces in the collective unconscious that are moving *both* superpowers toward a *single* objective. Thus, it is vital to recognize and work with those collective dynamics that are moving both nations and political systems in order to facilitate a new world order and the preservation of life, or the process can founder on the horns of that dilemma, to the peril of us all.

In this regard, I have taken what has been for me the more difficult road of trying to bridge the old superpower psychology with the new. The reader will find this evident especially in the third chapter, some of which may come across as "out-of-date." I have done so because some of the psychological dynamics of the old relationship still lurk in the background ready to pounce at some future point when the new relationship hits some serious ruts in the road—as it surely will. It is axiomatic in psychoanalysis that major psychological issues not *consciously* worked through and integrated are not resolved (although one may think they are) and can intrude into one's life at some future time. This is no less true of relationships between nations.

IT HAS BEEN a fascinating process over the six years it has taken to complete this work, to see where I began and where I have ended up. I became a Jungian analyst because, among other reasons, I can think of nothing more fascinating and gripping than the mystery of the human psyche. Having begun this work in the frame of mind and feeling that I described above, I have found it a labor both burdensome and redeeming, profane and sacred, at one and the same time. It has renewed my fundamental conviction that although life—and God as well—is at one and the same time nihilistic and committed to the preservation of life, the latter track has held, and still holds, the edge.

The substance of this book was completed in the spring of 1988. Since that time there has been an American election and a change of administration. The cumbersome process of editing and finalizing a book has permitted limited editorial insertions along the way, such as the updating of references to political administrations in the United States (i.e., President Bush and former President Reagan). For this reason some content references may seem a bit behind those political changes which have taken place since the completion of the book.

I do wish to acknowledge that I am aware that some readers may be put off by what appears to be the "sexist" language of the book. However, war has always been and remains the work of men who are its instruments. I have chosen to retain "archaic" patriarchal language because, in the context of this book, it reflects psychological truth.

Finally, I recognize that the number of footnotes in this book is unusually large. There was considerable discussion with the publisher, who was concerned that the number of footnotes would make for unaesthetic pages. On balance, I insisted on keeping them in.

This book employs Jungian theory to reinterpret the superpower relationship and to analyze the major dynamics influencing the evolution of civilization. Although rapidly growing in popularity, Jungian theory is not well known in non-Jungian circles. Even less understood is how some of its ideas could work in a practical political context. Similarly, Jungians are noted for their highly interesting symbolic interpretations of clinical material, but often fall short in being able to transpose theories into mundane terms so that they may be used on a practical level. Some have also tended to deny the applicability of Jung's theories to the political realm. I have employed content footnotes to ground theoretical and symbolic material for both camps—for those interested. However, it is emphasized that anyone wishing to read the book without reading the footnotes may skip them and will find that the content holds together quite well without them. As a reader of content footnotes, I find it maddening to flip back and forth between the page that I am on and the end of the chapter (or the book) in order to read the content footnotes. Therefore, at the sacrifice of aesthetics I have insisted that they remain on the given page. The indulgence of the publisher is appreciated.

Acknowledgments

First and last, I wish to acknowledge the sacrifices that my family made so that this book could be written. It has been exceedingly difficult to write a book of this complexity while maintaining a full-time private practice, completing my six-year term as vice chairman of the board of the C. G. Jung Institute of New York, and being an invested husband and parent. In fact, it could not be and was not done without much time taken away from family. That sacrifice was accepted most of the time with love and respect for the fact that the writing of this book was not altogether a free choice.

My wife, Susan, in addition to sacrifices of time and energy, personally read and reread and reread the manuscript and at critical points in the writing pointed me in new directions. Her capacity to retain an objective critical eye was impressive and invaluable. Without her loving support throughout, the completion of this book would not have been possible.

I wish to express my appreciation to my patients for their investment in the completion and outcome of this work and for the contributions a number of them made—knowingly as well as unknowingly.

I particularly wish to acknowledge my parents who, in ways unknown to them and to me, have contributed to this work. Always in the background has been the Russian blood that flows in my veins. Sometimes I was aware of it and sometimes not. Both of my parents are Russian immigrants. Some of the Russia that I have written about they have known; much of it they have not. I am grateful that they have lived to see the healing that is taking place in the Russian psyche and between Russia and the United States. They have carried antipathy toward Russia for far longer than anyone should have to—a testament to the depth of the deprivation and emotional wounding they experienced as Jews in their homeland.

I wish to thank my son Matthew David for his suggesting the Kleh cartoon in the chapter on primary cooperation and to thank the fourth-grade class at Sidwell Friends Lower School, Bethesda, Maryland, and Mrs. Alfandre ("Mrs. A") and Mrs. Verdin ("Mrs. V"), their teachers, who provided it in their enlightened social studies unit.

Thanks too to my son Eric Bernstein, M.D., who was my informal consultant on technical points involving the so-called hard sciences.

During the first two years I worked on this book, I had many doubts about my ability to complete it. The subject matter was in a field about which I knew little more than the next guy. In 1983 I sent an early draft of a working paper (I didn't know then that it was to become a book) to Professor George Kennan. His response—that he and I arrived at several of the same conclusions coming from different directions and that I develop my paper further—was very positive and encouraging. That encouragement came at a time when I was considering abandoning the venture altogether. I am grateful for his support.

Not long after, when I was receiving rebuffs from the political psychology and psychohistory disciplines and other professionals and groups already working in the field, I was invited by the Newport Institute (its board consists mostly of retired military personnel) to participate in a full-day panel discussion entitled "Communicating with the Russians." I was surprised at the positive reception a number of my ideas received from the military members on the panel. About a year later, I was invited to participate at Brown University in another symposium under the auspices of the institute with a First Secretary of the Soviet Embassy and a representative of the Arms Control and Disarmament Agency of the U.S. State Department. My participation in these symposia, as well as others under other auspices, were both encouraging and provided stimulation for the further development of my concepts. I am grateful to the Newport Institute for those early opportunities and particularly to Col. William (Fred) Long, Jr., USA (Ret.), for his encouragement and support. I wish to thank Robert Bosnak for recommending me to Fred Long.

My appreciation to Mrs. Antoine de Laire for her enthusiastic interest in my work and her attempts to gain it entry into the field of arms negotiations.

My thanks to Aryeh Maidenbaum, Ph.D., Executive Director of the C. G. Jung Foundation of New York, for introducing me and my work to the publisher and for his efforts to get it a timely reading.

My warm thanks to my friends Edward C. Whitmont, Sylvia Perera, Pat Finley, and Charles Taylor, who, for many years, have given me loving support for much that I have engaged in in my life. I wish to thank Charlie Taylor in particular for his warm support of this specific work and his suggesting an interview regarding it with the *Boston Globe*.

I wish to acknowledge the successful efforts of Thayer Greene, Jungian analyst, in getting the first National Conference of (American) Jungian Analysts to have as its theme the nuclear threat.

My thanks to my long-time friend and colleague Lori Paulson for her suggestions for a suitable title for this work.

I wish to express appreciation to Emily Hilburn Sell, my editor, for her precise, yet kind, red pencil, her sense of humor, and her ability to insist on what she knows is right even when I intimated that divine inspiration may have written the part she wanted me to cut and that she might indeed go you-know-where if she insisted that it be cut! In the end, I think almost without exception, I concluded she was right.

Genuine appreciation and thanks to Glea Humez, the copy editor, for her attention to detail, improving my syntax (and even my meaning), and her incredible intuition about what I probably meant instead of what I wrote.

Marvin Pace, Carolyn Williams, and Sharon Levin have provided me with valuable support as research assistants at various points along the way. Their patient pursuit of sources, citations, the elusive professor who said something or other I needed to quote, and just plain drudgery enabled me to devote my energy to the writing itself. To Sharon in particular I would like to express my deep gratitude. Her hanging in there through the ungratifying pursuit of permissions for cartoons and other research and "go-fer" work made it possible for me to meet publication deadlines. If I had a medal to give her, I would. Thanks too to Howard Alexander for some last-minute scrambling during the crunch of final editing.

If I have forgotten to mention anyone who should be acknowledged here, my sincere apologies.

Power and Politics

① Introduction

The advent of nuclear weaponry has irretrievably ruined war as a means for asserting national and regional power ambitions and settling disputes, or as an instrument in the evolution of civilization. The age of Clausewitz and his philosophy that "war is the pursuit of policy by other means" is moribund.[1] In the nuclear age any war, no matter how small, no matter who the antagonists, is a potential trigger for a much larger confrontation that will ultimately involve the superpowers and the risk of nuclear exchange.

While helping to avoid nuclear holocaust, our deterrence technology has also resulted in the amassing of enough nuclear weapons to destroy the planet many times over. But the development of the nuclear ballistics missile and other deterrence weapons has also brought with it the profound shock that man's ego is not a limitless source of solutions to perceived problems. Indeed, we have been forced to recognize that the "solutions" devised are potentially more dangerous than any of the problems they were intended to solve. It is a profound mistake—a potentially fatal mistake—to see these issues as just new complications of an old problem. These facts change *everything* and require a radical redefinition of the problem we think we are dealing with.

In the future, "winning" wars will mean not fighting wars at all and ending with the utmost speed those that are started. "War" and "winning" are not the only definitions that are changing in the thermonuclear age. Our concept of "peace" must change as well. It is essential that peace be addressed in its active and dynamic form, not just as the absence of war. There is likewise an urgent need for a fully developed peace technology that goes beyond the limits of deterrence theory and arms reduction—

---

[1] "We see, therefore, that war is not merely an act of policy but a true political instrument, a continuation of political intercourse, carried on with other means. . . . The political object is the goal, war is the means of reaching it, and means can never be considered in isolation from their purpose" (Carl von Clausewitz, *On War* [Princeton: Princeton University Press, 1976], p. 87).

Also, in 1827, he wrote, "War is not an independent phenomenon, but the continuation of politics by different means." Ibid., p. 7.

one that deals with the dynamics that generate and perpetuate conflict between the superpowers. It is growing increasingly evident that a major allocation of our technical resources will have to be shifted away from building "deterrence" arsenals to developing a "peace technology," if we are to survive at all.

It is important to note that *all* of the above statements apply to mankind and civilization as a whole. None of these problems or objectives or "facts" is more or less true for any one or a collection of peoples or nations. They are all as true for the United States as they are for the Soviet Union and, for that matter, for Burkina Faso, Singapore, or Iceland. Like it or not, the fact is that all nations of the world and all governments, most especially the United States and the Soviet Union, have been put into the same survival boat regardless of real ideological, economic, social, political, and religious differences.

"Survival" too is being redefined by the thermonuclear age. We are arriving at the recognition that survival above all else means inter*dependence*. The old Darwinian notion of the survival of the fittest—at least in terms of nations, and most especially the superpowers—has become as passé as nineteenth-century Clausewitz. Even the Burkina Fasos of the world, in their utter economic and technological impoverishment, as well as nationless peoples (for example, the PLO), or the disempowered (for example, Blacks of South Africa), could conceivably precipitate a nuclear confrontation between the superpowers through nuclear terrorism and other means.

The superpowers are being forced to join together in a search for a mutual defense against their respective arsenals and to radically change their behaviors toward one another. We will have to embrace our mutual problem of survival and make it our mutual priority *above all others* in our struggle to contain our instinct to war. This means that in spite of ourselves and the myriad real and tangible differences and antagonisms that have dominated the relationship between the superpowers on a day-to-day basis since 1917, we will have to override, transform, and contain them in favor of the abstract goal of "survival." This is a monumental task. It has been much easier and more immediately gratifying to become aroused about the Soviet occupation of Afghanistan and the U.S. threat to Sandinista Nicaragua on a day-to-day basis than it is to subordinate those and other "real" issues to the abstract goal of surviving in the world together.

Until very recently, we have behaved as if technological solutions will save us and the species will somehow survive. But missiles and warheads are not the problem; rather, they are the symptoms of a deeper problem. That deeper problem is human nature itself and, more specifically, the underlying psychological dynamics of the relationship between the Soviet Union and the United States. In the end, the source of our destruction or our salvation will be the human psyche. Consequently, the problems wrought by the thermonuclear age require the elevation of the science of psychology as a major, if not indispensable, technological tool on a par with political, military, and weapons technology in making possible the survival of the human species.

THIS BOOK POSITS a new way of looking at Soviet–U.S. conflict and the nuclear peril. It presents a comprehensive analysis that differs significantly from the analysis of and solutions to the conflict as it has come to be viewed typically within the foreign policy, intelligence, military, and political fields. A thesis of this book is that there is an entire psychological stratum involved in generating and perpetuating the conflict between the superpowers that is not seen (that is, it is unconscious) and therefore not taken into account. This is Carl Jung's concept of a "collective unconscious," which holds that there are universal psychic parameters that motivate human behavior, collectively as well as individually, and that, because they are universal, transcend cultures. These dynamics are primary, though not exclusive, manipulators of Soviet-American conflict.

It is well established in psychology that forces that are unconscious are potentially the most powerful motivators/manipulators of human behavior because, being unaware of them, we are easy prey for acting out their dynamics. It is also axiomatic in psychology that unconscious dynamics are almost always projected onto others, groups as well as individuals. Thus, in its most fundamental terms even in the wake of *perestroika* and *glasnost*, the United States and the Soviet Union project a great many of their respective negative qualities onto each other, perpetuating deadly conflict between them. To the extent that this is true, then in our struggles to wrestle with the problem, we may be dealing more with symptoms than with the underlying causal dynamics. For example, while we focus primarily on reducing the number of missiles (a *symptom* of the problem) the underlying dynamics that continue to perpetuate the arms race lie essentially untreated and continue to generate the need for ever more deterrence systems, which themselves threaten our survival.[2] The nuclear

---

[2]In the wake of the signing of the INF Treaty to eliminate the class of intermediate-range nuclear missiles in 1988, the United States and, to a lesser degree,

threat is forcing the superpowers to probe for and address the powerful underlying psychological dynamics that are perpetuating superpower conflict and the resultant threat to the survival of human life.

Moreover, it is forcing a constructive relationship where one has not been wanted. The two superpowers traditionally have been more comfortable than not in dismissing each other as the center of all evil in the world. Not only is the nuclear threat forcing us to live together, it is forcing us to deal with one another at increasingly deeper levels of intimacy.

Since this book presents new conceptual glasses through which to look at the problem, analyzing the material herein primarily from within a standard political science/rationalist standpoint will not give the reader an understanding of this new theoretical framework or the kinds of possibilities ensuing from it. *Therefore, it is emphasized that the primary focus of this book is the psychological dynamics underpinning superpower conflict. It is crucial to its understanding that the reader be open to the working hypothesis that some of the causal dynamics of the conflict between the Soviet Union and the United States are psychological and archetypal, as well as political and rational.*

---

the Soviet Union have proposed new and/or expanded nuclear weapons systems that would more than make up for the missiles eliminated under that treaty.

② Jung's Theory of the Collective Unconscious and Archetypes

Since the publication in 1900 of Freud's *Interpretation of Dreams*, the Freudian view of the personal unconscious has become the primary basis for our understanding of the psychological nature of man. Virtually no one disputes that unconscious contents and personality dynamics can influence, if not predominate, in determining *individual* human behavior. It is known, for example, how a phobia—an unconscious emotional block— can dramatically prevent a person with an otherwise strong will and determination from carrying out a desired action (for example, flying in an airplane).

On the other end of the scale, in the instance of kleptomania, the strongest personality might be overruled by unconscious contents and be compelled to carry out behavior which he or she personally abhors (that is, compulsive theft). Other examples are hysterical blindness, amnesia, and psychogenic sexual impotence.

Freud's concept of the unconscious has found growing acceptance even within the professional political community, where it has been applied in the growing field of "conflict resolution" to attempt to develop techniques to help resolve domestic and international conflict ranging from labor-management negotiations to the macro-conflicts between the United States and the Soviet Union.

In 1934 Carl Jung published an essay entitled "Archetypes of the Collective Unconscious" and in 1936 two essays, one entitled "The Concept of the Collective Unconscious" and another entitled "Wotan," wherein he described with great accuracy the eruption of the ancient Teutonic myth, Wotan, in the German national psyche in the form of Hitler and Nazism. Subsequently, he published extensively on the subject of the collective unconscious and the nature and influence of archetypal energies in human psychology. A rudimentary understanding of the concept of the collective unconscious and the theory of archetypes will assist the reader in understanding the chapters that follow.

In his concept of the "collective unconscious" Jung asserted that mankind in general, and all cultures in particular, as well as individuals, are subject to nonpersonal unconscious contents that do not derive from personal experience and that are antecedent to personal and collective experience. These collective psychic forces are not directly knowable but are experienced through their manifestation in collective and individual behavior through universal psychic forms which he called "archetypes." Archetypes are also manifested symbolically through myths and fairy tales.[1]

Some examples of archetypes are the archetype of the mother, the archetype of the father, the child, the hero, the healer/doctor, the wise old man or woman, the witch, and the archetype of war, among others.

A given archetype may have myriad symbolic representations that are influenced by cultural and personal factors, but the archetypal form itself is universal. For example, there are many different hero myths throughout the world, which tell different stories of heroic exploit. But the basic behavior of the "hero" is essentially the same in all hero myths. When we talk about any archetypal form, its fundamental meaning is universal. The terms *hero* or *priest* or *wise old woman* or *god* have universal meaning across all cultures, even though the particular style or incarnation in which the archetype expresses itself will vary in details among cultures.[2]

---

[1] In Jung's words: "The other part of the unconscious [in addition to Freud's notion of the personal unconscious] is what I call the impersonal or collective unconscious. As the name indicates, its contents are not personal but collective; that is, they do not belong to one individual alone but to a whole group of individuals, and generally to a whole nation, or even to the whole of mankind. These contents are not acquired during the individual's lifetime but are products of innate forms and instincts. Although the child possesses no inborn ideas, it nevertheless has a highly developed brain, which functions in a quite definite way. This brain is inherited from its ancestors; it is the deposit of the psychic functioning of the whole human race. [Therefore it also brings with it the cumulative learned *capacities* (not content) that man has acquired over the millennia: for example, the ready capacity to learn reading and math.] The child therefore brings with it an organ ready to function in the same way as it has functioned throughout human history. In the brain the instincts are preformed, and so are the primordial images [archetypes] which have always been the basis of man's thinking—the whole treasure-house of mythological motifs. It is, of course, not easy to prove the existence of the collective unconscious . . ." (C. G. Jung. *The Collected Works*, vol. 8, pp. 310–311).

Also see the work of Rupert Sheldrake for a discussion of "collective memory": his six-part essay "Morphic Resonance and the Collective Unconscious," beginning with the Fall-Winter 1986 issue of *Psychological Perspectives*, and in his books *A New Science of Life* (1981) and *The Presence of the Past* (1988).

[2] For example, if one analyzes the dynamics of the Greek myth of Theseus and the Navajo myth of Monster Slayer, one will find that they are identical (not simi-

One may encounter individuals who are "naturally" heroic types, or patriarchal personalities, ebullient extroverts, or goddesses like Marilyn Monroe, for example. The same is true of cultures: the Latins are extroverted, by and large, Swedes generally are introverted, the Swiss are thinkers and the Italians are feelers, and so on. The implication is that the behavior of individuals or whole societies can be explained, in part, in terms of archetypal energy.

Thus, archetypal energy might push one toward becoming a healer, but what kind of healer depends on the individual's culture, his personal qualities, and his free will. One person might become a priest, another a physician.

However, Jung's theory of the collective unconscious and his system of depth psychology have been slow to catch on in Western society, and particularly in the United States, because of modern man's overidentification with his rational faculty.

Since the Age of Reason we have overdeveloped our rational function. It is as if everything emanates from our rational thought processes and as though nothing derives from unconscious forces. We readily acknowledge the individual unconscious, but have enormous difficulty acknowledging the idea of a collective unconscious because it challenges the ultimate supremacy of our rational ego.[3]

Hitler and the Third Reich are a dramatic example of collective identifi-

---

lar, but identical) hero myths. The cultural content in which they are dressed are radically different, but the psychic contents of the myths are identical. (There is a version of the Theseus myth wherein he has a twin brother, as does Monster Slayer.) Of course, there appears no basis at all for contamination between Greek and Navajo culture. Thus we have an example of the archetype of the hero manifesting itself independently in two identical myths in two extremely divergent, unconnected cultures.

[3] It is man's ego that stands between him and his more primitive instinctual nature. The ego has developed man's rational capacity as its supreme defense against his instinctual drives. As Harding puts it, "Man, like the other animals, is originally simply the puppet of instinct." (M. Esther Harding, *Psychic Energy.* [Washington, D.C.: Pantheon Books, 1947], p. 204.) On the one hand, his ego has enabled him to rise above his animal nature and to claim the positive fruits from his development of culture and civilization. On the other hand, that same ego defense has pushed his still-present instinctual side further into the recesses of his unconscious. Thus man becomes increasingly alienated from, and unconscious of, his instinctual nature and, most particularly, his instinct for aggression.

Whitmont points out that "our human problem lies in the fact that our basic instinctual urges are polarized; they include both social and antisocial drives; the desire to give and receive mutual support as well as the tendency to envy, greed

cation with an archetypal dynamic—the German hero myth—one that went awry with catastrophic consequences. In the Nordic myth, the world goes from the golden age to dissolution and corruption, with the death of Balder, the light hero, and the punishment of his adversary. This drama is followed by *Ragnarok*, the doom or twilight of the gods, a mythological destruction of the world.[a] It is evident how Hitler and Nazi Germany brought about a literal instead of symbolic *Ragnarok*.

Mircea Eliade points out how Marxism takes its one-sidedly rationalistic roots in the messianic Judeo-Christian myth. He says:

> Let us . . . consider . . . the mythological pattern of communism . . . and the meaning of its popular success. For whatever we may think of the scientific claims of Marx, it is clear that the author of the *Communist Manifesto* takes up and carries on one of the great eschatological myths of the Middle Eastern and Mediterranean world, namely: the redemptive part to be played by the Just (the "elect," the "anointed," the "innocent," the "missioners," in our own days by the proletariat), whose sufferings are invoked to change the ontological status of the world. In fact, Marx's classless society, and the consequent disappearance of all historical tensions, find their most exact precedent in the myth of the Golden Age which, according to a number of traditions, lies at the beginning and the end of History. Marx has enriched this venerable myth with a truly messianic Judaeo-Christian ideology; on the one hand, by the prophetic and [salvation] function he ascribes to the proletariat; and, on the other, by the final struggle between Good and Evil, which may be compared with the apocalyptic conflict between Christ and Antichrist, ending in the decisive victory of the former.[b]

On the one hand, it is obvious that "atheistic communism" as we have known it in the pre-Gorbachev era had no notion of the mythologic and archetypal roots of its ideology. On the other hand, it is that very archetypal/mythological underpinning that may be serving as a psychological impetus for the rapprochement between East and West in the Gorbachev era.[4]

---

and hostile destructiveness" (Edward C. Whitmont, *Return of the Goddess*. [New York: Crossroad, 1982], p. 11).

The other issue is fear. Man's addiction to rational/cause-and-effect explanation of himself and the world in which he lives is so great that the mere suggestion that psychologically he is still subject to instinctual drives (which have no antecedent cause) evokes the greatest fear. This is particularly true in the case of his instinct for aggression. The very idea of man's ego not being in control of life itself (as well as his own personal life) can leave him so unsettled as to feel as if his world were coming apart. This can lead to paranoid reactions and psychopathology.

[4] Archetypally speaking, it is not accidental that rapprochement between East

Archetypal energy can be not only an influence on individual and collective behavior, it often is a primary energy source behind patterns of individual and collective behavior. (The following chapters on the archetypes of the Shadow, the Hero, and War will amplify this point further.)

One can view this phenomenon from the standpoint of figure and ground. Against the figure of man going his way with a seemingly accurate rational view of himself and the world he lives in is the background of his instinctual drives, which influence his choices and his behavior. The more unaware of the latter he is, the more subject to those drives he becomes. In the case of Hitler and Nazi Germany *unconscious* identification with the myth, only partially understood and embraced, resulted in disaster.[5] On the other hand, consciousness of predominating myths that are influencing individual and collective human behavior, permits awareness of where the archetypal dynamic is trying to take us and therefore affords the opportunity to exercise ego control over human destiny. That is what Carl Jung was endeavoring to do when he wrote his essay on Wotan— warn the world of the literal Ragnarok that was approaching.

Notwithstanding man's conscious commitment against violence, our lives, to our dismay, are full of violence at personal and collective levels. One need only look at this week's *TV Guide* or the most frequented movies to verify our fascination with violence, or today's newspaper or TV news to see the degree to which our day-to-day lives are filled with it. Jung stated it well: "Instinct has been domesticated, but the basic motive still remains instinct. There is no doubt that we have succeeded in enveloping a large number of instincts in rational explanations to the point where we can no longer recognize the original motive behind so many veils. In this way it seems as though we possessed practically no instincts anymore."[c]

The power of our instincts in the background of our conscious ori-

and West under Gorbachev is taking place at the time of the jubilee celebration in Soviet Russia of one thousand years of the Russian Orthodox Church and that, despite sometime denials, the Soviet government itself is consciously participating in the healing of the schism between church and state that has existed since the 1917 Revolution.

[5] In the case of Nazi Germany, unconscious identification with the most primitive elements of Teutonic myth resulted in a mass psychotic regression of virtually the entire German population, portrayed most vividly in the 1936 Nuremberg torchlight rally involving tens of thousands of Germans chanting oaths in cadence, reminiscent of primitive rites practiced over a thousand years ago. The Nazi stiff-armed salute was patterned after the salute to the emperors of ancient pagan Rome.

entation serves as a trimtab[6] in the psychological reality of our lives—exerting silent and subtle, but inexorable, influence on our perceptions, our choices, and our behavior. To make matters worse, the more our egos sense us as being off course, the more we exert rational control, blind to the presence of our instinctual trimtabs, leaving us more at their mercy.

A depth-psychological approach to the psychology of human conflict can make a profound difference. For example, if the archetype of the scapegoat is a strong force in a conflict situation, the antagonists can strive valiantly to solve what they perceive as a mutual problem—a territorial dispute, for instance—without affecting significantly the underlying archetypal problem. They may even reach an agreement. But if the underlying tendency to scapegoat each other is not dealt with, some other dispute is extremely likely to develop. Or the original dispute may erupt once again—even years after a settlement has been reached. One need only count the number of Middle Eastern truces negotiated in recent years to see this dynamic.

In such situations, what the antagonists perceive as problems are really symptoms. Until the underlying scapegoat dynamic is consciously dealt with, they will remain negatively engaged, like Br'er Rabbit stuck to Tar Baby.

Using a depth-psychological approach, the two antagonists would find themselves both sitting on the *same* side of the table viewing their *mutual* problem—chronic conflict resulting from their mutual identification with the scapegoat archetype—sitting on the *opposite* side of the table. From this standpoint, the entire dynamics of the relationship would be changed over time. Both parties would come to perceive that each had been victimized—not so much by the other as by a psychic phenomenon. The impersonal nature of archetypal energy would permit the antagonists to

---

[6] Harold Willens describes this factor well: "On airplane wings, and on the keels of racing yachts, trimtabs are small adjustable flaps that assist in balancing and steadying the motion of the craft. The principle of the trimtab also applies to a ship's rudder. In explaining the trimtab factor, Buckminster Fuller used the image of a large oceangoing ship traveling at high speed through the water. The mass and momentum of such a vessel are enormous, and great force is required to turn its rudder and change the ship's direction. In the past, some large ships had, at the trailing edge of the main rudder, another tiny rudder—the trimtab. By exerting a small amount of pressure, one person could easily turn the trimtab. The trimtab then turned the rudder, and the rudder turned the ship. Thus, the trimtab factor demonstrates how the precise application of a small amount of leverage can produce a powerful effect." (Harold Willens. *The Trimtab Factor* [New York: Morrow, 1984], p. 27).

have a freer dialogue, because no one can be blamed for an archetypal problem—archetypes exist a priori.

Furthermore, since each archetype contains within its own dynamic structure the very mechanisms needed to disengage from its influence, a number of specific techniques could be devised for disengaging from an archetype that is causing trouble between political entities.[7]

One way to demonstrate dramatically how this dynamic manipulates both the Soviet Union and the United States would be to take the 1968 Soviet intervention in Czechoslovakia and the 1983 U.S. intervention in Grenada and portray them as space-age dramas projected four hundred years into the future. Although none of the essential facts in either situation would be changed, all names, places, nationalities, et cetera, would be fictionalized so that the two events could not be identified as such. They would be portrayed in historical terms without ideological or political interpretation. Quotes of the Soviet Union and the U.S. in justifying their respective interventions would be transposed into futuristic language for the dramatization.

Policymakers and political representatives from both countries would be shown each drama and asked to describe in political terms what they saw. (Preferably the high-level personnel involved in making the decision to intervene in each country would participate.) It is likely that Soviet decisionmakers would see *both* situations as popular revolutions against oppressive imperialist forces, while the American decisionmakers would see

---

[7] For an astonishing, albeit unconscious, portrayal of this dynamic, see the Soviet novel *The Day Lasts More than a Hundred Years* by Chingiz Aitmatov (Bloomington: Indiana University Press, 1983). This book, which soon after publication went through pre-Gorbachev Soviet society like wildfire, depicts how the Soviet Union and the United States bridge their enmity and come together in a matter of two to three days in a joint military venture to defend their planet from another planet in another galaxy. The traditional paranoia and tendency to scapegoat one another is projected onto a third entity, the planet Lesnaya Grud. In the doing, both countries pointedly decide to abandon and banish from Earth a cosmonaut team, consisting of one Soviet and one American, previously put together to research the potential for joint Soviet-American mining of mineral and other natural resources in our solar system. This team is then stranded on the alien planet—a literal scapegoat ritual. Also see Sylvia Perera, "The Scapegoat Complex," *Quadrant* 12,(2) (Fall 1979).

In symbolic irony, at the first summit meeting between the two in 1986, former president Reagan told Mr. Gorbachev that if the Martians landed, Washington and Moscow would quickly mend their differences and cooperate. (As reported in the Institute for Soviet-American Relations' *Surviving Together*, November 1986, no. 10, p. 29.)

both situations as leftist subversions of legitimate governments. Why each would interpret the scenarios in these particular political terms is amplified in the discussion of the Shadow archetype. What is important is that each would see both events in the same light, irrespective of its own ideological standpoint.[8]

As a training technique, it would be crucial that participants have no prior indication of the nature of the exercise. To the extent that this technique will have been effective, the discovery that archetypal dynamics would have appeared to have manipulated each party to see its own respective incursion in the same political light as the other's could be profoundly jarring and could call into question the entire rational framework used by each to justify its own policies. The insight that the rational justifications for many political and military decisions made by both sides often are not what either party thinks they are, and that each is indeed manipulated by archetypal forces of which it is unaware, is the ultimate goal of the exercise. Whether any particular invasion was justified will become of secondary importance if the exercise is successful.[9]

---

[8] Relatedly, S. Plous and Philip G. Zimbardo, conducted a survey wherein they claim to have demonstrated that "it is difficult or impossible to discriminate between unlabeled Soviet and American actions" (Scott Plous, "Psychological and Strategic Barriers in Present Attempts at Nuclear Disarmament: A New Proposal," *Journal of Political Psychology* 6, no. 1 (March 1985); cited in *Psychology Today* (November 1984), p. 50). Although they appear to have demonstrated that educated middle-class Americans could not reliably distinguish between events like the Soviet invasion of Hungary and the U.S.–backed Bay of Pigs invasion when some identifying data were removed, their study does not demonstrate my thesis that each superpower will tend to perceive its own as well as the other's behavior *consistent with its own ideology and ideological outlook on the other.*

I would maintain this view notwithstanding the Soviet reassessment in November of 1987 of its intervention in Czechoslovakia. However, should General Secretary Gorbachev remain in power and his policy of *perestroika* remain operative for another two to three years, this example might not suffice to demonstrate this psychological phenomenon because of shadow integration on the part of the Soviets. (See Chapter 3 for the meaning of "shadow integration.")

[9] It is recognized that one exercise (or even several) of the type outlined above will likely not be sufficient to change entrenched ideological perceptions, prejudices, and national biases. Psychological research has shown repeatedly that deeply held beliefs and prejudices are not readily subject to change as the result of logical argument or standard educational approaches.

However, the first step toward bringing about changes in perceived reality is having doubt cast on those that one holds. The advantage to the exercise proposed above is that the individual would not have been argued with about his perceptions, but in effect would *himself* have challenged, as it were, his own perception of reality.

The emphasis here has been on demonstrating how an archetypal approach to dealing with crucial conflicts in the thermonuclear age can lead to totally different perceptions and analyses of the problem, as compared with standard rational analysis.

Based on this depth-psychological approach to the resolution and management of human conflict, some generalizations can be made:

1. Recognizing the archetypal forces that are at play in international conflict can free each protagonist from unconsciously acting out those dynamics and from having to see each other as responsible for the crisis. It posits a new and third point of view. Without this, blame hovers over and usually intrudes upon the rational negotiations.

2. It is not known why a given archetype predominates in a given situation. We cannot pick our archetypal identification, but we can endeavor to be more conscious of the deeper psychological dynamics that move us, individually and collectively. Simply put, awareness of prevalent archetypal forces = greater power in dealing effectively with the issues that concern us.

3. Archetypes represent transpersonal psychic energy. Therefore they cannot be explained away.

4. Since the scapegoat dynamic is central to any conflict between nations, archetypal theory can be used to help the conflicting nations to stop scapegoating each other. Usually, it is the archetype of which they are unconscious that is scapegoating them and that they must come to see as their *common* adversary that poses the greater threat to stability.

5. Archetypal energy is always bipolar, having a positive and negative aspect. Identifying with one pole of an archetype invites a powerful compensatory response from the other pole—a strong hawkish stance on nuclear weapons early in the Reagan administration was a catalyst for the rise of the Nuclear Freeze Movement.

6. Since archetypal energy is universal, then "speaking through the archetype," as it were, can provide a *common* psychological language and frame of reference that transcends cultural and religious values. Both parties can thus approach their mutual problem from a common standpoint instead of from intransigent ideological and political positions.

7. An archetypal problem between two parties, be they individuals or nations, almost always involves a *mutual* problem, because each of the two sides is identified with one pole of an archetype that calls forth and energizes the other pole, keeping them both in perpetual conflict. For example, you cannot have a bully without a participating victim and you cannot have a victim without a participating bully. The one literally calls

forth the other. Not only will a bully search out a victim, but a victim personality will unconsciously search out a bully.

8. Archetypes do not operate singly. Usually two or more archetypes operate in conjunction with each other, although one usually will appear to predominate.

For example, in the foreign policy of the United States, one can inevitably find the archetype of the hero operating in concert with the archetype of power. One can see the heroic image of Prometheus the light-bringer in the United States' perpetuation of its at-times-repressive hegemonic dominance of the Western Hemisphere. While pursuing a legitimate archetypal role of protecting and furthering the tenets of democracy, the United States often falls into its own power complex, violating the very principles it is pledged to protect and preserve: for example, Chile 1973.

③ The Archetype of the Shadow

If you know the enemy and know yourself, you need not fear the result of a hundred battles. . . . If you know neither the enemy nor yourself, you will succumb in every battle.
　　　　　　　　　　　—Sun Tzu, *The Art of War*, c. 400 B.C.E.

Cartoon by Tom Toles, *Buffalo News,* March 8, 1987. Reprinted by permission.

In depth-psychological terms, the shadow represents the psychological and emotional facts about ourselves that are incompatible with our own self-image and that, as a result of this incompatibility, we unwittingly repress into our unconscious. (This also includes material never before realized overtly.)

We can most readily recognize our personal shadow when, for example, we walk into a room at a social gathering and have an intense negative emotional reaction to a total stranger after having exchanged only two or three sentences with him. A close examination of the particular qualities we dislike in that person will in most cases give us a graphic description of our own repressed negative side. A feeling of "that guy is too arrogant and opinionated for me" should be heard as "*I* am too arrogant and opinionated for me!" It is the intensity of the reaction that is the tip-off that this stranger we dislike carries qualities that we particularly dislike in ourselves.

One can pick up the newspaper any day and read about shadow dynamics that are acted out unconsciously: the congressman concerned with ethics in government who is caught taking bribes; the illegal acts of J. Edgar Hoover, our anticrime hero; the self-righteous fundamentalist minister—a Jim Bakker and his PTL Ministry—who passionately crusades against the evils of the flesh and pleads for the neediness of the poor, who is found to be morally and materially corrupt, et cetera.

It is axiomatic in all psychological theory that repressed emotional contents usually are projected unconsciously onto others.[1] Simply put, shadow projection means that we see our own negative qualities in the other person while not being able to see those same qualities in ourselves.

From a depth-psychological standpoint there is a *collective shadow* that is projected onto groups and nations as well as an individual shadow that is projected by one individual onto another. Jews as the object of the shadow projections of Nazi Germany is one obvious example. Thus, as nations, we are constantly projecting our primitive sadomasochistic instincts. Instead of experiencing these impulses as ours, we perceive them

---

[1] As Whitmont puts it: "The fundamental law of preservation of energy applies to psychological functioning as well as to physics. What is expelled, repressed from individual [and collective] consciousness, reappears in projection upon another person, group or figure." (Edward C. Whitmont, *Return of the Goddess* [New York: Crossroad, 1982], p. 63.)

Clinically speaking, untenable positive qualities as well as negative qualities may be projected onto others. This is a crucial psychological fact, as we shall see in the case of the Soviet Union.

as objective evil, embodied in an external other. We perceive "evil empires" and the evils of "capitalist imperialism" in the other.[2]

To make matters worse, the more we try to deal with shadow dynamics purely with rationality and willpower, the more we fall into its grips. The rational function ends up constructing all manner of rational frameworks that explain and justify why "the other" is an intractable enemy. Although many of these explanations and rationalizations may be true about the other, the fact doesn't help *self*-awareness of our own shadow dynamics. Indeed, more often than not, it further reinforces our self-righteous view of "the enemy" and "his" intractableness. Ultimately this leads to isolation, paranoia, and a vicious circle, and sometimes overt conflict or war with the perceived outer enemy. The enemy within becomes even more removed from reality, more encrusted in paranoid defense.

Projected shadow dynamics not only determine a distorted view of how we perceive the other, but they also bring about a self-fulfilling prophecy

---

[2]This is not to equate "evils," for there are indeed profound qualitative differences in the "evils" of the two respective systems and countries. The point here is one of psychodynamics, not a political, philosophical, or moral one.

The Soviet Union and the United States are two halves of a psychic whole. The Soviet Union represents the primitive, collective, repressive, instinctual shadow of the United States; the United States represents a material and ideological utopia, and its drive for national and personal individuation, of the Soviet Union (Jerome Bernstein, "Power and Politics in the Thermonuclear Age: A Depth-Psychological Approach," *Quadrant* [Fall 1985]: 11–12).

We can see a clear example of a piece of the primitive national self-definition of the Soviet Union in an incident that occurred on September 18, 1986, in Jurmala, Latvia, U.S.S.R. At a conference involving more than 250 American participants, jointly sponsored by the Soviet government and the New York Chautauqua Institution, a Soviet official stated that authorities "could not guarantee the physical safety" of seven Latvian-Americans attending the conference because they distributed to locals pens bearing the flag of independent Latvia and had visited friends and relatives in the area (apparently without "permission"). An editor of Hearst Newspapers and a director of the Chautauqua Institution, "said a Soviet security official asked him to pass the warning on to the Latvian-Americans. . . ." In addition, three of the Latvian-Americans had their hotel rooms searched and several articles were taken. Also, some of the local friends they had visited were called in by the KGB for questioning.

For a government to threaten the lives of individuals without accusation or trial is not only contrary to American laws and traditions, but it harkens to a more primitive period in the development of Western civilized nations: that is, pre–fifteenth-century English common law. Moreover, such behavior, by American standards, is morally outrageous and is "proof" of the primitive nature of Soviet society and law as well as of the nation's inherent evil.

wherein we are perceived consistent with our own repressed shadow qualities. Often we, as individuals and collectively as nations, stimulate some of the very evil behavior we perceive in the enemy with our insistence that he claim his evil nature while we self-righteously deny the existence of our own.

In this regard, shadow integration requires three essential qualities: rational awareness, psychological maturity and sophistication, and moral consciousness.[3] It is the last of these that is the most difficult, because it is so humbling. It takes enormous personal security, ego confidence, and personal courage to stand up and say, "Not only are you right, but I am wrong." And it is crucial that those last three words—"I am wrong"—be claimed.[4] Without them, the ego can slip out from under having to face up to its own negative characteristics that it is committed to not seeing, and can use the words "you are right" as a paranoid defense to avoid having to confront its own shadow. Moreover, and of crucial importance, over time, the claiming of its negative shadow by one antagonist makes room for the other antagonist to do the same. The Soviet Union has been quite active in claiming parts of its negative shadow side in recent years. There is evidence that this process within the Soviet system is stimulating more dynamic shadow integration on the part of the United States (as well as heightening some American paranoia).

If this is difficult at the individual level, it is awesomely difficult at the collective level. It has been axiomatic in international relations that nations *never* say they were wrong about any policy. Often a nation will change unworkable policies, but always under the guise of improving the old policy or simply announcing a new one while denying that it is a departure from the old one. For example, in February 1984 the Reagan administration announced that it was "redeploying" U.S. marine contingents garrisoned in Lebanon to offshore ships for "logistical" reasons, rather than admit that its policies in Lebanon had failed.[a] After two or three months of the ships remaining off Lebanese shores and after news coverage dwindled away for lack of news, the ships one day simply sailed away. From the standpoint of shadow integration, little was learned from

---

[3] Moral consciousness will be discussed at greater length in Chapters 7 and 9.

[4] An absolute example—"You are right, I am wrong"—has been used here for purposes of emphasis. In fact, such a black-and-white situation is seldom the case, and usually both parties are right *and* wrong to greater and lesser degrees. The emphasis is that both sides of this equation must be claimed if genuine shadow integration is to occur.

the episode, with the danger that a similar policy would be tried else-where in the world.[5]

In conjunction with the archetype of the scapegoat and the archetype of power, the shadow probably has been the most active, disruptive, and dangerous psychic energy operative between the United States and the Soviet Union.

SHADOW PROJECTION IN THE PRE-GORBACHEV ERA OF SOVIET-AMERICAN RELATIONS

During the present period of unprecedented relaxation of tension be-tween the Soviet Union and the United States, it is tempting to ignore altogether the shadow dynamics between the two superpowers. (Liter-ally, "Why look for trouble?") However, since shadow dynamics are ar-chetypal in origin, they may wax and wane, but they do not go away. In-deed, from this *psychological* perspective, these are dangerous times, for if we ignore the shadow dynamics between the two countries, they can arise again—much to our surprise—in another form. Just as likely, those shadow dynamics can be projected onto a new target by either side or both.

A brief historical look at the respective shadows of the United States and the Soviet Union is revealing in terms of the psychodynamics that governed Soviet-American relations from 1917 to 1985.

Because neither side considered its own power ambitions fully consis-tent with its stated ideology, each denied them and in doing so projected them onto the other. "*We* do not wish to dominate anyone; we *must* enter into alliances, build missiles, use spies, plan for war, because *they* want to dominate others." Although there have been and remain profound dif-ferences in ideology between the two countries and systems, a primary source of the negative power projections onto each other has been the in-compatibility of the respective power drives of each with *its own* ideology.

Each side has believed that the political system of the other is the source of all social injustice and evil in the world. As a result, each has been ideologically committed to the elimination of the sociopolitical sys-tem of the other. This standpoint has put each in instant conflict with its own self-image of supporting world peace and freedom, since, short of

---

[5] One could draw analogies between the Reagan administration's Lebanon pol-icy and failed attempts in 1988 to topple the Noriega regime in Panama.

going to war, each side has used tactics of subversion and violence to bring about the demise of the other's system—wherever it exists. (The Soviet military invasion of Czechoslovakia in 1968 to abort that country's popular political liberalization and the United States–engineered overthrow of the democratically elected Allende regime in Chile in 1973 are but two examples.)

The degree to which each side denies and lies about its complicity and the actual reasons for its actions represents prima facie evidence of its feeling that the action taken is inconsistent with its ideological self-image. Perhaps the archetypal example of this phenomenon in contemporary terms was the 1986–1987 Iran-Contra affair, wherein the United States covertly sold arms to Iran in exchange for the release of American hostages and illegally used the funds obtained to support the Contras in Nicaragua—all of this in the face of a vociferous official policy of opposing negotiations with terrorists and terrorist nations as well as the shipment of any arms to Iran. Not only did government officials lie to the American public—even after the basic facts were known—but the president himself apparently lied on several occasions.[6]

It is important to recognize that, psychodynamically, shadow projection has more to do with domestic self-image than it does with the nature of the perceived enemy, although there may be many truths in the content of the projection. When the United States government denies CIA involvement, and otherwise lies about the U.S. role in mining Nicaragua's harbors in 1984 and the sinking of a Russian freighter by one of those mines, for example, the lie is not told for the consumption of the Nicaraguans or the Russians, both of whom, in the age of satellite surveillance and supersensitive electronic eavesdropping, surely know the nature and source of the act. The lie is told to protect *domestic* self-image in the United States. Most dangerously, particularly in a democracy, it is also

---

[6] In a nationally televised address on November 13, 1986, Reagan said: "We did not—repeat, did not—trade weapons or anything else for hostages—nor will we . . ." (as reported in the *Washington Post*, November 14, 1986, p. A1). Subsequently, at a press conference on November 20, 1986, Reagan acknowledged that he had indeed approved arms sales to Iran to gain the release of hostages and went on to say, ". . . I think that what we did was right, and we're going to continue on this path" (*Washington Post*, November 20, 1986, p. A1). In the same news conference he asserted, ". . . all of the shipments of the token amounts of defensive arms and parts that I have authorized or condoned taken in total could be placed aboard a single cargo aircraft. This includes all shipments by the United States" (ibid., p. A23). Subsequent testimony at the Iran-Contra hearings in 1987 revealed this statement to be false as well.

told to manipulate the Congress and the public into supporting a policy that it would otherwise oppose. The Gulf of Tonkin Resolution of August 7, 1964, is a case in point.

When the Soviets lie about the nature of the facts that led up to its 1979 invasion of Afghanistan, for example, it is doing so for its domestic self-image, not because it believes that the United States and the rest of the world will believe its lie.[7]

---

[7]Although it is true that Soviet government control of the press has limited the need to which it must address its people at all, in the age of global communication and powerful and cheap technology, the man in the street has much more access to the information he wishes to have, even in the Soviet Union. In more recent times, General Secretary Gorbachev's policy of *glasnost* has begun to open up communication, not only between the larger elements of Soviet collective leadership and the United States government, but, more important in the long run, between the Soviet government itself and the Soviet populace-at-large.

Moreover, because of its historic and severe inferiority complex as a superpower, the Soviet government has been much more prone than the American government to "preserve" its self-image for its own self-respect. There is the story about how, at the SALT I negotiations, American negotiators persisted in demanding accurate numbers from the Soviets regarding the number and placement of Soviet missiles. Finally, when the Soviets would not produce the data, American negotiators proffered it. With great embarrassment, a senior Soviet official took aside a senior American negotiator and, while admitting the accuracy of the American data on Soviet missile placements, in hushed tones begged him not to reveal those data in open meeting since that kind of information was simply not made available to any but a select few governmental and military personnel in the Soviet Union.

It is ironic that information that our government *knows* that the Soviets have is still kept secret from the American public. In numerous confrontations with the American press, where spies working for the Soviet Union have been arrested, the United States government has taken great pains to suppress "leaks" to the press about the nature of the particular espionage. This "policy" seems to be uniform, no matter what administration, Democratic or Republican, is in power. Indeed, so great is the paranoid protection of the national shadow that the federal government has gone to court to prosecute publishers of material dubbed classified or "against national security interests" and has threatened others with prosecution when the material in question had already been published, some of it in U.S. government publications, and was available through public libraries and other easily accessible public sources.

On November 24, 1987, the Association for Responsible Dissent (ARDIS) announced its formation to campaign for an end to covert activities on the part of the United States in the wake of the Iran-Contra affair. The group is composed of over fifteen CIA spies, spymasters, and analysts. In a press conference on November 26, 1987, Philip C. Roettinger, president of ARDIS, said, "We are going to try to expose covert action. We're going to try to get it legally banned because we can

In this regard, the Grenada incident of 1983 represents a lost opportunity because of the unanimity of bipartisan and public support for military intervention by the United States and the low risk of adverse consequences, politically or militarily. If the United States could have been more forthright concerning what appeared to be the predominant reasons for that invasion and had not claimed that the *primary* reason for intervention was the ostensible threat by a left-wing government to American medical students on the island, a piece of our shadow could have been owned and thereby removed from the dynamic that perpetuates conflict with the Soviet Union. (In official Washington circles it is openly acknowledged that military intervention would have occurred with or without the presence of the medical students. Notwithstanding, the official governmental position as of December 1984 was that military intervention was dictated primarily by the imminent threat to life of American citizens [that is, the medical students].)

The more compelling reasons for American intervention in Grenada were the need to send a strong message to the Soviet Union and Cuba that the United States would not tolerate the proliferation of left-wing Cuban-style governments in its hemisphere of the world—especially if those governments come to power by other than democratic means and if they posed a military threat to other nations in the area or to the United States—an opportunity for the United States to have demonstrated that as a superpower it was no longer operating under a post-Vietnam national retrenchment and no longer would it be overly cautious about the use of our military power to back up its perceived national security interests. Last, it appears that the Reagan administration wished to demonstrate that the post-Watergate crisis of self-confidence was over and that the executive branch of government—namely, the President as commander-in-chief—would not be afraid to use American military power to protect the nation's interests.

The problem with openly stating these reasons is that some in and out of government would have perceived them as inconsistent with the professed democratic ideals and historical traditions of the United States. Ultimately, the administration in power might be thwarted in its given foreign policy/power initiative. In the contemporary era of American

---

find no reason, no justification, for covert action on the part of the U.S. government in the name of the American people." Roettinger, a former CIA case officer, participated in the overthrow of Guatemalan President Jacobo Arbenz in 1954 (David Ottaway in the *Washington Post,* November 26, 1987, p. A21).

presidential politics it would appear that "no" is not viewed as an acceptable answer on some foreign policy initiatives.

However, if the United States government were willing to take a more open and honest stance with respect to its actual power needs and ambitions, *and if it had been willing to face the arguments that some aspects of that power stance might be inconsistent with its own professed ideology and traditions*, a significant portion of the unconscious power shadow could have been redeemed, with the result that the United States could be measurably less prone to projecting it onto the Soviet Union (and vice versa).

In the case of Grenada, the United States government might have found itself in the position of having to say "Yes, our military intervention in Grenada does run counter to *some* of our democratic ideals;[8] yes, Grenada does represent a necessary exception; yes, we do reserve the right to act inconsistently with our political ideals and traditions in limited situations when we perceive our national survival or our system of government as being materially threatened; yes, there *are* real limits to what we will accept in our own hemisphere, even when imposing those limits may appear to conflict with our own self-concept of democratic government," et cetera.

The United States might have to declare openly, for example, that Soviet military ties that would provide the basis for an offensive military capability *will* be grounds justifying military intervention by the United States *and* acknowledge that such a policy stance does violate Nicaragua's sovereignty and is at odds with America's own democratic ideals, but that the perceived gravity of threat to American interests justifies actions repugnant to its political creed.[9]

---

[8]The United States was asked to intervene militarily by Grenada's neighbors, *not* by the country it invaded—an act inconsistent with professed American democratic ideals.

[9]A report of a virtually unanimous bipartisan committee, participated in by past and present State Department personnel, pulled together to assess the impact and implications of the Grenada incident, issued by the Kennan Institute of the Woodrow Wilson Center, Washington, D.C., on August 8, 1984, entitled "Soviet/Cuban Strategy in the Third World after Grenada," authored by Jiri Valenta and Herbert Ellison, stated:

"Above all, the Grenada experience demonstrates that the U.S.S.R. avoids contracting military alliances with more vulnerable Communist and Third World radical nations, particularly those adjacent to the U.S. periphery, where Washington is willing to protect its interest with military force. . . . While there was no conclusive evidence of an immediate threat to U.S. security interests in Grenada, cir-

In fact the Reagan administration almost took this exact position in November of 1984 when it stated publicly that it would consider the delivery of Soviet MiG fighters to Nicaragua as grounds for military intervention. However, what the Reagan administration did not do was to follow this up with a clear *public* policy statement that it would not permit Nicaragua to develop offensive military capability in the future, nor did it otherwise define the nature of "offensive" military capability. However, it is a virtual certainty that these very positions were communicated quite explicitly to Nicaragua by the United States through "unofficial channels."[10]

This obfuscation of the true policy stance of the given administration in power, particularly as it involved covert American military action and the support of antigovernment forces (for example, the Contras), reinforces shadow projection on the part of both policymakers and the public as well as on the part of the Soviet Union. It also muddies communication among the various protagonists and makes unclear what the real terms for a settlement might be—dangerous complications at a time when it is crucial that communication be clear.[11]

---

cumstances in Grenada prior to the intervention . . . made the U.S. and East Caribbean security forces' intervention an extraordinary yet necessary measure" [p. 6].

"U.S. negotiations with Cuba and Nicaragua should be based on reciprocity, verifiable agreements, and monitoring. *Soviet and Cuban military ties with Nicaragua or other radical regimes in the basin should be non-negotiable*" [Pp. 7–8, my emphasis]. [It should be noted that this is exactly the position taken by the Soviet Union in Eastern Europe.]

"The Grenada operation was . . . popular in the U.S. . . . it may have signaled . . . a major recovery from the Vietnam syndrome" [p. 21].

[10] Of course, it is recognized that such a policy will "work" only if the United States does not cry wolf too often—threatening a given action and not following it up. Some would argue that such an approach would take away one of the most potent diplomatic and political tools—bluff and threat. That is a valid argument. At the same time, one would have to weigh the degree of "success" as a result of bluff and threat (for example, in Lebanon, Nicaragua, Panama) against the long-term value of having policies that are clear, definitive so that the antagonist will not be confused as to consequences of its actions, *and* accompanied by wide congressional and public support.

[11] Indeed, a case could be made that the covert nature of America's true policies toward Nicaragua (and elsewhere in the region) and the inconsistency of American behavior in that region have built considerable "bad press" and resistance in the public and in the Congress to those policies and therefore work against the approach taken by the administration in power.

With regard to foreign policy, notwithstanding the fact that the Reagan administration always stopped short of meeting the full and essential requirements of consciously withdrawing shadow projections—that is, openly acknowledging

Politically, in the United States a more forthright position would be difficult to take initially because of dissenting positions in the Congress and would risk negative public opinion. However, the dialogue that would ensue, both within the executive and legislative branches of government and between the two, might significantly raise overall consciousness about the complexity of real American power needs and ambitions, as well as the assumptions underlying them. The result might be a clearer foreign policy, less confusion on the part of adversaries about American limits and response, more public confidence, both domestically and among allies, in the integrity of American government, the establishment of greater trust between the Congress and the President with respect to the War Powers Act and the meaning, limits, and integrity of the concept of "national security needs," and therefore less need for covert military operations, and, finally, less projection of the American shadow onto the Soviet Union. Also, it would probably result in somewhat more constrained power options in some situations on the part of a given administration in power. However, the trade-offs in terms of a probably more stable regional and international climate would appear to be justified from a long-range perspective.

When such dialogue between the executive and legislative branches is lacking, however, then it is left for the Congress to carry that piece of the shadow or piece of consciousness that the executive branch is not willing to address. The result often is confused or paralyzed foreign policy, confusion on the part of the American public, confusion on the part of the nation that is the object of the policy, perhaps wrongly enticing it to press limits unacceptable to the U.S., and, ultimately, possible miscalculation on the part of the Soviet Union with disastrous potential. An obvious example was Reagan administration policy on Nicaragua, culminating in the Iran-Contra scandal of 1987–1988.

This approach has significant implications for United States policy else-

those aspects of its policy stance that are at odds with the American national self-image, ideals, laws, and treaty obligations—it did more, albeit unintentionally, than any other administration since World War II to provoke dialogue and consciousness-raising necessary for ultimate recognition of shadow projections. Despite the fact that the Congress repeatedly caved in to presidential pressure on the final votes, the depth and intensity of congressional debate and challenge of the claim of "national security" needs regarding aid to the Contras in Nicaragua by the executive branch is one example of how shadow contents are raised to consciousness. The Reagan administration also provoked the raising of overall public consciousness to unprecedented levels regarding foreign affairs, as reflected in national polls of public sentiment and as a result of the Iran-Contra hearings of 1987.

where in the Caribbean and Central and South America, especially with regard to bringing about negotiated settlements to problems that affect United States security interests and long-term stability of the region.

One of the dangerous consequences of shadow projection between the superpowers is that both the Soviet Union and the United States have been seen as being more negative, dangerous, and aggressive than either really is. Shadow projection also distorts each country's view of itself and prevents insight into destructive tendencies that, in some instances, can be as destructive as, if not more so than, those perceived in the adversary. (This point is further amplified in Chapter 4.) Nuclear annihilation looms in our age, and gross distortions in perception, such as exaggerated perception of threat, are extremely dangerous because they increase the possibility of miscalculation and misunderstanding. Until the advent of the Gorbachev administration in the Soviet Union, we have lived in a time when shadow projection on both sides was at its height.

Moreover the dynamics of mutual shadow projection are self-reinforcing. The more one side projects negative contents onto the other, the more it will tend to become self-righteously inflated by the "positive" content of its own distorted self-image.[12] In addition, each side needs the other as the "bad guy" to receive its negative projection, and thus each has an unconscious investment in the other side's remaining at least as negative as perceived. Therefore, movement away from the status quo creates an unconscious psychic imbalance, which moves one side or the other to take aggressive action that will reestablish the equilibrium.

For example, when the United States did not keep pace with the Soviet Union in the production of nuclear armaments during the decade of the 1970s, a new psychic tension and anxiety may have been created and the Soviet Union may have continued arms development in part as a result of uncharacteristic behavior by the United States. This action, in turn, served as a stimulus to the aggressive counterreaction by the United States in the form of its unprecedented accelerated arms buildup during the 1980s. By limiting production in the 1970s, the United States had acted "out of character" with regard to the Soviet image of the United States as imperialist warmongers. It is likely that this behavior in turn contributed to an unconscious increase in Soviet anxiety, resulting in ac-

---

[12] Not only does it inflate the self-image of a given nation, but that inflated self-image gets projected onto others in a self-serving way. An example of this was President Reagan's referring to the Nicaraguan "Contras" as heroes and the moral equal of our "founding fathers"—hyperbole at best, and dangerous psychic inflation at worst (*New York Times*, March 2, 1985, pp. 1–4).

tions that manipulated the United States into behaving in a manner consistent with the Soviet's shadow projection onto the United States. This result worked against the long-range interests of both the Soviet Union and the United States and significantly increased the risk of accidentally triggering nuclear annihilation.

Apparently, any planned reduction in arms development must always be consciously negotiated with the other side, even if it is to be a unilateral reduction, so that the other side will be party to the decision to act uncharacteristically. When there is "danger" of one side or the other agreeing to what the other "wants," this danger heightens paranoid projection, because the other side will have to face a piece of its own projection handed back. What does the United States do with a Soviet Union that doesn't behave like an "evil empire"? What does it do with the sins for which it insists the Soviets are responsible and that justify so many of American actions and policies? What does the Soviet Union do with a United States that doesn't behave like an imperialist warmonger? How will it justify to the nations of Eastern Europe the need for the Warsaw Pact (and the stationing of Soviet troops on their borders)? The shadow of one side always suspects the motives of the other side—it must, for its own needs as well as for the "facts."

Another example of how the Soviet Union and the United States unconsciously manipulated themselves and each other into maintaining the status quo in their conflict with each other was reported by Edward L. Warner, senior defense analyst with the Rand Corporation, Washington, D.C., who pointed out that when the Carter administration, as part of the SALT II (Strategic Arms Limitation Talks) negotiations, proposed to the Soviet Union that strategic nuclear delivery vehicles (SNDVs) on both sides be limited to a maximum of 1,800, the Soviets were incensed, and then Foreign Minister Andrei Gromyko "went up in smoke," stating that the American proposal proved that the United States was not serious about the negotiation. Later, when the Soviets offered the identical proposal as their initial position in the 1982–1983 abortive START (Strategic Arms Reduction Talks) negotiations in Geneva, the United States rejected "the Soviet position" as unacceptable. Warner also asserted that the United States rejected the figure *because* it was acceptable to the Soviets.[b]

Another glimpse into this dynamic is provided by J. M. Joyce, former science advisor to the U.S. embassy in Moscow, who reports, "The Soviet offer made by Brezhnev October 6, 1979 [under the Carter administration] to negotiate on tactical nuclear weapons was perceived by most policy-level people in the U.S. not as an acceptable way to attain our original goal, reduction in the SS-20s [Soviet intermediate-range nuclear missiles targeted on Western Europe, China, and Japan], but rather as a threat to our new goal, deployment of LRTNF [Long Range Theater Nuclear Forces: for example, the Pershing II missile stationed in Western Europe and targeted at Soviet Russia]. We feared that our allies would be enticed by the Soviet offer and waver in support of LRTNF." ". . . Most policy-makers in the U.S. government saw Brezhnev's October 1979 offer to withdraw unilaterally 20,000 troops from Central Europe as duplicity. Whether or not any of these perceptions were correct is perhaps less important than the fact that, given their image of their opponent, the perceivers could have come to no other conclusions. The structure of hostility is so rigid it interprets even troop withdrawals as signs of hostility." [c]

Deadly Gambits, by Strobe Talbott, has provided a more detailed view from the American perspective of how the two superpowers unconsciously manipulated themselves and each other into maintaining the status quo with respect to their shadow projections onto each other. In it, Talbott asserts that a significant and dominating element in the Reagan administration believed that ". . . the United States would do best with gambits at the negotiating table that would lead to diplomatic stalemate; that way the United States might more freely acquire and deploy new pieces on its side of the board and position itself, if necessary, to make winning military moves against the Soviet Union." [d]

An almost humorous example of this phenomenon concerns the issue of civil defense programs in both countries. Since American intelligence sources reported early in the Reagan administration that the Soviet Union was building a massive civil defense system that would be capable of evacuating large numbers of its citizens, some highly placed American officials became convinced that the Soviets were planning for a "first strike capability" against the United States and urged commensurate planning within the United States defense establishment. Why else would the Soviets need such an elaborate civil defense system unless they were planning a "first strike" against the United States and were preparing for a retaliatory strike by the United States?

At the same time, since the United States had virtually no civil defense program to speak of and was planning none, some highly placed Soviet officials became convinced that the United States was planning a "first strike" against the Soviet Union and urged appropriate action on the part of the Soviet defense establishment. What other reason could the United States have for not developing a civil defense program to protect its population unless it were planning a "first strike" and therefore would not need one?[e] As of the fall of 1988, this issue still had currency in the Gorbachev and Reagan administrations.

Here, totally opposite and contradictory "logic" was used by each side to justify its own shadow projection onto the other. Indeed, there has been a twenty-year history of "flip-flopping" between the two super-powers in arms reduction negotiations.

From a psychological point of view, it does not matter who is right and who is wrong. In most cases, both are right and both are wrong. Shadow projections produce profound distortions of perceived reality and thus augment war-inducing tensions between the antagonists. Unless these shadow projections are worked through and withdrawn, rational negotia-tions between the two will be of only marginal and short-term value be-cause the most powerful issues lie unseen in the unconscious and remain undealt with. Shadow projection is an unconscious phenomenon and therefore is almost never affected by negotiations over "objective" issues (for example, arms control), but can negatively impact on such negotia-tions between the superpowers. Therefore a psychological resolution of shadow issues must take place before long-term transformative political resolution is possible. The superpowers, after years of arduous work, may indeed finally negotiate an arms reduction treaty (for example, the two Strategic Arms Limitation agreements—SALT I and II—and the INF Treaty of 1988). However, without psychological resolution of shadow issues, new weapons systems (for example, the MX missile, SS-20 mis-siles, "Midgetman," and SDI technology) will come into being, thus vitiating past agreements[13] and requiring that the process be started all over again.

One other important observation is crucial to understanding the nature

---

[13] Other examples include the refusal by the United States Senate to ratify SALT II, exaggerated charges and countercharges regarding cheating on existing treaties, and unilateral American "reinterpretation" of the Anti-Ballistics Missile (ABM) Treaty to suit its own defense research objectives (that is, continuing with a full "Star Wars" [SDI] research program, components of which would clearly vio-late the ABM Treaty). The latter attempt was abandoned by the White House after failing to obtain United States Senate support for the proposed reinterpreta-tion of the treaty.

The Center for Defense Information reports that in 1988, after the signing and ratification of the INF Treaty, there were plans for deploying of unneeded new nuclear weapons in Europe, such as the Lance missile. Of particular note and con-cern were the attempts on the part of both the Soviets and the Americans to in-crease significantly the deployment of long-range cruise missiles ("After the INF Treaty: U.S. Nuclear Buildup in Europe," *The Defense Monitor*, 17,[2] (1988)).

of shadow projection and how that dynamic might be dealt with: until the advent of the Gorbachev administration, the Soviet Union has made an ideal "hook" (receptor) for the projection of the American national shadow and, vice versa, the United States for the Soviet shadow, for the very reason that both do hold opposite ideologies and values. Americans value individual rights above the collective; Soviets value collective rights above those of the individual; Americans insist on the free exercise of religious convictions; Soviets are officially atheistic, et cetera. A closed collective society is antithetical to American self-image and therefore is repressed into the American shadow. On the other hand, an open society that places its highest value on the rights of the individual is incompatible with the Soviet self-image and is therefore part of the Soviet shadow. The American shadow is, in part, fascistic, repressive, and collective—witness Watergate and the Iran-Contra scandal. The Soviet shadow is, in part, capitalistic and democratic. Poland's Solidarity, and its press for democratization, has been an active aspect of the Soviet shadow.

It is not necessary at this point in history to argue the above thesis. The American shadow is evident. As of this writing (winter 1988), the Iran-Contra trials are getting under way, with the president and vice president claiming that the biggest lawbreaker, Colonel Oliver North, is a national hero.

Evidence of the burgeoning of the seeds of democracy and capitalism in the Soviet Union (and in the People's Republic of China) is as clear as the bright yellow McDonald's arches in Moscow and the government-sponsored press conferences by Andrei Sakharov with the Western media. Also see *The Day Lasts More than a Hundred Years*, by Chingiz Aitmatov, for a poignant portrayal of how deeply religious conviction and a yearning for individual rights and freedom have lived in the soul of pre-*glasnost* modern-day Russia. The fact that this novel, with its criticism of Stalinism and the archaic repressive controls characteristic of the various Soviet regimes over the years, was published under the pre-*glasnost* system, testifies to the seeds of democratic reform that had lain hidden in the Soviet shadow during the many years of a much more repressive Soviet regime.

This observation is highly important and needs to be understood by American political, foreign policy, and military analysts because, in the case of the Soviet Union, it demonstrates the archetypal dynamic of the positive shadow operating from within deep layers of its psyche. In the case of *glasnost* and *perestroika*, the positive shadow is bringing forth psychological and political dynamics never before experienced in the Soviet national psyche.

There are many in the United States who attribute the accession to power of Mr. Gorbachev and his policies of *perestroika* and *glasnost* as a kind of short-lived fluke. In the waning days of the Reagan administration, no less than the secretary of defense and the vice president (now president) as well as other notables such as former Defense Secretary James Schlesinger warned of the limitations of Soviet reforms and even of conscious duplicity on the part of Mr. Gorbachev. Such a view would characterize Mr. Gorbachev as either some kind of master deceiver or as an interloper usurping the Soviet system against its will. Ironically this put post-Moscow summit Mr. Reagan, the arch-proponent of the "evil empire" view of the Soviet Union throughout most of his administration, as the liberal pitted against the more conservative elements of his own administration![14]

Mr. Gorbachev did not suddenly arrive on the scene[15] as an outsider in 1985 to take over the reins of the cumbersome and repressive Soviet system. He came as an insider and spent more than twenty years rising to the top of that same system. Presumably he brought with him many of the ideas for democratic reform that he has implemented since coming to power. The conclusion is inescapable that Mr. Gorbachev was elected to power within the Soviet collective system *because* of many of the ideas for reform that he brought with him, notwithstanding the considerable resistance to those reforms within the system as a whole and on the part of many of the Politburo members who voted him into power. Indeed, the very nature of that system assures, perhaps more than any other in the world save outright dictatorships, that Mr. Gorbachev represents conscious and unconscious elements within that selfsame system. Otherwise he would not have been selected as General Secretary and would not have been able to retain his position to date. (He can be removed at will by the Politburo and the Communist Party, unlike the case with American presidents, who have the rest of their term to retain power, notwithstanding the feelings of the electorate.)

In the short run prior to the advent of the Gorbachev administration, the People's Republic of China may have reflected more of this capitalistic

---

[14] During the Moscow summit, Mr. Reagan, when asked, said that he no longer considered the Soviet Union an "evil empire" and said that that characterization fit another era and previous Soviet leaders.

[15] As some might say Jimmy Carter did in the United States in 1976.

and democratic shadow than the Soviet Union did, because most of the overt hostility and shadow projection by the Reagan administration had been onto the Soviet Union to the exclusion of the Republic of China. (Indeed, since the days of the Nixon administration, the United States, if anything, has been in alliance with the People's Republic of China against the interests of the Soviet Union.) This fact has afforded a comparatively calmer, slower evolution of the underlying layers of the Chinese national psyche without the intrusion of the kind of heightened paranoia stimulated by heavy American projection onto China as is the case with the Soviet Union. It is to be remembered that not ten years ago, the People's Republic of China was hurling vitriolic invective at the Soviet Union for being too "revisionist" and "deviationist" from orthodox communist doctrine: that is, too capitalistic and democratic.

However, if the Gorbachev administration survives into the decade of the 1990s with its policies of *glasnost* and *perestroika* intact, it appears that the Soviet Union will have demonstrated the most comprehensive and radical transformation, without revolution, of a political and economic system of any nation within the twentieth century.[16]

---

[16] In the fall of 1988, as I edit this section, which was initially drafted in November 1982, I cannot help but comment at the reaction I received then to my observations about the democratic and capitalistic shadow components of the Soviet (and Chinese) national psyche(s). For the most part they met with incredulous and sometimes mocking disbelief. One colleague commented that I simply did not understand the concept of the archetype of the shadow if I could make such observations. Others said that it was wishful thinking on my part to make such an assertion about the Soviet shadow, since there was no evidence for it.

One highly placed CIA official commented that in all of Russian history there were no historical elements that could serve as a historical reservoir from which such political dynamics could be drawn. When I pointed out that that was my precise point—that an archetypal dynamic can generate specific contents never previously experienced by a national psyche (that is, political entity), he said that it made no sense. All in all, with the exception of my wife, Colonel Fred Long (Ret.) of the Newport Institute, and private correspondence with Professor George Kennan, from whom I received positive critical analysis and his interest in seeing the work further developed, this notion was essentially met with disbelief. My attempts to get my manuscript published in the relevant professional journals were met with sometimes not-too-polite rebuffs.

In the wake of the earthshaking events taking place in the Soviet Union (and, to a less dramatic degree, in the People's Republic of China)—that is, the profound structural changes being made at all levels of the Soviet sociopolitical system as a result of General Secretary Gorbachev's policies of *glasnost* and *perestroika* (whether Gorbachev survives or not)—I cannot help but say, "I told you so!"

By definition, the shadow represents the inferior, less developed, repressed, and unconscious facts about an individual or nation that are incompatible with its national self-image, *as well as* aspects, including positive qualities, of its psychic identity that have not yet been realized: that is, a country's national potential. (A clear example of this was Japan's potential to become one of the strongest capitalistic countries in the world—a fact not guessed at by either Japan or the rest of the world until late in the post–World War II era.) This latter is important psychodynamically in the conflict between the Soviet Union and the United States, because it contains the seeds of points of future connection and cooperation between the United States and the Soviet Union where psychic as well as political cooperation may be possible.[17]

Carl Jung made an important observation that has critical bearing here:

> It has become abundantly clear to me that life can flow forward only along the path of the gradient. But there is no energy unless there is a tension of opposites; hence it is necessary to discover the opposite to the attitude of the conscious mind. It is interesting to see how this compensation by opposites also plays its part. . . . Seen from the one-sided point of view of the conscious attitude, the shadow is an inferior component of the personality and is consequently repressed through intensive resistence. But the repressed content must be made conscious so as to produce a tension of opposites, *without which no forward movement is possible.* The conscious mind is on top, the shadow underneath, and just as high always longs for low and hot for cold, so all consciousness, perhaps without being aware of it, seeks its unconscious opposite, lacking which it is doomed to stagnation, congestion, and ossification. Life is born [and growth takes place] only of the spark of opposites. [My emphasis.][f]

With intense paranoid projection *between* the two superpowers, the *internal* tension that is necessary for the internal psychic growth of each nation has been misdirected toward an outer "other": that is, the Soviet Union or the United States. Thus, to the extent that the internal psychic tension that Jung states is necessary for forward movement is displaced onto the "other," internal growth has been thwarted.

In 1982 I wrote:

> Given the autonomous and unconscious nature of the shadow, the single most effective thing the United States could do to undermine the Soviet system

---

[17]This notion will be discussed at length in Chapter 7.

would be to remove itself as the projection screen for the Soviet shadow, thereby taking advantage of one of the most powerful dynamics in the Soviet national psyche. Were the United States to do this, the Soviets would suddenly be left with their own Solidarities which they would have to deal with. They would no longer be able to use the United States as their primary excuse for repression, not only within Poland, but within Soviet Russia herself. However, to do that, the United States would first have to recognize and take responsibility for its own shadow.[18] But ideological warfare and name calling between our opposing systems does not bring about real change. On the contrary it optimizes shadow projection and ideological intransigence on both sides, *reducing* the possibility of ideological and political evolution.

The psychological fact is that opposites attract. In the case of the United States and the Soviet Union, that attraction is so powerful that each is driven to attempt to change (subvert) the other—even at the risk of mutual suicide. The physical and economic survival of all of us depends on a mutual recognition of the need to pull back our shadow projections.[g]

In suggesting that the United States remove itself as a projection screen for the Soviet Union it is *not* meant that it should take an uncritical or passive stance with regard to the Soviet Union. Indeed, it is crucial not to do that.

When the United States realized that the Soviet Union continued its offensive buildup in missiles during the decade of the 1970s in the face of détente and an American slowdown in defense allocations, it could have put the Soviet Union on notice that it would match and outpace the Soviet "defense" buildup without having to launch an unprecedented anti-Soviet campaign depicting them as the source of all evil in the world. The latter could only lead to extreme paranoid projection on both sides, heightening the arms race to the extreme. The hypothesis should be considered that the Soviets might have backed off from their arms buildup had U.S. determination been *demonstrated* without the inflammatory rhetoric.

---

[18] Some important steps in this direction have already been begun within the U.S. State Department. "Two-Track Diplomacy," an approach designed and implemented by William D. Davidson and Joseph Montville, aims at utilizing group dynamics to couple psychoanalytical and psychohistorical techniques with standard negotiating and conflict-resolution techniques to assist diplomats and other negotiators to see the issues from the psychological and emotional perspective of the other side. Although this approach is a major step forward in the technology of conflict resolution, it is not undertaken jointly with the Soviet Union, operates under the political and bureaucratic constraints of the U.S. State Department, and lacks an integrated archetypal perspective so that it leaves out a major psychic stratum operative in macro-conflicts: for example, between the United States and the Soviet Union.

For sure, there are domestic political considerations in building up the image of the Soviet Union as not only a threat to world peace, but the source of all evil in the world. The appropriations process necessary for an arms buildup does call for appropriate images of that need in order to gain public support. However, the approach of the Reagan administration suggested that, in addition to believing a lot of its own rhetoric, it also did not credit the American people with the capacity to see the need for an arms buildup in objective terms without picturing the Soviet Union as an "evil empire" out to destroy the world. In the last analysis it might not be possible to sell such a need without excessive rhetoric. But I would suggest that the American public may be ready for a more objective and enlightened presentation without having to have their minds and emotions manipulated as if Madison Avenue had "just" another product to sell. The long-term stakes are too high. It takes a long time and enormous resources to undo the results of the kind of shadow projection that had been characteristic between the Soviet Union and the United States from the mid 1970s to the end of the Reagan administration.

Ironically since 1982, when I wrote the essay quoted above, it has been the Soviet Union, not the United States, that has made the most strides in shadow integration.[19]

Given the structural nature of the changes already introduced by the policies *glasnost* and *perestroika,* there is little doubt that Soviet society and the Soviet Communist system itself have been already sufficiently "contaminated" that they can never return to their former primitive state. By this I do not mean that there will not be regressive pulls by conservative elements within the Soviet system, particularly on the part of the oligarchical bureaucratic machinery, toward the status quo ante. Consciousness once tasted can be repressed—for a while, but the human psyche, having realized that what it craves deep within is accessible, will have its way in the long run. This is not just wishful thinking, but a demonstrable clinical fact of human nature.[h] We can see this dynamic in the democratic and capitalistic reforms struggling for permanent integration within the fabric of the system of the People's Republic of China. Individuals are sacrificed in the struggle between progressive and regressive elements in the society, but the psychic imperative for change and the ideas generated by it hang on with tenacity. This will be no less true of the Soviet system, which ultimately may have to sacrifice Mr. Gorbachev himself as it did Nikita Khrushchev before him.

---

[19] See Chapter 7, note 8.

Regarding the speculation as to whether Mr. Gorbachev and the reforms he has instituted are "real" or "cosmetic" or even a cynical political ploy to dupe the United States, *structural* changes—changes in the very nature of Soviet economic and political system—are aimed at Soviet domestic needs, not American demands and notions of "linkage." One would wonder just what would constitute "real" reforms of the Soviet system if those currently under way are merely cosmetic. Such views reflect not only American political conservatism but, more important, insistent American shadow projection and paranoia.

It is important at this stage to distinguish between what is being attempted on the part of the Gorbachev administration and how well those efforts succeed. To date, the effort to experiment with elections of local party officials with a slate containing more than one candidate (unprecedented under the Communist system) has been something less than a smashing success. The point here is not the success of a given reform effort, but the goal and genuineness of the effort. Clearly, the kind of overhaul of the Soviet system through *perestroika* and *glasnost* of which Mr. Gorbachev speaks will take many years. Between here and more in-depth democratic reforms, there will be a lot of one-and-a-half-steps-forward and one-step-(sometimes three steps)-back behavior and half-baked efforts and bumbling on the part of a system and society that has no historical precedent for much of the reforms it seeks to make.

In a two-month period the Soviet government permitted an open demonstration at the Kremlin wall by Tatars seeking more ethnic and regional autonomy and broke up a small demonstration of refuseniks in Moscow on December 13, 1987, the same day when a large demonstration in support of Soviet Jewry took place in Washington, D.C.

It might do well for Americans to remember the many years of internal struggle and strife (including violence) it took to obtain the civil rights legislation of the 1960s and the regressive tendencies in the decade of the 1980s to undo that progress.

In the first three years of the Gorbachev administration, fundamental issues affecting all levels of Soviet society were addressed in the areas of political reform, revisions of the criminal code, economic theory and practice, trade, significant lifting of censorship, stimulating debate at all levels of society, revising official records of Soviet history to present the facts as they occurred rather than as a function of Communist propaganda, among many others.[20] Perhaps most important of all is the psychological message

---

[20] In a move unprecedented in modern times, the Soviet government in June

to the Soviet people: that is, the Communist system in the Soviet Union does not work as it has been practiced over the last seventy years. The message is sometimes subtle, but it is there and is being felt increasingly by the Soviet people: "We need democracy not to show off and not to play democracy. We need democracy to rearrange many things in our life, to give greater scope to the creativity of people, to new ideas and initiatives."[i]

Clearly a number of the reforms already instituted in the Soviet system have resulted in elements of the American shadow being handed back. Ironically, during the Moscow summit between General Secretary Gorbachev and former President Reagan, Gennady Gerasimov, spokesman for the Soviet foreign ministry, said on U.S. television, "We are going to do something awful to you. We are going to deprive you of an enemy."[j]

As of November 1988, this has not been received with alacrity.[21] Although some of the reticence of American officials to become "too" enthusiastic about reforms (long called for by American governments) taking place in the Soviet Union is understandable, given the history of Soviet-American relations over the years, one can also detect in some quarters a subliminal feeling of anxiety that they just might be genuine. Psychologically and clinically speaking, some of this anxiety is due less to a resistance to actual changes in the Soviet system than to an unconscious anxiety over components of the American shadow that we have succeeded in avoiding facing through the convenience of a Russian scapegoat.

1988 announced that it was temporarily canceling all history examinations in the country. The *Philadelphia Inquirer* of June 11, 1988, reported:

"The Soviet Union, saying history textbooks had taught generations of Soviet children lies that poisoned their 'minds and souls,' announced yesterday that it had canceled final history exams for more than 53 million students.

"Reporting the cancellation, the government newspaper *Izvestia* said the extraordinary decision was intended to end the passing of lies from generation to generation, a process that has consolidated the Stalinist political and economic system that the current leadership wants to end.

"'. . . The guilt of those who deluded one generation after another, poisoning their minds and souls with lies, is immeasurable,' the paper said in a front-page commentary.

"'Today, we are reaping the bitter fruits of our own moral laxity. We are paying for succumbing to conformity and thus to giving silent approval of everything that now brings the blush of shame to our faces and about which we do not know how to answer our children honestly'" (p. 1-A).

[21] This point will be discussed in greater detail in Chapters 7 and 8.

Carl Jung's theory of psychological types offers unique insights into the communication problems between the Soviet Union and the United States and can provide a powerful new tool in resolving shadow problems between the two superpowers. In his theory of psychological types, Jung identifies four functions present in individuals that govern the way people perceive and react to information and events: Thinking, Feeling, Intuition, and Sensation.

Jung proposed that people are innately predisposed to developing one of these as a predominant or "superior" function, much as a person is innately left- or right-handed. These innate predispositions can be seen in varied reactions to a single event.

In witnessing a car accident, the person who is a *Thinking type* would instinctively provide the police with an *analysis* of what happened: for example, the car, although not speeding, was going too fast for weather conditions.

The *Feeling type*, witnessing the same accident, would instinctively respond out of *feeling judgments*, often without *apparent* supporting data to back up the feeling judgments, and might say that the driver of the car was reckless and not paying attention.

The *Intuitive type* would simply *"know"* the cause of the situation without being able to state how he or she knew: for example, "I bet that driver recently got his license and was new at driving in inclement weather."

The *Sensation type* would instinctively respond in very *concrete detail* without necessarily drawing any conclusions: for example, the light turned red as soon as the driver entered the intersection, the streets were slick, the tires on the car were not in good condition, and the other car had begun to pull into the left lane without giving a signal.

All four might be correct in their perceptions, each perceiving the situation in terms of his or her own predominant psychological function.

To the four functions, Jung observed, must be added the "Introvert-Extrovert" dimension.

The *Introverted* type is naturally more inner-directed, experiences phenomena subjectively, and experiences the world as "other." He or she knows it in terms of his or her subjective *impressions* of it. Others often have a hard time getting to know the "real" nature of the introvert.

For the *Extroverted type*, reality is what this person experiences in the outer world. Often he or she has great difficulty knowing his or her own inner subjective state. These types know the world is *as they see and ex-*

perience it and are often surprised to find out that things are different from what they appear to be. Although others often think they know the extrovert well, extroverts may feel frustrated—because their "true depth" is not appreciated.

Combining the four functions and the Introvert-Extrovert dimension, there is a total of eight types of people. Four examples are provided below. (Examples of Introverted and Extroverted Intuition and Sensation types are not needed for purposes of the discussion of the dynamics of the Soviet-American relationship.)[1]

For example, the *Extroverted Thinking type* (for example, President Bush) is quite generous with his analysis of a situation and is ever ready to provide ample data to support his analyses.

The *Introverted Thinking type* (for example, Henry Kissinger), on the other hand, may provide one summary statement on a situation, not revealing the real depth of his analysis, which often is quite extensive.

The *Extroverted Feeling type* (for example, former President Reagan) can hardly withhold his feelings about people and situations, which seem sometimes to flow out of him without containment. (During Reagan's presidency, his staff exerted great efforts to keep his availability to the press as limited as possible.) As was evident in the case of former President Reagan, persons of this typology are not readily persuaded by contrary data from deeply held feeling convictions.

The *Introverted Feeling type* (for example, former President Ford) may have a profundity of feeling about a situation, but because his feelings lie so deep within him, few may get expressed, and he may sometimes appear to be cold, aloof, unfeeling, or confused and slow in getting his thoughts together.[22]

The four psychological functions as described by Jung and outlined in Figure 1 represent two pairs of opposites: Thinking and Feeling are opposite functions, as are Intuition and Sensation. Each individual is predisposed toward a typological dominance (his or her "superior" function), which becomes naturally more developed and used. The opposite function, his or her "inferior" function, is the less developed, the most perplexing, and the source of a chronic blind spot. Thus, for the Thinking type, his or her feeling function usually is the most undeveloped (inferior) function, and vice versa.

---

[22] For example, Ford's famous gaffe during one of the 1976 presidential debates with the Democratic candidate, Jimmy Carter, where he asserted that Eastern Europe was not under the domination of the Soviet Union, a position that clearly was opposite to the one he himself held.

FIGURE 1. FOUR PSYCHOLOGICAL FUNCTIONS

In Jungian terms, the dominant typology of the United States is *Extroverted Thinking,* and the dominant typology of the Soviet Union, the Slavs in particular, is *Introverted Feeling.*[23] The two societies are typologically opposite, and consequently each has continually spoken to the other's inferior function, talking past the other.

As a generalization, the Introverted Feeling type (the Soviet Union) may appear to his typological opposite (the United States) as impossible to communicate with, cold, unemotional or too emotional, easily offended, judgmental, irrational, stubborn (if not dogmatic), intellectually dull because of an inferior thinking function, intellectually slow, unable to let go of the past, morally self-righteous, unduly suspicious, inaccessible, condescending, hostile, unsociable, and generally unreasonable.

On the other hand, the Extroverted Thinking type (the United States) may appear to his typological opposite (the Soviet Union) as heady, a know-it-all, dogmatic, arrogant and glib, superficial, egocentric, too abstract, unemotional and insensitive, morally dogmatic or immoral, hostile, very materialistic, unprincipled, exploitive, and fickle.

A given typological predisposition determines the way we hear others and the way we communicate emotionally as well as intellectually. These factors transcend language. Negotiators cannot rely simply on understanding each other's language or having good interpreters. If the *manner* in which they *process* the information they receive is profoundly different, grave misunderstandings may exist without either party's even knowing it.

For example, the late Premier Brezhnev, on several occasions, broke down and wept openly when talking about the prospects of nuclear anni-

[23] My conclusions about Soviet typology are based on a sampling of Soviet literature, music, and poetry, observations of public behavior of Soviet officials, discussions with Soviet expatriates and with Soviet government officials, discussions with American officials in the Department of State, the Central Intelligence Agency, the National Security Council, and the military, as well as individuals within American "think tanks" and other private groups that have had direct experience in working with and negotiating with Soviets on a regular basis.

hilation.[1] Mr. Brezhnev's weeping over the prospect of nuclear holocaust might be taken erroneously by an American president as a sign of weakness. Mr. Reagan's rhetoric about the evils of Communism, particularly during the first three years of his administration, might have been misunderstood as a serious indication that the United States might countenance a first strike against the Soviet Union.

During the abortive INF (Intermediate-Range Nuclear Forces) talks in 1983, Paul Nitze, the American negotiator, in discussing the relative advantages over aircraft of unmanned cruise missiles, noted that the latter "can sustain much higher rates of attrition" (because they are unpiloted). He added that they (the missiles) are "infinitely courageous," a characterization from which the Soviets took great offense because they considered his wry comment as a denigration of the bravery of Soviet pilots, which it was not.[m] Most Americans, because of typological sameness, would have understood Mr. Nitze's comment as one about the ironies of warfare, not as an aspersion on the bravery of Soviet pilots.

Because of these typological differences, the Soviets have tended to perceive the United States as overly concerned with data and details and not sufficiently concerned with "substance," as glib and superficial and unable to stick to the issue, as seeking to go beyond the limits of the issue at hand, as uncommitted to negotiating because of shifting positions in response to irrelevant detail, and as condescending. The Americans have tended to perceive the Soviets as concerned only with generalities and not committed to negotiating specific issues (for example, reductions in missiles), as slow and foot-dragging, as exploitive by using emotional issues to avoid the "real" issues, as stubborn and inflexible, as paranoidly suspicious.[24]

It is not suggested here that all issues between the United States and the Soviet Union are due to typological differences. But it is suggested that added onto the cultural and political differences between the two countries (as well as the complications of language) are the complex prob-

---

[24] These perceptions of the respective attitudes of the two superpowers toward one another have been gleaned from interviews with State Department, CIA, and military personnel, a number of whom were participants in SALT negotiations, official reports and press statements, and discussions with Soviet Government representatives as well as from *Deadly Gambits* by Strobe Talbott and "Living With the Soviets" by Paul H. Nitze, head of the U.S. delegation to the Intermediate-Range Nuclear Forces (INF) negotiations and presently special representative for arms control and disarmament negotiations, in *Foreign Affairs* 63,(2) (Winter 1984–85):360–374. This stereotype has shifted somewhat since the final negotiation and signing of the INF treaty in December 1987.

lems resulting from their being typological opposites. This fact, along with the mutual tendency of both parties to project their negative power shadow onto the other, causes misunderstandings of intentions and confounds the negotiating process between the two. One must wonder how the miscalculated Soviet assessment of the likely reaction of the United States to their invasion of Afghanistan was flawed because of typological differences that distorted their perception of anticipated American reaction.

Both sides need to train their policy and intelligence analysts as well as their negotiators to understand the psychological typology of both countries and the dynamics of how each is likely to misread and respond negatively to the other. Ideally, training would be jointly undertaken, and negotiating teams would be organized according to the individual typological makeup of members within a team and according to the makeup of members within the other team. Such organization would minimize the negative impact of typological differences and maximize agreement on real mutual objectives.

It is presently possible to identify, with extant testing instruments, the most problematical and efficacious typological combinations among United States policymakers and negotiators.[25] Doing this would enable American

---

[25] There are extant standardized psychological tests to determine individual typological makeup. One such test, the Myers-Briggs, is used extensively in the private sector and increasingly in government, but not extensively in the foreign policy, intelligence gathering, and military spheres. When it is used, it is primarily for administrative personnel purposes, not for the purposes outlined above.

A notable exception is the National Defense University at the National War College in Washington, D.C. Students (and often their families) at the university—usually professional military and foreign policy and intelligence personnel—are given the Myers-Briggs test as an enlightening exercise in psychological types. Although the university has identified (in the language of the test) the ISTJ (introverted, sensing, thinking, judging) and the ESTJ (extroverted, sensing, thinking, and judging) types as the best for dealing with the tensions and decision-making essential in preventing war, there is no indication that this "finding" has been carried over into any operational context in the selection of negotiators and commanders who will have ultimate decision-making for launching nuclear attack. (For example, under some conditions, American and Soviet submarine commanders may launch nuclear missiles if contact cannot be established with land-based command centers.) It is to be noted that the ESTJ and ISTJ typologies established by the Myers-Briggs test for most of the students at the National Defense University are opposite to those of the Soviets, who appear to be predominantly IFSJs (introverted, feeling, sensing, judging). (Emily Yoffe, "Study War No More," The *Washington Post Magazine*, November 4, 1984, pp. 17, 18, 21.)

agencies to pull together teams of negotiators and technocrats more highly suited to the task at hand and, equally important, to avoid typological combinations that would either slow the group's progress or augment shadow problems within the entire group.

Moreover, since, as suggested above, whole cultures tend to exhibit typological dominances, it would be possible as well to develop similar typological testing instruments that could be used effectively by the Soviets with their own policymakers and negotiators, so that the Soviet Union, too, could pull together typologically efficacious teams of negotiators and technocrats. It would then be possible to use such instruments in organizing American-Soviet negotiating teams. This would be particularly important for ad hoc and standing working groups composed of American and Soviet personnel (for example, those dealing with such issues as on-site inspection in conjunction with arms reduction talks or as the degree of compliance with terms of various treaties).

④ The Hero Dynamic

Another predominant archetypal dynamic in the conflict between the United States and the Soviet Union is that of the hero.[1]

The hero represents and carries forth the highest ideals of a culture—its aspirations, its pride, and its self-esteem. This dynamic is best depicted in hero myths such as those of Odysseus, Siegfried, Moses, Luke Skywalker, and Superman. Symbolically, the hero dynamic is constellated during periods of trial and stress. On him rests the hope for the future. He is an essential element of cohesion within any society, having the capacity to weld together the disparate elements within it during periods of national crises (General Douglas MacArthur comes to mind).

From a psychohistorical point of view, unlike any other civilized nation in the world, the United States was born at the hero level. Most other countries, particularly those of Europe, arrived at their herohood after many centuries of evolution from tribal societies, to small communities, to city-states and principalities, and ultimately to nationhood in the modern sense of the word. The United States, on the other hand, was essentially born a nation after a brief developmental period in the colonial era of less than two centuries. There was virtually no evolution as such; rather, the American experiment erupted and came into being over a period of twenty to thirty years.

The nature of the birth of the United States is crucial in understanding the role of the hero archetype in its national character and particularly in understanding its relationship to power. Revolutionary America was like an obstreperous adolescent, rebelling against a rigid and unreasonable patriarchal father: that is, King George III.

Psychologically speaking, a strong identification with its revolutionary and pioneering roots has left the United States stuck at the adolescent phase of the hero stage of development. Psychodynamically, the adolescent hero appropriately explores the nature of power, and particularly his own power, which he strives to develop to its fullest. Thus, there is a ten-

---

[1] Since I do not feel qualified to discuss the manifestation of that archetype from the Soviet perspective, it will be discussed only from the American standpoint.

dency to identify with power, and typically he identifies with the warrior. (This behavior can be seen on high school and college athletic fields—the modern-day jousting fields—almost any weekend.)

The warrior represents power, glory, pride, and the supremacy of force. Because the adolescent typically identifies with the warrior, he finds glory in sacrificing his life for the heroic cause. Thus, as a symbolic figure, the adolescent hero represents an *anti*-life force at the individual level. In most myths the warrior heroes ultimately die carrying out their heroic missions, as in the *Iliad*. At a collective level, the hero represents the defender and protector of life and culture. The adolescent hero tends to be swept up into causes and is highly ideological. It is not unusual in a myth or fairy tale to find a hero going off to a foreign land to defend the honor of an unknown king or princess about whom he has heard only five minutes before.

The mature hero, on the other hand, largely has come to terms with power, particularly its limits, and has seen over the horizon to the greater moral and ethical issues in life. He sees power as a means to an end and is not so taken with the "glory" of power—he is a statesman rather than a warrior.[2] The mature hero is committed to the life principle itself and therefore has a healthy mistrust of, as well as respect for, power. Above all, he is not identified with power.

For the adolescent hero, power *is* the objective of life. For the mature hero, power is the means to a higher and more moral end, rather than being an end in itself. Sometimes warrior power must be renounced directly by the mature hero in his quest for the higher goal.[3]

The late President Anwar Sadat of Egypt, in his dramatic flight to Jerusalem, is an excellent example of a warrior hero converted to a mature hero statesman. Sadat knew, of course, that first he had to fight the Yom Kippur War to establish his credentials as a warrior. Doing this enabled

---

[2]This may be why enormously popular Winston Churchill was turned out of office at the end of World War II—the public in Great Britain identified him with the warrior and, with the war nearly over, it may have felt another kind of statesman was needed in the postwar period.

[3]As I have used the term here, the "adolescent hero" may be any age (Lieutenant Colonel Oliver North comes to mind). It is emphasized that the terms *adolescent* and *mature* (hero) have no pejorative meaning in the context in which they are used. Both are legitimate and *essential* psychic energies. The question explored in this book is when each type of heroic energy is appropriate and functional and when it is counterproductive and hands us over to a destructive power complex.

him subsequently to turn and confront war as an illegitimate instrument of diplomacy in the Middle East. In so doing, he became a new symbol of moral consciousness as a national and world leader.

In the thermonuclear age, the archetype of the hero can be a dangerous psychic presence. The destructive force that can be unleashed by this dynamic is awesome. It is thus imperative to understand how this archetype is manifested in foreign policy and within the military establishment. The United States unquestionably has been *the* world power for the whole of the twentieth century. Americans are used to being "first" in most things and in taking American power for granted in the international arena. Until the advent of the thermonuclear age and the nuclear ballistics missile, no nation and no society carried the potential for challenging the American position as the world's most powerful nation. The Soviet Union is (and probably China will be in the twenty-first century) the only country that can pose a relevant challenge to American supremacy on the world scene. Consequently, along with the United States' collective identification with the warrior hero, it has been exceedingly difficult to bring about the needed transformation of American society and politics sought by former President Carter—a society operating as much out of its ideological and moral roots as on the basis of its economic and military power. The question that poses itself, then, is: Will America be psychologically disposed to letting the Soviet Union catch up domestically and as a world economic and political power? On this question alone could hinge the fate of the world, since it is unlikely that the Soviet Union will voluntarily accept a perpetual status of "second-rate superpower." If the answer to that question is no, the INF Treaty notwithstanding, the ensuing confrontation will inevitably lead to continued nuclear arms competition and large conventional-force capability as manifestations of the vying for power by the two countries.

Indeed, the Reagan administration seemed, prior to the succession of General Secretary Gorbachev as leader of the Soviet Union, intent on bringing the Soviet Union to its knees domestically and economically (but not militarily). This was most dramatically indicated by Mr. Reagan's 1982 speech before Parliament in London and his 1983 "evil empire" speech. Mr. Reagan's allegiance to SDI technology was as much a commitment to defeat the Soviet Union economically as it was a belief in an ultimate defense against a Soviet first strike against the United States. As recently as July 26, 1985, former Defense Secretary Weinberger called on conservative politicians worldwide to assist in "spotlighting the inherent evil" of Communism and the "philosophical and moral superiority" of the United States over the Soviet Union.

The point is not to discover philosophical "truth," since the latter is subjective relative to the philosophical standpoint of the observer. Rather it is one of *emphasis*. The two adversaries may believe what they wish about each other. But if the inherent "evil" of the one and the "moral superiority" of the other is what is emphasized in the relationship, then the net result will be splitting,[4] massive shadow projection, psychic self-inflation, heightened paranoia, and the inherent complications ensuing from such dangerous psychological states of being. On the other hand, if what is emphasized in the relationship is that which is necessary to live with a repugnant adversary and to actively contain tension and its symptom, nuclear arms competition, then the world will have been pulled back from the brink of nuclear holocaust—and perhaps economic ruination as well.

What is called for now is the highest form of the hero—one who will use warrior power with wisdom but who will also, like Sadat, contain power and take responsibility for channeling its use. He will turn and face power rather than be possessed by it. He will not serve it (which happens when one becomes identified with power), but will learn to channel it. This awareness comes from the realization that power *cannot* be mastered—ever—it can only be channeled and contained, at best. This is the issue that nuclear weaponry brings to man in the thermonuclear age. Survival depends on our recognition of this issue.

Former President Reagan's decision, in the face of vociferous protests from his most loyal conservative political constituency, to commit to the INF treaty eliminating intermediate-range nuclear missiles, reflects some element of this quality. It is not insignificant that Mr. Reagan, who talked publicly and privately of bringing the Soviet Union to its knees economically and diplomatically, took the more morally responsible position of rejecting further escalation of the arms competition and of demonstrating that it is possible not only to limit arms development, but to eliminate them as well. It is not known to what extent his hard-line, saber-rattling policies during the first six years of his administration were responsible for facilitating the accession to power of General Secretary Gorbachev or for bringing the Soviets around to a more rational stance on Intermediate-Range Nuclear (INF) Forces, but surely they played some, perhaps a highly significant, role.

---

[4] *Splitting* is a clinical term referring to the tendency to split people and ideas into parts, only part of which is related to by the ego. This can lead to seeing an individual (or nation) in categorical terms, that is, as good *or* bad, but being unable to see both positive and negative qualities in the same person or situation.

To what extent Mr. Reagan had the vision of the mature hero whom I described above, or was a less aware instrument of an archetypal dynamic prevalent at this point in history, is questionable. Certainly, Mr. Reagan's own words did not betray such vision. To the degree that the latter is true, we have been witness to the paradoxical way in which the hero archetype often chooses "unlikely" characters as agents for bringing about major shifts in psychoevolutionary direction.[5]

The mythological figure who best exemplifies this mature heroic quality is Athena. She is a warrior goddess, but also a goddess of the arts and of peace; she is the goddess of prudent intelligence, the goddess of wisdom. But most important, she uses her warrior power to settle disputes, unlike her brother Ares (Mars), who gets pleasure from making them; she also uses her power to uphold the law by nonviolent means, unlike her brother. What is important, she has the power to defeat Ares, the god of war—that is, she has the power to defeat him on the battlefield, not to destroy him. Thus she represents the potential for containing and channeling the wild and destructive instincts of the god of war. (In one encounter in the Trojan War, when she knocks him to the ground on the plains of Ilium, she says to Ares, as she looks down at him with contempt, "Vain fool! Hast thou not yet learned how superior my strength is to thine?" This theme will be amplified in Chapters 6 and 9.)[6]

It is relevant in the modern context that Mars (Ares) and Athena are brother and sister. It is as if we have been living out primarily the Mars

[5]Another obvious example was Richard Nixon, the archetypal anti-Communist and accuser of those who "lost China," as the president who opened the door to normalized relations with the People's Republic of China.

Moses himself, in Exodus, pointed out to God his many shortcomings and unsuitability (for example, his stuttering) as the heroic leader of Old Testament Jews. God, notably, was unimpressed—and apparently chose the right man for the job.

[6]Christine Downing, in *The Goddess,* says of her that "her martial aspect relates to her civilizing function. It derives from her original commitment to the royal citadel and then to the polis and, consequently, to their defense. Athene Promachus is a protectress, the helper in battle, the instructor in the art of war, not a battle-lusty aggressor [like her brother]. A beautiful relief of her leaning on her spear, her head drooping, pervaded with sorrow, introduces us to a very different Athene: the warrior goddess herself touched by defeat and loss. Farnell believes she is mourning some terrible national disaster and the deaths of all those who were killed" (p. 120).

She also points out that "Athene gives courage and confirmation, the sudden bright idea or the seasoned reflection. She does not actively take command over the men whom she supports but brings them into touch with their own highest potentiality. Thus, in the *Iliad,* when Achilles rashly moves forward to attack

aspect of the Mars-Athena archetype. The stressful transition from the Mars to the Athena dynamic in Western civilization's psychoevolutionary development is a very recent phenomenon, beginning with the advent of thermonuclear weaponry and the ballistics missile. One can view the conflict between the Soviet Union and the United States as a metaphor for that transitional process.

The Vietnam War was the turning point for the United States in its psychoevolutionary struggle to move beyond its identification with the adolescent level of the hero archetype.[7] Because the Vietnam War was the only war the United States has lost, it was the nation's first painful and humiliating experience of the humbling of its warrior ethos. The United States began to learn that its power is not unlimited and was forced to begin to move away from its identification with the warrior hero. The United States can no longer presume military superiority, as it has since the turn of the century. It must now question its use of power, assess its limits, and exercise its military might prudently.[8] Iran has demonstrated how the American hero can be humbled. Smaller nations, such as Kuwait

---

Agamemnon, Athene (visible only to him) holds him back and gives him that moment in which he can recall himself (p. 106). Christine Downing, *The Goddess* (New York: Crossroad, 1981).

Regarding the latter, in the thermonuclear age when miscalculation can launch an intercontinental missile unleashing nuclear holocaust in thirty minutes, the quality to contain hotheads and Martial passion is of no small consequence.

Graves observes: "Although a goddess of war, she gets no pleasure from battle, as Ares and Eris do, but rather from settling disputes, and upholding the law by pacific means. She bears no arms in time of peace. . . . Her mercy is great: when the judges' votes are equal in a criminal trial at the Areiopagus, she always gives a casting vote to liberate the accused. Yet, once engaged in battle, she never loses the day, even against Ares himself, being better grounded in tactics and strategy than he." Robert Graves, *The Greek Myths*. (Baltimore: Penguin, 1974), vol. 1, p. 96.

[7] It is reported that the *average* age of the men who fought in that war was nineteen! It was *truly* a war fought by the adolescent hero. (This average age was obtained from the Vietnam Veterans in Congress [VVIC] in the office of Congressman Thomas Daschle, South Dakota, and is supported by Gloria Emerson, *Winners and Losers* [New York: Random House, 1976]. Notwithstanding innumerable attempts to corroborate this average age with the U.S. Army and the Pentagon, no specific age could be obtained from those sources.)

[8] This point was dramatically put forth in a speech to the National Press Club on November 28, 1984, by then Secretary of Defense Caspar Weinberger, in which he listed six conditions that must be met before committing the United States to military action. One of these was determining with a high degree of certainty *before* undertaking any military adventure that American forces could prevail mili-

and Panama, have demonstrated considerable sophistication in manipulating the power of the American colossus.[9] In the modern era, heroic power simply doesn't work as it used to.

The United States is in the midst of a powerful psychoevolutionary struggle. There is an observable tendency to evolve into the "mature" Athenian hero, while at the same time, there is a powerful counterpull, due to psychic inertia, that keeps the United States identified with the warrior hero. The struggle between these two poles of the hero archetype manifested itself pointedly in the presidencies of Jimmy Carter and Ronald Reagan.[10]

In his inaugural address in 1977, Jimmy Carter spoke of "moral duties" and "moral strength" and of "humility." He spoke about power, as "a quiet strength based not merely on the size of an arsenal, but on the nobility of ideas." He also addressed the need to recognize the limits of our power when he said, "We can neither answer all questions nor solve all problems."

Jimmy Carter preached to, and alienated, a large portion of the nation. Ronald Reagan, on the other hand, spoke in his first inaugural address, in 1981, of not limiting the nation to "small dreams." He said very directly, "We have every right to dream heroic dreams." It was as if his inaugural address were a direct rebuttal to Carter's. Reagan also spoke of the "monu-

---

tarily. Historically, the United States was able to presume that its forces ultimately would prevail, no matter the task.

Further, the Reagan administration relearned this painful lesson in stationing American marines in Beirut and the subsequent humiliating withdrawal of U.S. forces and embassy personnel from Lebanon in February 1984.

[9]When first approached by Kuwait to reflag its tankers, the United States was cautious and hesitant. The minute Kuwait approached the Soviet Union to reflag its tankers—making sure, of course, that the United States knew it was doing so—the latter rushed in to take the bait. This vignette reflected underlying American insecurity regarding its previous unchallenged status as preeminent superpower. Through the end of 1987, there were no Kuwaiti tankers operating under the Soviet flag.

[10]We can also see the struggle between these two poles of the hero archetype by the number of democratic and repressive regimes in the world (those ruled by military men or those whose governing oligarchy remains in power as a result of military authority as opposed to some form of democratic consensus by the governed). The volatility of this struggle is seen within nations such as Argentina, Brazil, and the Philippines. It is noteworthy that the trend since 1980 seems to have been more toward the democratic Athena pole than toward the more authoritarian Mars pole.

ments to heroism" in Arlington Cemetery.[11] He was clearly identified with the warrior hero.

Reagan also spoke to the hero in the American psyche and reactivated it. Carter said in his inaugural address: "Your strength can compensate for my weakness, and your wisdom can help to minimize my mistakes." Although he correctly embraced the *ideas* associated with the Athena hero, he denied the hero in himself and the powerful heroic energy in this country as a whole. It would appear that his lack of personal heroic quality, more than Iran, inflation, or any other single foreign or domestic issue, cost Jimmy Carter the 1980 election. On the other hand, Ronald Reagan's general symbolic identification with the hero archetype, the Martial warrior hero in particular, contributed greatly to his election in 1980 (but not necessarily his reelection in 1984).

It appears that Jimmy Carter, notwithstanding his startling long-shot win of the U.S. presidency, did not adequately understand the formal dynamics, limits, and requirements of the power structure of U.S. government as a whole and the presidency in particular—a fatal limitation to which he fell victim. Power has its own rules, which must be taken into account. Those who plan to change the rules must understand them very well in order to know which rules are changeable, which are not, and, above all else, what must be offered up as a substitute. (If one dams a river without providing another channel for the flow of the water, there is likely to be much destruction and grief, not to mention the firing of the builder of the dam!)

Carter used power without sufficiently respecting it. (Mars can be put

---

[11] Reagan went on to quote from the diary of a World War I soldier killed in that war. The quotation from the diary reads in part: "My Pledge: America must win this war. Therefore I will work, I will save, I will sacrifice, I will endure, I will fight cheerfully and do my utmost, as if the issues of the whole struggle depended on me alone." This is an extraordinary statement to be included in the inaugural address of a president during peacetime and exemplifies this country's tendency, as symbolized by the election of Mr. Reagan, to identify with the warrior hero.

Another symbolic example of the overidentification with the warrior hero by American culture, and the Reagan administration in particular, is the fact that a total of 8,612 combat medals, badges, and/or decorations were issued in the wake of the Granada invasion (information provided by the Office of the Secretary of Defense). The largest number of U. S. forces present on Grenada at any one time during the intervention was approximately 6,500 (statement by Admiral Wesley L. McDonald, Commander in Chief, U. S. Atlantic Command, given before the House Armed Services Committee, January 24, 1984).

in his place by his morally superior and powerful sister, Athena, but he cannot be dismissed!) His Christian moralism pitted him against the very power he sought to wield. A cardinal rule for bringing about change in power relationships is a recognition that power as a force, like other forms of energy, has its own intrinsic properties, which, in the last analysis, make it ultimately a stronger force than any person(s) wielding it.

Carter did understand the problem of how power corrupts and erodes the very democratic ideals that symbolize the greatness of the United States. However, of the three essential qualities for being a change agent of power—a high degree of personal consciousness and maturity, humility with strength, and an appreciation for the autonomous (archetypal) nature of power—Carter lacked the last two.

At the same time, the principles of moral courage and the need to recognize the limits of power of which Jimmy Carter spoke in his inaugural address, *are* the crucial issues of our time, and limiting and channeling Martial power is the specific issue upon which hinges the survival of humanity. Looking at Carter's presidency in concert with Reagan's first term suggests that the journey toward the age of the mature hero must be led by someone who embodies wisdom and moral incorruptibility, as well as heroic qualities. One only hopes that the tension between these two poles of the hero archetype will produce a transcendent political leader.

In assessing these factors regarding recent world leaders, it would appear that Nixon lacked humility and incorruptibility; Carter lacked warrior power and overemphasized humility; Sadat lacked incorruptibility, and Reagan appears to have lacked incorruptibility and wisdom. Although it is yet too early to tell, it would appear that General Secretary Gorbachev may have all of the requisite qualities for bringing the Soviet Union and, to some degree, the United States as well, into a new age of power politics.

If one studies the *unlikeliness* along with the specific circumstances that resulted in their becoming presidents of the United States, along with the ironic role each played as president, one gets the impression that all United States presidents (including Ronald Reagan) since John F. Kennedy have had the hand of destiny very much involved in determining their personal role in the evolution of national and world destiny.[12] With the

---

[12] Obvious examples are Richard Nixon, the arch enemy of the "China lobby," and archfoe of Communism, stating that he considered his greatest accomplishment as president that of establishing diplomatic relations with the People's Republic of China. Ronald Reagan, the protector of the free world from the "evil empire" and the generator of the largest arms buildup in world history, as the

exception of Mr. Gorbachev, the American presidents since Johnson could be viewed in this specific regard as reluctant heroes relative to the conscious roles that they have played in history.[13] Each ended up as a major change agent in a manner opposite to his consciously claimed philosophical and political positions. In the case of Mr. Gorbachev, he appears to be a very conscious and enthusiastic modern-day Promethean light-bringer to a dark and, in many ways, primitive culture and its people. It is Soviet Communism, with its repressive bureaucratic system, and the Russian culture and people themselves that have been "reluctant" to enter a new age of political and moral enlightenment.

With regard to such enlightenment, as it concerns presidents and other leaders, it is the level of personal consciousness and maturity, coupled with a deep understanding of, appreciation of, and respect for power, when and how to use it, and the real limitations of the human ego to control fully or to constrain the power drive, as described above, that distinguishes a wise leader (Sadat) from a weak one (for example, Jimmy Carter), or one caught in the grips of a power complex (for example, Lyndon Johnson). It is also the distinguishing factor between a leader who is more an unconscious instrument through which the archetype of power works its will (Ronald Reagan), and one who plays a consciously decisive role in constructively altering the nature of man's relationship to power (a person as yet not apparent on the American political scene).

The Reagan administration, in its first term, set about a number of specific policies to address the post-Vietnam crisis of confidence in the wake of the Vietnam loss and the Iranian revolution and hostage crisis that took place under the Carter administration. These policies focused on reversing the dangerous impression that the United States would not use its military power to back up its national security (Grenada being one specific example); it took the next step (after the general amnesty of the Carter

---

signer of the first arms accord to abolish a class of weapons and as defender of the Gorbachev administration against the conservative wing of his own party. And Mikhail Gorbachev, a loyal Communist on the one hand and, on the other, a change agent for a recalcitrant Soviet Communism, bringing capitalistic practices into the Soviet economy and democratic reforms to its system of government.

[13] Joseph Campbell points out that "refusal" to accept the call to play a conscious role as a change agent in human history is a telling and universal characteristic of a heroic figure chosen by destiny to play such a role. (Joseph, Campbell, *Hero with a Thousand Faces*. [Princeton: Princeton University Press, 1973], pp. 59–68.) Moses' reluctance to accept his call from God in Exodus is so emphatic as to be amusing. It results in a running argument with God consuming several pages of the Bible!

administration) in ending the scapegoating of our Vietnam veterans by honoring and interring a Vietnam-era soldier in the Tomb of the Unknown Soldier at Arlington Cemetery, thereby symbolically healing the sense of national shame over that war; it demonstrated that the Soviet strategy of splitting the United States from its European allies would not work and that the United States must be dealt with directly on the issue of arms control, and it began to define in specific terms the conditions under which American military power will and will not be used.

Other administrations have drawn specific lines for using U.S. military might when those lines have been crossed. However, the ongoing controversy (*prior* to the commitment of forces on a significant scale) over the limits and use of military power in the Middle East and Central America, begun under the Reagan administration, served to raise overall consciousness and bring about an unprecedented level of dialogue on this issue. Unfortunately, much of the redefinition of the use of power by the Reagan administration was by default, as its policies backed by military might in the Middle East and Latin American failed, and was not the result of a conscious realization that America's relationship to its own power drive and its use of power needed fundamental redefinition. The Carter administration attempted the latter but failed.

A process of refining the limits of and the conditions under which U.S. power will and will not be used brings the U.S. to the threshold of its negative power shadow. It remains to be seen to what extent the latter can be raised to consciousness and reflected in U.S. foreign policy as well as strategic military planning.

One way of looking at the Reagan administration is that its role was to heighten tensions between the United States and the Soviet Union to the level where the dynamic of forced cooperation would have to come into play.[14] No other American administration has had a policy of a winnable nuclear war as did the Reagan administration up until 1983. Psychologically, it may have been necessary to think the "unthinkable," and even to formulate it into formal policy, to realize in feeling terms the horror and insanity of such a policy.

The Reagan administration, in the first term, appeared to have laid the foundation for "turning and facing" the power issue. It demonstrated America's willingness to be the warrior, when necessary, to protect its national interests. It also compensated for the post-Vietnam national crisis of confidence. Reagan's second term provided him with an unprecedented

[14] See Chapter 7.

opportunity to exchange the Martial warrior robes for those of the mature hero statesman. This opportunity was not unlike that fulfilled by Richard Nixon in his historic trip to China or Anwar Sadat in his flight to Jerusalem. Of course, with regard to superpower conflict, Mr. Reagan, as the leader of one protagonist nation, was one half of the equation.

The world has long been used to frumpy, aging, and unpolished leaders of the Soviet Union. The general attitude toward the Soviet Union was that it was a generally backward, still semifeudal nation, with a nuclear capability that gave it definite, but illegitimate, status as a superpower. It has been viewed as pathologically paranoid, powerfully resistant to change, politically stultified, and fundamentally dishonest in its dealings in the international community.

Thus, the advent of a progressive, wise, aggressive, youthful, intelligent, counterparanoiac, dynamic leader of the Soviet Union has taken the world, the United States in particular, by surprise.[15] It would be a major, potentially fatal, mistake to view Mr. Gorbachev merely as an aggressive political aberration within Soviet Russia. It is critical to recognize that the advent of a new *type* of leader within the Soviet system reflects the fact that something new is trying to emerge from within the national psyche of the Soviet Union.

Taken at face value, Mr. Gorbachev seems to fit the profile of the mature hero outlined above. Time will tell the extent to which Mr. Gorbachev does fit that profile, his capacity to survive in a system that will develop increasingly higher levels of political antibodies to the new and revolutionary political phenomenon it has spawned, and, most important, the degree to which the United States can support and not sabotage the syntonic components of the political revolution endeavoring to take place in the Soviet Union.

On the other hand, Ronald Reagan not only symbolized the hero archetype in the American psyche; he was literally its spokesman. As alluded to earlier, the language of archetypal energy is symbols, usually in the form of fairy tales and myth.[a] In the Western psyche, the archsymbol of the romantic hero for centuries has been the dragonslayer. In his farewell remarks to Mr. Gorbachev before departing from Moscow on June 2, 1988,

---

[15] During the first year of Mr. Gorbachev's tenure, a senior Soviet analyst in the U.S. intelligence community noted for his objectivity and openness with regard to the Soviet Union spoke of his astonishment at the progressiveness and comprehensiveness of Mr. Gorbachev's policy proposals and the speed with which he has moved to put them into place.

Reagan said: "I would like to think that our efforts during these past few days have slayed a few dragons and advanced the struggle against the evils that threaten mankind, threats to peace and to liberty."[b]

It would appear that Ronald Reagan had an archetypal mission for the United States as well as a political one. Regarding the former, his role may have been that of enacting a "last hurrah" for an archetypal dynamic that has served its purpose well in the evolution of the United States as a world power and defender of democratic principles. In this regard, it is not insignificant that he, as the oldest man to hold the office of president, was often referred to and symbolized as a cowboy during his first administration. If Reagan indeed symbolized the passing of an archetypal dynamic from predominance in the American psyche, then the question is posed as to what will replace it.

Whether the United States can be forthcoming with a transcendent leader who embodies the qualities of the mature hero remains an open question. Such a president will have to be capable of leading the nation with pride toward a new kind of power stance in the world community. He (she) will have to carry the ability to symbolize the heroic in the American national psyche without having to literalize it in the manner of Reagan. Unlike American presidents in recent history, he or she will have to be capable of educating, persuading, and "bringing along" his or her electoral constituency in the model of a Lincoln, rather than just serving a popular ethos for the sake of political expediency and being beholden to it.[16]

This president will have to be capable of seizing the opportunity to work with Mr. Gorbachev not only to bring about peace in old terms, but to usher in a new age of global politics with moral consciousness as an equal if not higher force, along with military and economic might. A related and critical question is the extent to which the years of the cold war, anti-Communist sentiment and rhetoric have so conditioned the American electorate against the Soviet Union that such a leader *could* get elected at this time in the American political system. Ironically, the ascendancy of Mr. Gorbachev has tended to lessen American fears of the "Russian menace," making such a possibility more plausible. A transcendent leader will have to be capable of leading the country out of its own

---

[16] Lincoln, in my view, is the quintessential example of an American hero figure who embodied the essential balance of warrior power at ready use coupled with an appreciation for the limitations of military power and the necessity of developing the art of moral consciousness as a higher political power. His assassination cut short his pursuit of the latter.

paranoid position—however justified it may have been, based on past Soviet behavior—to grasp and build upon the archetypal dynamics that are vectored at building a new global order based on peace. In 1988, George Bush, the vice president and Republican nominee, reinforced that paranoid position during the election campaign with repeated warnings of the continued Soviet menace.[c]

Archetypal forces pressing for the emergence of just such a leader on the American scene may have been at play in the 1988 election. To the extent that such a transcendent leader will emerge on the American scene before the turn of the century, he or she is likely to have the following characteristics. He would be either someone seemingly born to the role (a Roosevelt or Kennedy) or a relative unknown on the national scene prior to ascending to power. In the latter case, he would present an unimpressive persona, including probably not a large stature, and his leadership qualities in terms of changing the nation and the world's relationship to power would emerge suddenly and quickly and would appear to come without personal philosophical and behavioral antecedents. Or he would be someone seemingly lacking the qualities for such a role but who, upon assumption of the presidency, was profoundly impacted and transformed by the office itself. It is *unlikely* to be someone elected because he/she espouses such a policy.

The point that is being made here is that the impetus for fundamental change in the relationship between politics and power could come from an impersonal source, not a conscious ego with a specific plan. Ronald Reagan played a historic role in banishing a class of weapons for the first time in human history and in forging a new more positive relationship with a nation he had dubbed "the evil empire" not four years before— roles he neither desired nor sought, nor imagined for himself. The question poses itself as to whether the greater impetus for those specific roles that he played as president came more from his conscious ego or from collective (archetypal) psychological forces that moved him.

⑤ Power

In all that has been explored so far and in all that will follow this chapter, the archetype of power is an ever-present backdrop. As will be explored below, man's view of power has been profoundly affected by the thermonuclear age. Robert Oppenheimer expressed it poignantly in his spontaneous reaction to the first atomic explosion at Alamogordo, New Mexico, in July 1945. Quoting from the Bhagavad Gita, he said, "I am become death, the destroyer of worlds."[a]

The thermonuclear age has taught us that the power of the gods is awesomely frightful in the hands of man and that it must not be used. What we have not learned so well and are just beginning to come to grips with is the autonomous nature of power itself. This is a crucial factor. For if power does have its own intrinsic properties, which are subject to human control *only* to a limited degree, then to the degree to which we are unaware of those "immutable" properties, they can manipulate human behavior toward the very opposite ends sought by the human ego. Nuclear-deterrence arsenals are the best case in point.

The word *power* (as energy) is ultimately derived from the Latin *posse*, "to be able."[b] In psychic terms, I would define power as the impetus that produces the cycle of life-giving and life-destroying tension essential for the evolution and perpetuation of life, one that splits unity into opposites and that strives for the union of opposites.[1] The unabridged edition of the *Random House Dictionary of the English Language* defines *impetus* as "moving force; impulse" (p. 715), "an impelling action or force, driving onward or inducing motion" (p. 717). That "impetus" in inherent in the

---

[1] This definition specifically acknowledges the inherent paradox that the evolution and perpetuation of life are dependent on the atrophy and destruction of life forms.

Jung puts it that "every process is a phenomenon of energy, and that all energy can proceed only from the tension of opposites." Also, "Life is born only of the spark of the opposites." The *Collected Works*, vol. 7, pp. 29, 54.

Also, "Life, being an energic process, needs the opposites, for without opposition there is, as we know, no energy." The *Collected Works*, vol. 11, p. 197.

physics of life itself.[2] Given these definitions, it would be easy to slip into defining power as synonymous with "instinct." However, they are not the same.

We might distinguish the two by saying that instinct (or instinctual energy such as hunger and sex) is the form through which a great deal of power is made manifest. Power represents the means and the valence by which the instincts are carried.

It is important to recognize power as transpersonal force for change in its own right—a force that existed before Man. As a force carried by the species *Homo sapiens*, it existed before civilization, man's ego, his will, and his will to power. Without such a recognition, we tend to fall victim to seeing power only in terms of the "power complex." The latter refers to the condition where power is appropriated by the human ego for its own sake, to enhance the ego at all costs and to subject to ego control the instinctual forces of life.[3] Power manifested as instinctual transpersonal force recognizes that instincts themselves have force and direction[4] of their own, independent of man's ego.[5] Therefore the ego can be *somewhat*

---

[2] Fritjof Capra points out, "According to quantum theory, matter is . . . never quiescent, but always in a state of motion. Macroscopically, the material objects around us may seem passive and inert but when we magnify such a 'dead' piece of stone or metal, we see that it is full of activity. The closer we look at it, the more alive it appears. . . .

"Modern physics, then, pictures matter not at all as passive and inert, but as being in a continuous dancing and vibrating motion whose rhythmic patterns are determined by the molecular, atomic and nuclear [and, I would say, "psychic"] structures. . . ." (Fritjof Capra, *The Tao of Physics* [Berkeley: Shambhala 1975], pp. 193–194).

[3] The outcome, however, is usually the opposite: the individual is strongly influenced, if not taken over, by powerful instinctual drives to his own destruction, individually and collectively.

[4] The source of the directed goal or end point of instinct is not known and is better left to metaphysical and religious exploration. But that there is some kind of defining source is indisputable. If we speak of the "laws of nature," of "physical laws," of "evolution," we speak of an ordering principle (including the recent focus in physics on "chaos"). The sciences of biology, physiology, ethology, medicine, and psychology, among others, have amply demonstrated instinctual imprinting and its goal-directed nature.

[5] As Esther M. Harding put it: "In the early beginnings of the life of the race . . . the forces of instinct alone dominated the scene. But at some time there arose another power setting bounds upon the untrammeled desirousness of instinct, and this power is found to be at work in some measure at least, in all people, even the most primitive. This power we call will. Its energy is recruited

successful in bringing the instincts under control. When the limits to which power can be controlled are exceeded through ignorance and hubris, the instincts can "rebel" with cataclysmic results. Indeed, the instinctual components of power can overrule man's ego and place it in service toward its own ends.[6]

This distinction is important, because a view of power from only the standpoint of the power complex leads to a unidimensional, rationalist concept of power. Recognizing power as a transpersonal instinctual force that can be appropriated by the ego *to a limited degree,* acknowledges that power is involved at an instinctual (pre-ego) level in the life-generating or -generation, destruction-generating process that is the basis for the generation and evolution of all life forms. The one is a tautological circular argument, beginning and ending with man's ego. The other acknowledges the fact of purposive instincts—that is, goal-directed drives, the source of which is unknown.[c]

In *The Parable of the Tribes,* Andrew Bard Schmookler falls into this trap. He posits that "[power] is a sudden new phenomenon in the living systems of the earth" (p. 238). His theory is overly mental and reduces power to the "will," which, as he uses it, particularly in exercising "choice," reduces all power to an ego level. (Where was power prior to a developed ego—a psychic development less than thirty thousand years old? Did none exist? When we lean against an oak tree and feel its intrinsic power, are we just projecting onto the oak tree or is there something intrinsically powerful in the tree itself?)[7]

---

from the instincts which arose *pari passu,* as the instincts were tamed." She goes on to add, "Thus the emergence of the ego from the unconscious brings with it a new problem, the problem of the will to power" (Esther M. Harding, *Psychic Energy: Its Source and Goal* [Washington, D.C.: Bollingen Foundation/Pantheon 1947], pp. 192, 211).

[6]This has been an unstated, semiconscious psychological focal point of the nuclear arms and deterrence debate of the past ten to fifteen years. The proliferation of nuclear missiles along with uncontainable technological "advances" such as "launch-on-warning" capability, where computers would launch nuclear missiles without direct human action, have forced governments and men to question seriously whether the human ego could adequately control war technology or whether humans had to be protected from it. The answer, of course, is both.

[7]American Indians (and other primitive groups) know of the intrinsic power of the nonhuman world, and most tribes have words in their languages that recognize the intrinsic power in life, including inorganic matter.

In an enlightening essay distinguishing the difference between "power" and "force" in the context of military power, Edward N. Luttwak, a highly influential consultant on military and deterrence strategy during most of the Reagan admin-

Indeed, power as a force in human behavior goes back to instinct and the interface between the biological and the unconscious directing (rather than directed) drive for life between the animal and human, and indeed, the inorganic and organic drive for life. Jung states, "Instinct is a very mysterious manifestation of life, partly psychic and partly physiological by nature."[d] Although instinct and power are not the same thing, neither are they separable.

At the same time, there is no question that power negatively in service to man's ego is one of the most destructive forces in today's world. Schmookler's penetrating analysis of the dynamics of how power (that is, the power complex) corrupts and the implications for modern civilization is enlightening and opens up new avenues for exploration.

The point is that, psychologically, a major outcome of the nuclear age is that it has forced man to recognize that power is not something that begins with his ego and is completely subject to his will. This realization has profound implications for how we look at ourselves and how we perceive the nature of war and conflict.

This concept of what might be called two-track power—power as a directed force in service to man's ego, and power as unconscious instinct invisible in the background working to subvert the ego toward its own independent goals (positive as well as negative)—is in evidence in the hero dynamic explored in the preceding chapter, and will be explored further in Chapter 6.

---

istration, discusses power (and "force," which he distinguishes from power) as if it begins and ends with the human ego (Edward N. Luttwak, *The Grand Strategy of the Roman Empire from the First Century A.D. to the Third,* appendix: "Power and Force: Definitions and Implications. [Baltimore and London: Johns Hopkins University Press, 1976], pp. 195–200).

⑥ War

War is the father of all things.
—Heraclitus

WAR AS ARCHETYPAL ENERGY

War has always been with us. As Maurice R. Davie put it in *The Evolution of War*, "War . . . is universal. It has affected every part of the earth's surface where men have come into contact or collision." Indeed, it is so prevalent in man's nature that from 1496 B.C. to A.D. 1861, a period of 3,357 years, there were 227 years of peace and 3,130 years of war. That is thirteen years of war for every year of peace. From 1500 B.C. to A.D. 1860, more than eight thousand treaties of peace were concluded, all of them meant to last forever. The average time they remained in force is two years.[a]

As of 1985, the twentieth century has already experienced 207 wars, with an estimated 78,000,000 lives lost, more than five times as many war deaths as in the nineteenth century. Two-thirds of the world's countries, representing 97 percent of the world's population, have participated in at least one war since 1900.[b]

More recently, from 1980 to 1983, six new wars started, while only two ended. Many ongoing conflicts escalated dramatically. In 1983 there were approximately 40 major and minor conflicts in the world, involving 45 nations. Over 4,000,000 soldiers were directly engaged in combat. Estimates of the total loss of lives during this period ran from more than 1,000,000 up to 5,000,000. The Iran-Iraq war alone, conservatively, resulted in an estimated 1,000,000 casualties. In 1981 the 45 nations involved in those wars spent over $528 billion on their armed forces.[c]

These figures are staggering—to the extent that the mind can image them.[1] One could amass reams of statistics and documentation to support

---

[1] However, Robert Bigelow in *The Dawn Warriors* (London: Hutchinson, 1969) points out that ancient warfare was more "personal," being fought not for ideological reasons, but for the literal survival of the group itself. Wars took place between neighboring groups within a small radius, in one's backyard, so to speak, as op-

the fact that war is universal and fundamental in man's nature throughout his existence.[d] Indeed, war has been essential to life and an integral part of the evolution of civilization.[2] Yet we continue to behave as if war were an aberrant condition of man and of nations. The fact that we genuinely abhor war does not mitigate against our fascination with it or the fact that it is a natural characteristic of postagricultural, deritualized man. Indeed, it is remarkable to what lengths we will go to deny one of the most prevalent and stable facts of man's condition.

It would behoove us to accept and take responsibility for war's role in our collective character and psychology, despite the repugnance of such an idea to our Judeo-Christian self-image. To do so would focus our attention where it needs to be: that is, on man's inherent nature and his psychology as well as on the collective psychic forces that impel us to war.[3] Otherwise we will continue to see the problem of the threat of nuclear annihilation as only external to our collective psychology and will continue to focus primarily on technological and diplomatic solutions to the exclusion of the psychological factors that often have greater power in governing our behavior as individuals and as nations.[4]

---

posed to distant places miles away or across oceans. Battles five thousand years ago were on a smaller scale but more frequent and "personal," usually involving the entire community—men, women, and children. Per capita casualties may have been higher in prehistoric times.

[2]The role of war in man's history and in the evolution of civilization is reflected in the work of Froebinius, Davie, Bigelow, Stevens, Whitmont, and others.

[3]Jung pointed out, "Instincts are typical modes of action, and wherever we meet with uniform and regularly recurring modes of action [such as in the persistence of war], we are dealing with instinct, no matter whether it is associated with a conscious motive or not" (Collected Works, vol. 8, p. 135, the original in italics).

[4]Bigelow (The Dawn Warriors) makes a plausible case for the existence of warfare more than a million years ago. The essence of his thesis is that "the ability to learn cooperation was actually favored by the selective force of warfare. The highest human qualities were demanded by the 'lowest' human qualities, with such force and constancy that the size of the [human] brain trebled very rapidly [over 2–3 million years]. Cooperation [for warfare] requires communication. Communication is achieved through signs and symbols, and symbolic thought is required for higher mathematics." Thus, warfare, through its requirement of intragroup and later intergroup cooperation, and the symbolic language necessary for communication, resulted in a vastly expanded brain capacity.

He takes to task those who put forth the popular view, held by many anthropologists, that warfare is a relatively recent advent in the evolution of man, and that warfare began in the cities of Sumer only a few thousand years ago. He cites a find by Kathleen Kenyon of a settlement at Jericho wherein the charred remains of a walled city were radiocarbon-dated to 6800 B.C., offering objective evidence

Notwithstanding the horrors and ravages of war, war has been an inextricable instrument in the advancement of civilization. It has been a primary means for bringing about acculturation, new forms of government, new kinds of art, agriculture, economic growth and diversification, new inventions, industrialization, and advances in medicine. It has imposed the rule of law over the rule of indiscriminate fighting and, with it, the development of mores and moral codes, including codes of conduct between nations, as well as codes governing the nature of warfare itself. With the practice of taking slaves, war began to place value on the individual human life. It imposed abstract religion in lieu of religious practices involving human sacrifice, cannibalism, and blood revenge, and other practices resulting in the treatment of human life merely as chattel or fodder for mass slaughter.[5, e]

Bigelow defines warfare as "an *intergroup* conflict with intent to kill on both sides." By definition, warfare would involve intergroup cooperation. My definition is "the instinct to aggression overlaid with symbolic meaning, manifested in intergroup conflict with intent to kill on both sides."

This is an important distinction, because if we are to understand more fully the psychology of war, we must search deeper into the instinctual, religious, and symbolic dimensions of human psychology that drive a given nation or ethnic or cultural group to aggressive behavior leading to warfare.

---

for warfare being a much earlier and more deeply rooted aspect of man's nature than had been thought previously (ibid., p. 189).

"Objective proof" of warfare dating back tens of thousands of years is lacking primarily because physical evidence such as skeletal remains and weapons have long since decayed or have otherwise been reabsorbed into Nature's bosom. However, Bigelow offers considerable inferential "proof" (the only kind available to us) for his thesis: for example, the sudden and widespread appearance of Cro-Magnon Man twenty thousand to thirty thousand years ago and the equally sudden disappearance of Neanderthal Man during the same period, suggesting that the former killed off the latter.

[5] An example here is the Nazi murder factories of World War II. Although Germany, the land of Goethe, Heine, and Beethoven, acted out of the most primitive human instinctuality in the mass slaughter of Jews and other minority groups, with no regard whatsoever for human life, the ultimate outcome has been a raised human consciousness on the part of many civilized states with regard to the value of the individual human life and the bestial instincts that lurk in the darkest recesses of man's psyche.

The Soviet Union repeatedly cites the painful loss of 20,000,000 of its citizens in World War II as proof of its commitment to the avoidance of war with the United States.

Schmookler, in his concept of "the parable of the tribes," argues persuasively that when any *one* group opts for warfare, by definition it co-opts the choice for peace on the part of any groups that are their targets for war. However, the presence of intergroup cooperation as an intrinsic dynamic of war still would apply, since the "other" group would make the choice of fighting or not fighting.

Although conflict (as opposed to warfare per se), in one form or another, probably has existed for thousands of years and perhaps as long as man has been on the earth, its nature has evolved over the millennia.[f] With regard to very early man, it would be better to refer to man's "instinct to aggression," rather than to "warfare" in the formal sense of the word, since the intergroup cooperation necessary for "warfare" per se probably would have been limited and short-lived: that is, coming in spurts, probably lasting a few hours or even a few minutes. This would be so because of the small population size of ethnic groups, greater dispersal of groups over a wider geography, limitations in mobility, and a more primitive emotional makeup, thus a limited capacity to carry a grudge over a sustained period of time. The character of primitive "warfare" would be quite different from the warfare we know in the context of civilization.[6]

I have been referring here to preagricultural man with his hunting instincts intact. Hunting and territoriality on the part of early man were not only necessary means of finding food and fuel and protecting his territory and shelter for survival, but were also a means of acting out primal aggressive instincts inherent in most primates. For him, acted-out aggression was a natural, inseparable aspect of his day-to-day life.

We can infer from archaeological, anthropological, historical, ethological, and psychological research that instinctual aggression in humans made a radical evolutionary change with the process of socialization and acculturation that took place with man's shift from hunting and gathering for survival to agriculture and the subsequent move toward living in ever-larger communal settings.

A necessary and massive repression of human instinct into the collective unconscious occurred over time as man became more "civilized" and was accompanied by, and was a function of, an increasing capacity to sub-

---

[6] This factor too would make it extremely difficult to find proof of the existence of "warfare" on the part of preagricultural man.

Sue Mansfield, in *The Gestalts of War*, says, "My guess is that weapons were not specifically made in order to wage wars until the Neolithic period, about 13,000 years ago, when some people abandoned hunting and gathering and turned to agriculture" (quoted in *Psychology Today*, June 1982, p. 58).

ordinate his urge to aggressive behavior leading to warfare. It does not follow from this inference that either the frequency or ferocity (as measured in destruction and numbers killed) of warfare would (or should) have diminished with the advance of civilization, as a number of researchers in the field have argued. The capacity to subordinate the instinct to aggression changes the conscious and some of the unconscious motives for warfare. In my mind, the evidence is inconclusive as to whether modern warfare is more or less destructive, in relative terms, than ancient warfare. It is important to note that cooperation for war requires an increasing capacity to *not* act on one's instinct, but to subordinate individual aggressive urges to the attack plan of the group. Like all other learned behavior, this behavior leaves on the human brain its imprint, which is passed on phylogenetically, to be built upon by the learning of successive generations.

The cooperation necessary to live productively became progressively competitive with the energy and resources required to make war. This resulted in increased repression of the instinct to aggression, building up a massive "instinctual reservoir" in the collective unconscious. The walls of this "instinctual reservoir"—that is, human consciousness and the human ego—could retain the buildup of aggressive libido but for so long. When the instinctual reservoir would become full—that is, after periods of diminished warfare—the reservoir would overflow again and there would be an upsurge of warfare, usually in many places at once,[7] to permit a siphoning off of the instinct to aggression, making room again in the collective instinctual reservoir for the repression of the instinct to make war.

---

[7] Hence, historically, the psychological (as opposed to political) impetus for the foreign "alliances" attendant to conflicts between two parties. The collective unconscious is just that—"collective." The instinctual reservoir referred to above as containing aggressive libido transcends national boundaries.

Although there may indeed be rational grounds for joining another nation or group at war (for example, the United States declaration of war nearly three years after the start of World War I), a deeper and sometimes more compelling factor for such "alliances" is the buildup of excess aggressive libido in the collective unconscious. The degree to which this dynamic is determining is a function of the length of time overt aggressive behavior (that is, warfare) has been repressed *and* the degree to which the instinct for aggression remains unconscious. We cannot do something about a problem we do not perceive.

This is crucial in the present context of Soviet-American conflict because the dynamics that have changed since 1985 have been the rapidly increasing awareness of both superpowers concerning the nonpolitical dynamics that impel them to overt conflict. This dimension will be explored in greater depth in Chapters 7 and 9.

These cycles of warfare and "peace" have repeated themselves predictably over the millennia, and have been observable in the modern era. In this manner the repressed human instinct for aggression has been manifested, historically, through the "archetype of war." Thus, beneath all "rational" acts of war in the modern sense, is the archetype of war that exists a priori.[8]

The advent of agriculture and the resulting development of the village required greater and more sophisticated cooperation within a given group to be able to cultivate the land and to protect the community from foreign attack at the same time. This intragroup cooperation gave rise to intergroup cooperation against some foreigners, the development of the walled city, more sophisticated weapons, and progressively longer periods between attacks.[g]

In addition, aggression and the outer expression of anger and violence are essential in the early (pre-oedipal) development of ego strength and self-assertion and self-esteem. As indicated in the chapter on "The Hero Dynamic," the adolescent stage of the hero is a necessary phase in the development and consolidation of a healthy masculine ego.[h] Acted-out aggression on a limited scale is a critical and necessary aspect of this stage of ego development. Without it, the masculine ego would not have learned the extent of the self's impulse to aggression and how to control and channel its energy into more constructive avenues.[9]

With postagricultural man, we must talk of war, in part, as the result of repressed aggressive instincts[10] and their expression within the setting of

---

[8] Jung put it thus: "The question of instinct cannot be dealt with psychologically without considering the archetypes because at bottom they determine one another" (Collected Works, vol. 8, p. 134).

[9] But in its healthy form, it is *only* a phase, and the mature male works through that particular phase, moving on to a more mature form of masculinity. This has subtle, but far-reaching, implications in a world still operating more often than not under patriarchal authority, and for men in positions of leadership and authority in government and the military, many of whom are stuck at an adolescent level of the hero phase of ego development. Many such men operate out of narcissistic rage deriving from feelings of powerlessness that end up being reflected in "policy" positions backed up, sometimes, by the enormous power of the state—and the state's nuclear arsenal. However, this is too complicated a subject to be explored in greater depth in this context.

[10] Whitmont points out, "Ethologists have come up with impressive evidence that aggression is phylogenetically preprogrammed in the biological organism of animals and, hence, probably also of humans. . . . Aggressive . . . pathways are interlinked in the lower brainstem." Edward Whitmont, *Return of the Goddess* (New York: Crossroad, 1982), p. 18.

civilization—always within the context of a defined "rational" cause, and subject to man's power complex: that is, war as we know it today.

However, civilized man, by definition, is highly invested in seeing himself as having domesticated and divorced himself from his primitive instinctuality. In civilized societies, man subject to primitive instinctual drives is seen as pathological—sick. Any suggestion that he carries such a nature in his (collective) unconscious and that his behavior is influenced by it, calls forth intense personal fear, denial, and paranoid projection. This fact is ironic because it is at the instinctual level that there is an in-built genetic regulating and moderating element that furthers survival of the species, serving as a natural limit on the expression of aggressive instinct. By divorcing himself from his instinctual roots, modern man has made himself more subject to unbridled aggressive instinct and consequently more prone to warfare and, unlike lower forms of life, to killing off his own species.

Modern man's tendency to see himself and his creative work—civilization—as fundamentally good and devoid of instinctual aggression, and himself as being in full ego control of his destiny, heightens the tendency toward unconscious aggression. The more we repress our instinct to aggression, the more it is likely to sneak up on us from behind (like a dammed river), leaving us baffled as to how we got into this or that situation. One would think that the amassing of more than fifty thousand nuclear warheads[i] in the name of preventing aggression might raise some question about man's unconscious nature and the actual extent of his ego control over his destiny! That fact is not just a failure in the SALT or ABM treaties and the like. Treaties fail because the human ego fails. And, it must be pointed out, the power of the willed constraint by the human ego is not unlimited. In the last analysis, these failures ensue from man's fundamental unconsciousness about his own aggressive nature and the real limits of the ego to repress and contain powerful instinctual drives.[11]

Thus, a primary function of the "defined rational cause" in relation to war is to remove modern man as far as possible from the recognition that a

---

[11] Schmookler's theory of anarchical power as the sole culprit in causing man's destructive aggression offers only a partial, albeit important, explanation. Organized power may be new—"a sudden new phenomenon in the systems of the earth"—but aggression is not. They are not the same thing. His denial of the evidence supporting the fact of instinctual aggression and his assertion that pre-civilized man was essentially peaceful are not supportable, notwithstanding the research he cites in these fields, in the face of other extensive ethological, psychological, and anthropological research. (See nn. 2 and 4.)

probable primary cause in his behavior is his instinct of aggression. As Whitmont put it, "Though we may find it unpalatable, violence, far from being merely a response to frustration, is one of humankind's most profoundly moving experiences. It is fascinating as well as terrifying, and closely akin to sexuality and creativity." [12]

Unlike other primates, man has an intellectual capacity and an evolving capacity for cumulative learning that have given him an extraordinary ability to adapt instinctual behavior to directly serve rational (and irrational) goals that go far beyond subsistence survival. In the context of civilized man, some of these are religion (for example, the Aztec War of the Flowers, the Crusades, the Iran-Iraq War), the acquisition of property other than land (for example, women and slaves, natural resources including precious and other metals), blood revenge, human sacrifice and headhunting, development of trade routes, et cetera. Over the millennia, such "adapted aggressive instinctual behavior" (that is, warfare in service to a religious or political idea) became a primary means for the evolution of societies (as well as their destruction) ultimately leading up to the civilization(s) of the modern era.

At the same time, Maurice Davie reports a number of tribes and cultures where warfare supposedly does not exist. These include the Vedda people of Sri Lanka (Ceylon), the Eskimos of Greenland, the Similkameen Indians of British Columbia, the Aurohuacos of Colombia, the Lapps, the Hierro people of the Canary Islands, the Makalakas of South Africa, and the Todas of south India, among others. [13] These findings would appear to argue against an archetype of war as a universal instinct of our species.

However, closer scrutiny of the facts reveal that the Todas, although they use no weapons and are unacquainted with the formal concept of war, use the bow and arrow and club in their ceremonies. The Vedda have been recorded as participating in a fight with a neighboring group over disputed property. The Aurohuacos have a practice of settling disputes by having individual disputants go to a tree or rock and beat it with a staff, the first to break his stick being the "victor," betraying an underlying aggression that requires expression. [14] Although the Eskimos of Greenland

---

[12] Whitmont, *Return of the Goddess*, p. 17. In the 1987 movie *Top Gun*, one of the aircraft carrier pilots sent aloft to intercept Soviet fighters approaching the carrier exclaims that he knows that the enemy is near, even though he can't see them, because he has an erection.

[13] Davie, *Evolution of War*, pp. 46–54. Sue Mansfield, *Gestalts of War*, also cites the Hopi Indians in this category.

[14] These would appear to be constructive ways of channeling and displacement

do not fight, probably because of the sparseness of people to fight with and because the harshness of the environment necessitates that all energy be devoted to subsistence and survival, the Alaskan Eskimos have a history of constant conflict with neighboring groups. As Bigelow points out, a number of tribes like the Vedda were surrounded by warlike groups and their "peacefulness" was imposed on them by force.[j] Apparently, their "peaceful" nature is a result of a forced sublimation of their instinct to aggression into more ceremonial and ritualized forms. Physical survival always brings out man's most highly adaptive skills—psychologically, as well as physiologically.

Thus, of the known tribes and cultures for whom war is not an overt practice, it would appear under closer scrutiny that many, if not all, of them sublimate the instinct to war either through ritual and sham wars, or that their reported history of nonparticipation in warfare is not as total as reported.[15] Apparently the germ of the instinct to make war does exist in their group psyches. This would apply in the modern context as well.[16]

Schmookler argues that "conflicts between primitive human groups is of a ritualized, almost ceremonial display of hostility which produces a minimum of injury or damage":[k] that is, not warfare at all. But the *psychological* point is not the nature and degree of injury and damage, but whence warfare takes its roots and why there is ritualized and ceremonial display of hostility at all. There would be no "ritualized [or] . . . ceremonial display of hostility" in primitive man if there were no need for it, and if it were not a ceremonial vestige of a psychic and instinctual historical fact. The human psyche, no less than human physiology, is highly purposive and adaptive in its function. Indeed, psychological adaptation usually takes place much more rapidly than physiological adaptation. Ritualized and ceremonial display of conflict was and is present in primitive human groups for a reason—that is, adaptation for survival—as well as other religious, cultural, and psychological needs. It has served for

---

of aggressive behavior. They are one of thousands of subtle but effective examples of the human psyche's ability to adapt for survival and to sublimate the instinct of aggression.

[15] Alas, we recently discover, the wonderful peace-loving innocence of the Tasaday tribe of the Philippines turns out to be a sham. (Source: "The Tribe That Never Was," "20/20," ABC News transcript. Show #632, August 14, 1986.)

[16] This would also include the Hopi Indians (whose name literally means "peace"), who perform dances and other rites that involve clubs, bows, and arrows, and whose stories and myth involve intergroup conflict.

most of man's existence as the primary means for regulating the instinct to aggression.

Anthropological studies have demonstrated that when human societies diminish below a critical number (generally under two hundred members),[1] social extinction is imminent and irreversible. It seems likely that the instinct to aggression *had* to be sublimated into ritual and ceremony in some primitive societies (never large in numbers to begin with) to avoid social and cultural extinction. If man were inherently peaceful prior to the advent of power, which Schmookler claims arose at the dawn of civilization ten thousand years ago, and there were no inherent instinct to aggression, then there would be no need for ritualized and ceremonial conflict and none would exist.

Whether warfare in the formal sense arose with the advancement of civilization or existed in prehistory (since we cannot know and can only infer), two things must be said.

1. The psychic and instinctual roots of intercommunal aggression were present in man, whatever form they took: that is, literal warfare and/or ritual enactment of an inner psychic impulse.[17]

2. The psychic and instinctual roots of aggression play a significant role in the modern tendency toward warfare.

In contemporary terms, survival is dependent upon the realization that was (as opposed to warfare) is an archetype: that is, that its primary source is in transpersonal and instinctual energy,[18] not in the rationalization of external events.[19] Since, according to the law of conservation of energy, instinct and symbolic forms of energy[20] characteristic of the human psyche cannot be abolished, war as archetypal energy, manifested as warfare, is here to stay. In the context of archetypal theory,[21] warfare as we know it is

---

[17] It seems to me that this *psychological* conclusion is unavoidable.

[18] Anthony Stevens, M.D., an English psychiatrist, in his forthcoming book *The Archetypes of War,* asserts that an instinct to make war is a *biological* fact of life in many primates, including man, and offers evidence that a biological basis exists in the primitive "reptilian brain" of modern man—the limbic system—for explaining the dynamic of an archetype of war as part of modern man's psyche. Also see Stevens's book, *Archetypes: A Natural History of the Self* (New York: Quill, 1983).

Bigelow, Davie, Whitmont, and others also suggest a biological basis for an instinct to war.

[19] Can we imagine warfare without the presence of aggressive human instinct?

[20] As reflected in ritual, myth, and fantasy.

[21] Archetypal theory has been most fully developed in the context of modern psychology by Carl Jung. See my Chapter 2 and the bibliography for a list of references.

the form through which man historically has acted out this archetypal energy. In other words, the archetype of war stands behind the act of warfare. They are not the same thing.

I have used the terms *instinct,* biological and symbolic *urges* for aggression and war in some places, and have used the term *archetype of war* in others. The latter certainly contains elements of the former—Stevens would argue that the genes carry the mandate of the archetype. (In the literature, the "instinct to aggression" and an "instinct to war" become muddled, and often they are used interchangeably. I do not subscribe to the position that there is a specific genetic instinct for war; I do subscribe to the position that there is a genetic instinct for aggression. I have described above how the instinct to aggression becomes transformed into manifest warfare.)

However, there is a crucial difference between a biological instinct and an archetypal "instinct" or psychic mandate. A biological urge for aggression is just that—an undiscriminating and primitive survival urge, genetically grounded, which becomes acted out. The archetype of war, while influenced by instinctual drives, at the same time seeks *symbolic* embodiment and *meaning* of psychic content, giving rise to various rationales for war.[22] It is through the archetype of war, then, that man has come to learn about and reflect upon his warlike nature, giving rise to the possibility of relating *to* it, and thus changing his relationship with it. Ironically, recently it has been through reflection on his "rationales" for war that war has come to be perceived increasingly as irrational.

At best, we can only manage warfare, but never abolish the impulse to make war.[23] In managing the conflict between the Soviet Union and the United States, we have to address the archetype of war directly, as well as our warring behavior. The essential point is not that all war is purely instinctual, rational or symbolic but rather that there is an instinctual substratum that is ever-present and that is only momentarily quelled after periods of large-scale warfare (particularly world wars).

An example of how this dynamic can intrude upon a situation where

---

[22] Which may or may not be consonant with the goal of the archetype, as we shall see.

[23] Oliver La Farge reports that when the British pressed one group of Cherokee Indians to make peace with another, the former stated that unless they were at war with *some* tribe, "they would not know what to do with themselves." La Farge asserts that they tried not to "spoil a war by winning it, or to subjugate or drive other tribes from their territory." "The Enduring Indian," *Scientific American* 202 (1960): 37–45, as reported in Bigelow, p. 99.

conditions are ripe for war and can determine which way the scales will tip—for or against war—is World War I, known also as "the war no one wanted." Much has been written about how the various nations caught up in that drama tried repeatedly to avoid conflict and how, once hostilities began, they wondered aloud as to how "this" could have happened.

It is important to recognize that the cyclic psychic nature of warfare, as I have outlined it above, is dependent upon there being survivors somewhere to fight the next war. (See La Farge's observation in note 23.) Psychologically, a primary aim of aggression is connection. If that instinct, biologic and/or symbolic, is inherently cyclical, then the obliteration of warfare would go against the nature of the archetype of war itself. Paradoxically, it would follow, then, that the archetype demands a world in which aggression *can* be enacted[24] on an ongoing basis: that is, a world that will not act out nuclear annihilation. Nuclear annihilation is antithetical to the archetype of war. The thermonuclear age has brought humankind to the point where warfare itself, because it risks nuclear annihilation, is no longer tenable. Humanity finds itself facing a dilemma—war, which has brought it to the brink of self-extermination, at the same time demands that nuclear annihilation not be acted out. Where do we go from here?

THE CULTURAL/SYMBOLIC VERSUS THE INSTINCTUAL TRAP

At a meeting on August 31, 1987, the American Psychological Association endorsed the "Seville Statement on Violence," which concludes that "humanity can be freed from the bondage of biological pessimism . . . the same species who invented war is capable of inventing peace."

The Seville Statement goes on to say:

> The fact that warfare has changed so radically over time indicates that it is a product of culture. Its biological connection is primarily through language which makes possible the coordination of groups, the transmission of technology, and the use of tools. War is biologically possible, but it is not inevi-

---

[24] Enactment is a symbolic process (for example, ritual) that regulates and controls human behavior; it is not the same thing as "acting out": that is, unmediated externalization of inner impulses through overt behavior. Enactment is always somewhat conscious and at least partially subordinate to the will of the ego. Acting out is not.

table, as evidenced by its variation in occurrence and nature over time and space. . . .

It is scientifically incorrect to say that in the course of human evolution there has been a selection for aggressive behavior more than other kinds of behavior. In all well-studied species, status within the group is achieved by the ability to cooperate and to fulfill social functions relevant to the structure of that group. "Dominance" involves social bondings and affiliations; it is not simply a matter of the possession and use of superior physical power, although it does involve aggressive behaviors.[m]

Given the history between the superpowers over the past ten to fifteen years, particularly the pessimism bordering on despair that developed during the early years of the Reagan administration, the advent of the Seville Statement on Violence and its popularity within the scientific community is not surprising.[25] However, for reasons stated above and below, I believe that its impetus is tainted by emotion and that some important conclusions drawn from the scientific data are therefore biased and inaccurate.

Indeed, the Seville Statement is so tainted with emotion as to be coercive to anyone differing with its "conclusions." Ironically, the *APA Monitor,* an organ of the American Psychological Association itself, seems to acknowledge this fact. Because of the extreme importance of the Seville Statement on Violence and its potential impact on future research on the subject,[26] I have included the rather long quotation from the *Monitor* article:

---

[25] Popular belief on the part of the scientific community as well as the public at large on both sides of the Iron Curtain during the early 1980s was that nuclear war between the superpowers was close at hand and inevitable. At one point, the Union of Concerned Scientists displayed a clock showing two minutes to go before nuclear warfare would break out between the superpowers. At the same time, a number of highly regarded public figures in the United States expressed concern that the United States was planning a strategy for a winnable nuclear war, and some expressed concern that the United States was planning a first strike against the Soviet Union.

[26] The Seville Statement on Violence has been endorsed by the American Anthropological Association, the Americans for the Universality of UNESCO, Canadian Psychologists for Social Responsibility, the Czechoslovak UNESCO Commission, the International Council of Psychologists, the Mexican Association for Biological Anthropology, the Polish Academy of Sciences, Psychologists for Social Responsibility (U.S.), the Society for Psychological Study of Social Issues (U.S.), the Spanish UNESCO Commission, and the World Federalist Association, among others.

The Seville Statement on Violence—a document that *seeks to wipe out* any belief that humans have inherited a tendency to make war from our animal ancestors, was unanimously endorsed by the APA Council of Representatives at its August meeting . . . [author's italics].

. . . Surveys in Finland, Great Britain and the United States indicate that a large number of young people believe that war is intrinsic to human nature.

The Seville Statement was brought to APA's attention by Neal Miller, professor of psychology at Yale University, who wrote to the Board of Scientific Affairs (BSA) in February urging the association's endorsement of the statement.

Miller wrote, "Although human nature certainly does contain innate factors that can lead to violence, psychological evidence on the modification and redirection of anger and anthropological evidence that different societies have lived together peacefully, in some cases without even any weapons of warfare, shows that wars are not an inevitable consequence of human nature."

BSA and the Board of Social and Ethical Responsibility for Psychology (BSERP) voted to endorse the statement. The BSERP vote was unanimous. [Apparently the vote of BSA was not.]

In urging Council to follow suit, BSA wrote, *"The document is not attempting to address the issue of inherited behavioral traits leading to violence and war in a scholarly manner, but is instead a social statement analogous to similar statements on race that were circulated all over the world several decades ago"* [emphasis added]."

The minutes of the APA Board of Scientific Affairs meeting of May 2 to 4, 1987, that endorsed the Seville Statement specifically stated, "While BSA strongly endorses this social statement in spirit, *it would like to point out that certain statements are misleading and from a scientific perspective, many scientists would disagree with some of the phrases*" (my italics). As a statement endorsed by the Board of *Scientific Affairs* of the APA, it is shocking if not outright unethical.

Although the Seville Statement contains a number of important scientifically valid points, distortions of the research findings to date, the emotionalism of the statement, and its coercive tone render it counterproductive.

In recent years considerable debate and two opposing camps have emerged in the literature concerning whether preagricultural man was warlike. Bigelow, Davie, Stevens, Whitmont, and others argue persuasively that warfare, per se, has existed virtually as long as man has existed and that it has a strong instinctual basis. At the other extreme are the persuasive arguments of Service, Lionel Tiger, Schmookler, Steven

Kull, and others to the effect that warfare did not exist at all in primitive man. Kull, in discussing war, carries this argument to an extreme and cuts war off from any destructive instinct, per se, by asserting that its goal is symbolic, not literal physical destruction. As he puts it, "Rather than seeing violence as a regression to an earlier, instinctual mode, I think we must see it as a by-product of a developmental process . . . [of] newly emerging human motivations."° He goes on to say that warfare was preceded by the archetype of world destruction the goal of which is a wholly symbolic destruction, not a literal one (pp. 578, 582–583).[27] I believe that it is *both* literal and symbolic.

While I agree with Kull's conclusion that war as we know it is to a large degree part of a developmental process, cutting off the archetype of war from its instinctual roots and addressing it only in symbolic or sociocultural terms artificially dichotomizes and distorts the issue. It does not follow that because the archetype of war carries *a* symbolic and developmental goal and *a* religious imperative that it does not contain a substratum simultaneously instinctual and literally destructive. Nor does it follow that, because warfare per se is not genetically programmed in the human brain, instinctual aggression does not play a significant, even causal, role in the persistence of warfare.[28] Aggressive instinct is reflected symbolically in the human psyche. But it does not follow that symbolic representation is the only manifestation of aggressive instinct. Nor does it follow that Kull's brilliant and, I think, accurate formulation of a religious imperative of the archetype of war is the only imperative.

In drawing parallels to human psychology from the work of Lorenz and other ethologists, Whitmont observes, "*Regulation of aggression demands both expression and inhibition*" (author's italics).[p] It also requires contact[29] in an age of abstractions where weapons no longer permit contact (for example, the jousting lance, or even the gun, where the holder of

---

[27] In generalizing from Emil Durkheim's work on suicide, he says, "When we speak of self-destruction, the self being destroyed is not the body per se, but a particular image or experience of the self in a state of disunity." Steven Kull, "Nuclear Arms and the Desire for World Destruction," *Political Psychology* 4 (3) (September 1983):579. That is true. But at the same time there are tens of thousands of literal suicides each year.

[28] The Seville Statement on Violence waffles back and forth between talking about "war," "warfare," "violence," and "aggression," some or all of which are equated at different points in the Statement. Also, diplomatic, political, and military language of all nations tend to equate and to use the words interchangeably. Again, do we imagine the possibility of warfare without instinctual aggression?

[29] Since one goal of aggression is connection.

it could physically see his enemy—and see him die), and takes the form of missiles (land, sea, and air), which are fired from miles distant at a depersonalized blip on a radar screen. On the one hand, this is a real problem in the modern era, intruding on the functional release or channeling of aggressive libido. On the other, as discussed in Chapter 7, if we can find other forms in which to sublimate direct aggressive contact between enemies, they may also be our salvation.

The Seville Statement on Violence notwithstanding, the evidence does support the fact that violence and aggression, per se, trace back to the most elemental of human instinctuality—indeed in primates as a whole. Men in particular, as the nearly exclusive carriers of the archetype of war, have a particular relationship to aggression. John Bancroft, a behavioral endocrinologist at the Medical Resource Council in Edinburgh, Scotland, says, "There are behaviors likelier to occur in boys than in girls, and they are partly attributable to the effects of hormones. Testosterone is influencing not just male sexual behavior but male behavior—things like dominance and aggression. The two are not separate."[q]

Nature itself is violent in its essence, as can be seen from solar flares to earthquakes, volcanic eruptions, and tidal waves, to plagues (historic and contemporary). The life cycle is not only one of death and rebirth; it is also (but not exclusively) violent and aggressive.

Aggression in nature is reflected in all of its creations: from the vine that chokes another plant to the amoeba that "swallows" its own kind as well as alien protozoans, to the well-known aggressive violence of species *Homo sapiens*. In the case of primates, that "natural" violence is carried through the instincts. And, as we know from biology, "ontogeny recapitulates phylogeny."[30] Thus aggressive and violent instinctuality, albeit repressed and overlaid with other evolutionary adaptive mechanisms—the power drive in particular—is carried biologically in higher forms of the order. Those instincts don't just "go away."

Modern man finds himself in a struggle with the duality of nature reflected in his own nature, which is *simultaneously* destructive of life and committed to the perpetuation of life. Animals and other species of primates inherently and functionally carry this balance at a biological instinctual level. This is why the various species—except man—avoid killing themselves and each other off. Man's case is different because species *Homo sapiens* has been singled out to do God's work: that is, build civiliza-

---

[30] Each successive biological species repeats the developmental stages of lower level species.

tions, develop a self-reflecting ego, and to have the capacity to love—to be a feeling and emotional creature.[31] However, to carry out his "higher" mandate, species *Homo sapiens* has overdeveloped his rational function and in doing so has cut himself off from his instinctual roots, which still are powerful unseen motivators of human behavior.

As Jung explicates in his "Answer to Job," it is man's lot to have been chosen by God to bear *consciously* the conflict, pain, and struggle inherent in nature. In Western civilization this means wrestling with the essence of a powerfully violent, destructive, and conflicted Judeo-Christian godhead, which is the common psychoreligious heritage of the United States and Russia.[32]

Ironically, it is man's capacity to feel and to love that gives modern civilization its incredibly bloody mark, as much as anything else. It is that quality that gives the power drive its valence, that gives passion to rationally devised ideologies, that gives rise to hate (the other end of the love-hate continuum of emotions), and that gives rise to the capacity for emotional wounding, in some cases giving rise to the need for revenge.

Thus it is the rational (abstract thinking) function so highly developed in Western man, coupled with the development of complex emotions, that has made the dubious bridge between previously intraspecies-contained aggression and warfare. Ironically, those same capacities rapidly are giving rise to moral consciousness as a powerful constraint on the archetype of war. (This will be discussed in greater depth in Chapter 7.)

I shall propose in the following section that the "archetype of war" derives from the instincts—including violent destructive aggression, along with a religious (or transcendental) imperative, the eros principle, and intergroup cooperation—subsumed under a symbolic contextual framework. The archetype does call forth a higher form of conscious human development—what Kull calls "newly emerging human motivations." But,

---

[31] In this context, *feeling* is defined as affect that has meaning to a self-reflecting ego, unlike some lower species of primates that have affective responses but that do not have a self-reflecting ego.

[32] In this context, the word *Russia*, instead of *the Soviet Union*, is used advisedly to refer to that part of Russia, particularly its ruling class, that has Christian psychocultural roots (as opposed to others such as Muslim republics within the Soviet Union).

C. G. Jung, "Answer to Job." The *Collected Works*, vol. 11, pp. 357–470. "Job who expected help from God against God. This most peculiar fact presupposes a similar conception of the opposites in God" (p. 358).

Also see Charles Taylor, "Apocalyptic Power and Human Care," *Yale Review* 73, no. 4 (1984).

and this is important, nature's violence at one and the same time is regressively impersonal and counterdevelopmental, *as well as* progressively developmental and life-committed. I can think of no better symbol of this developmental-counterdevelopmental aspect of nature than the nuclear bomb. In the thermonuclear age, whether we know it or not, all of humankind is betting on its capacity to reconcile and consciously hold the tension of that duality that threatens to destroy us all.

RITUAL CONTAINMENT OF WAR IN THE NUCLEAR AGE

As presented above, evidence suggests that primitive man, when he could, managed his warlike instincts primarily through ritual. This was particularly true of small tribes whose numbers could not sustain constant attrition through war lest they face social extinction.[33] As civilization evolved, warfare became increasingly tied to the achievement of materialistic goals; acquisition, in and of itself, became a primary rationalization for war. Previously manifested primarily as an archetypal energy that was regulated and controlled through group ritual, warfare became an increasingly destructive implement in the hands of increasingly materialistic and rationalizing men. It became separated from the rituals that had previously governed it, and the rituals themselves eventually atrophied.

---

[33] This would be true also of other societies who "feel" the threat of social extinction in their national psyche. Two examples of the latter might be post–World War II Germany and Japan, both of whom faced social extinction and whose present-day preeminence as world economic powers might be seen as a modern version of ritual warfare. The terms *economic warfare* and *trade wars* are commonly used in the international economic and political arenas, particularly in relation to Japan. The specter of the United States, which had so humiliatingly defeated and occupied Japan after World War II, repeatedly pleading with Japan to reduce her exports in order to protect the American economy and its technological and industrial base must provide no small degree of satisfaction to the Japanese psyche.

It is worth noting as well that the Geneva Convention, which promulgated formalized rules governing future warfare between modern states, was written after the awesome destruction of World War I (which left many individuals and a number of nations with a *feeling* of having faced the threat of social extinction). The United Nations and its charter were established in the wake of World War II, and the Nuclear Atmospheric Test Ban and Non-Proliferation Treaties were signed by the Soviet Union and the United States in the wake of the Cuban Missile Crisis. These latter conscious efforts to contain warfare can be seen also as unconscious attempts to ritualize warfare.

I propose that ritual, once man's primary and most powerful constraint on his instinct to make war, can again serve this vital function in the thermonuclear age. One way of approaching this imperative is to reconnect warfare with its ritual roots. Research needs to be undertaken on past and present rituals used to control and manage the archetypal energy released through war. Past rituals are available through histories, myths, archaeology, anthropology, et cetera. Present rituals can be identified through studying modern armies, urban youth gangs, negotiation behaviors between groups and nations, and those few remaining primitive tribes that engage in ritualized warfare or in which some of the rituals may be still practiced without physical combat.

For example, as recently as the 1950s, among members of the Kapauku tribe of New Guinea, warfare with other groups resulted when disputes could not be settled by other means. Fighting, however, would take place only under fixed ritual rules of warfare, and peace negotiations would be commenced when both sides were tired of fighting and the number of dead was equal on both sides. If the number was not equal, then the side with the *fewer* casualties (what we would call the "winning side") would pay "blood money" to the other side. Thus the function of ritualized warfare was not to win per se, but rather was to discharge excess aggressive energy. The "war" would always conclude with a rebalancing of psychic energy.

Another example of ritual warfare occurred in the Plains Indian tribes of the United States. Fighting with "coup sticks" (long staffs with curved ends) was an alternative to killing with more lethal weapons. Often battles would be fought only with coup sticks. The objective would be to knock an opponent off his horse, knock him down, disarm him, et cetera, but not kill him. Different points were credited for the varying types of coup struck. "Counting coup" was a point of honor on both sides and there was no "cheating." Sometimes an enemy was killed accidentally. Less credit would be given for such a blow than for unmounting or disabling an opponent. Thus, war rituals were powerful devices that actually limited and prevented killing. H. W. Turney-High reported that although Plains Indians knew how to make stone arrowheads, they often used headless arrows with blunt shafts during their warfare. At the end of the battle they would pull out the shafts that had embedded in their bodies, leaving usually superficial wounds, and live to fight another day.[r]

The Kiowa tribe, for example, had an elaborate system of credits for counting coup. They and some other Plains tribes chose their leadership to a large extent on the basis of counted coup.

The Omaha Indians had a practice of sham fights where no one was attacked.[5]

The Ba-Mbala of East Africa have a similar practice, which they call *kutana* or "small war." They clear a special arena, and the opposing sides, armed only with bows and arrows, march in single file to the appointed spot, insult each other, then shoot and maneuver until they have had enough. Usually no one is killed and there are seldom serious injuries.

Similarly, the Euahlayi tribe of Australia have sham fights with boomerangs. Battles are arranged to test the strength of the tribe and for displaying their skill in the use of their weapons and to prove their bravery, to the warriors of their own tribe as well as to the enemy with whom they may be "fighting" this arranged battle. Lives are risked but seldom are lives sacrificed.[t] Similar practices have been reported with regard to Koreans, Polynesians, and tribes of New Zealand, as well as other groups. Some sham wars would take place between enemy groups and others would be held within a given group or tribe, the two "sides" being chosen from within the group itself, not unlike modern-day war games held by the armed forces of the United States and the Soviet Union.

James Moriarty observes that during the Middle Ages the tournament was a substitute for warfare.

> The supreme recreation of the noble during the Middle Ages was the tournament. It is the best substitute for war that could be devised and in its earliest forms differed very little from actual warfare. Early in the 11th century tournaments were . . . miniature wars and they were fought over rather large areas. Two rival armies were generally formed and a district would be indicated as a field of honor. There would often be as many as several hundred men participating. . . . This early form of the tournament differed from actual warfare only in that the lives of the contestants were spared.[u]

The war games conducted by NATO and Warsaw Pact countries could be viewed as a kind of sham warfare. Although at a conscious level these war games are conducted for the purpose of training *for* war, unconsciously they may also serve as a psychological means of containing the archetype of war in a manner similar to that of primitive tribes.

The *energy* expended in war ceremony and ritual, and in sham wars, is powerful. These are not merely staged dramas. They mobilize the entire energies of the people(s) involved, which are whipped to a fever pitch. Enormous anger is invoked, insults and curses are hurled, there is wild frenzied shouting, dancing, and jumping about, and weapons are used to threaten and beat upon the "enemy." They constellate the full rage and fury at an enemy and evoke the urge to kill. In primitive cultures, occasionally the entire population of the group would be involved—men, women, children, and old ones. Often some individuals would be seriously wounded in these frays, and occasionally a handful of individuals are killed. This is also true in modern-day war games.

However, it is important to note the power of ritual to contain what would otherwise be unbridled primitive instinctuality resulting in the loss of scores of lives, if not whole social groups. *Psychologically,* that is the express purpose of these rituals—they serve as a means of dissipating the energies that build from the instinct for aggression while minimizing the loss of life and preserving the cohesion of the groups and societies involved. Whitmont puts it, "By virtue of propitiatory inhibition and redirection, ritual helps sublimation. It has been serving as a civilizing and acculturating factor in transforming raw and brutal energy into humanly cooperative forms." [v]

At the same time, they serve another subtle, but crucial, psychological function—to bring instinctual aggression under the control of the ego. What is harnessed by the ego and called forth at will usually can also be put back into psychic containment through an ego decision. As most alcoholics who are members of Alcoholics Anonymous can testify, powerful unconscious drives cannot be contained by an ego decision alone. The ego needs to be bolstered by a spiritual connection. Ritual can provide this connection.

Ritual is a powerful vehicle through which a deep spiritual connection can be made. Unlike prayer in isolation, ritual constellates the psychic energy of the group and of the collective unconscious, which often is sufficiently powerful to contain psychic energy as well as to connect with a spiritual dimension (Kull's point). Individual ritual (for example, prayer) often will not suffice. We can see this in numerous contexts if we just look about us—the huddle on the football field is but one example. Every sports fan and player knows that the team playing in its home stadium is more likely to win because of the tremendous libido evoked on behalf of the team by the fans in the stadium. Basic training in the military constantly evokes the group psyche through ritual chants and cadences. Every drill sergeant knows, either consciously or intuitively, the power of ritual.

Virtually all primitive tribes have or have had specific rituals for putting the warrior back into the vessel of the collective unconscious. Some American Indian tribes had specific rituals for evoking the warrior before battles, and specific rituals for depotentiating the warrior and returning that energy to the collective unconscious. Turney-High puts it: ". . . The victory dance restored the equilibrium of the ante-bellum frustrations and those caused by the war as well. They were also a necessary rite of passage indicating the return to normality of statuses which had been seriously disturbed by the war."[w]

We have learned the very painful cost of not having rituals for putting the warrior jinni back into the bottle in the case of our Vietnam soldiers. Many have had their lives destroyed by the fact that they cannot contain the killer-warrior unleashed in basic training and further whipped up by commanders and combat in the field. I have yet to talk with a Vietnam veteran who would deny that he lives in fear that his inner warrior/killer may "escape" ego control and run amok. This group includes "well-adjusted" veterans who lead "normal" lives and show no overt signs of such inner psychic tension. The veterans I have treated in private practice have acknowledged that there was an inexplicable ritual component in their killing of the enemy. This ritual theme shows up repeatedly in their dreams as well. One Vietnam veteran, struggling, years after his return to civilian life, to contain his urge to kill, reported that one day he was fighting in the jungles of Vietnam and thirty-six hours later, he was walking the streets of Los Angeles in civilian clothes—decommissioned and left with his own warrior-killer to contain.[34]

---

[34] With one Vietnam veteran with whom I worked clinically, when I questioned, after two years of therapy, why he had not mentioned one thing about his time in Vietnam, he said he wasn't ready. As time passed, I began to realize that his Vietnam experience was where the clinical work had to go. Yet, I could not gain access. Over time I began to feel the shadow of his warrior-killer present in the room during our clinical sessions. Then I began to have fantasy images during our sessions of him standing between myself and my patient, legs spread apart and arms folded across his chest, in a stance that communicated that I was not going to be permitted to penetrate that forbidden ground. As a nonveteran, I was not an initiate, and it was forbidden to trespass.

I shared these thoughts and fantasies with him, but he still would not touch the subject area and he admitted to his resistance in the therapy. I asked if he would like to terminate his relationship with me and work with a therapist who was a Vietnam veteran. He was adamant about continuing his work with me. I felt stymied.

One day during a session, without warning or discussion, I challenged him to a wrestling match on the floor of the office. He grew instantly apprehensive and said he did not think it a good idea. I insisted and goaded him into combat. We moved the furniture and went at it.

I am 6'5" tall and weigh well over 200 pounds, but I am untrained as a combat warrior. Although my patient was a couple of inches shorter than I, he was at least

It took the collective ritual of the formal dedication of the Vietnam Veterans Memorial in Washington, D.C., on November 12, 1982, and the formal interment of the Unknown Soldier of the Vietnam War at Arlington Cemetery in 1984 to create a psychological climate wherein many of our Vietnam veterans could begin the difficult process of repressing their unleashed warrior so that they could come home again and rejoin the larger collective.

Davie connects these practices to the modern age:

> Civilized peoples are not very different from primitive men in this respect. Love of excitement is a powerful incentive in recruiting professional soldiers. It is played upon by the press and other agencies of publicity in mobilizing a nation for war. Military parades and trappings, martial airs, the honors accorded soldiers, and the like throw a glamour around warfare and mask its horrors. Military life affords a release for energies frustrated in monotonous industrial pursuits. In short, it still appeals to man—and to woman vicariously—as an exciting and glamorous adventure.[x]

It is significant that in the prenuclear age the rituals that played such an important role in inhibiting and channeling human aggression were face-to-face encounters between individuals and groups. However, A. Storr, as reported in Whitmont, identifies the crucial factors that interfere with that inhibiting impulse in the nuclear age: the tendency to paranoid projection, the invention of artificial weapons that depersonalize combat and prevent a face-to-face encounter with the enemy as vulnerable human beings, the aggregation into larger societies, which submerges individuality, the effects upon hostility of crowding.[y]

One of the more complicated and least recognized dangers that nuclear weapons and the guided missile pose to the survival of humankind is that they hold the potential for reducing the entire "war" to a matter of minutes—to a literal holocaust—making war, per se, less feasible because

---

ten years younger and in superb physical condition, and there was no question as to the outcome of the contest. I fought with all my vigor. He was forced to fight me. After a few minutes, I felt and saw his warrior come out. Instinctively, he wanted to kill me. There was a moment when we were stalemated in a hold, and I could tell that his instincts were telling him to go for the kill. I saw his struggle to resist. The fight ended moments later.

After that encounter, we spent the next three years working on the material from his war years, his personal day-to-day struggle with his warrior that still wanted to kill and his alienation in a society that he felt knew nothing of his struggle to stay alive. He said he still felt more secure and at home with his knife in the jungle than he did on the streets of Washington, D.C.

the threatened speed and totality of the blow would eliminate many of the rituals that have governed modern as well as primitive warfare. Some of these include consultations with other elements of government (for example, the Congress) and a nation's allies, formal declarations of war, the process of mobilizing armies, the issuing of threats and demands, flags of truce, and negotiated settlements. Paradoxically, they also exert enormous pressures on the superpowers to develop more effective and conscious rituals to contain the instinct to war.

Although various mechanisms, fail-safe systems, consultative and administrative procedures, and so on, have been devised by both the Soviet Union and the United States in response to this pressure, these lack the full archetypal potency of ritual. There is a profound difference between an administrative procedure and a ritual. The former is a rational construct of the ego that may have little or no connection to the vast reservoir of powerful psychic energy in the collective unconscious.[35]

Rituals, on the other hand, always take their source in the more powerful archetypal energy of the collective unconscious. The most dramatic example of the awesome archetypal holding power of ritual on a national scale was its skillful use by the Nazi regime prior to and during World War II, culminating in the famous Nuremburg rally of 1935.[36]

Ritual energy is adaptive instinctual energy aimed at protecting man from outer and inner forces that threaten his survival. However, ritual behavior does not change as rapidly as man's ego develops. Consequently, ritual behaviors that served a constructive adaptive purpose earlier in man's history may be out of date and even destructive in a contemporary context, if left unchecked. Examples of this type of instinctual adaptation are discussed in Chapter 8. Since ritual behavior in the context of civilized

---

[35] In the case of the shooting down by the USS *Vincennes* on July 3, 1988, of an Iranian civilian jetliner with the loss of 290 lives, one can imagine one shipman in the control room saying to another, "Hey man, I think that plane may not be hostile," and another saying, "He's coming straight at us. Shoot the bastard down!"—a violation of training and of combat administrative procedure. In the context of genuine ritual, such behavior would be extremely unlikely, bordering on the psychologically impossible.

[36] In contemporary terms we can see the power of ritual as it was reflected in the popular student demonstrations in South Korea during 1987. Thousands of chanting demonstrators snaked through the streets of Seoul and other cities over a period of several months. These largely nonviolent demonstrations, which had a clearly visible ritual quality, brought about major democratic reforms, culminating in the first free elections in seventeen years, in one of the most repressive regimes in the non-Communist world.

man is almost always unconscious,[37] ritual behavior can be as destructive as it can be helpful, ranging from the psychotic behavior of a serial murderer to the psychotic behavior of a nation (that is, Nazi Germany).

Although the source of ritual energy is the collective unconscious, ritual energy can be brought under significant control of the ego. This can be done for constructive purposes, as in the Olympic Games, or for destructive purposes, as was the case in Nazi Germany—it depends on the intent and conscious awareness of the ego (individual or collective). At most, ritual is always part conscious and part unconscious. Since ritual energy exists whether we are conscious of it or not, the only choices we have are to remain unconscious of this powerful psychic dynamic that operates in the individual and collective psyche, and thus to remain at its mercy, or to focus conscious attention on it and to take moral responsibility for it, as in the case of war. The latter approach could better enable civilization to harness a powerful psychological dynamic in the service of protecting humankind from its own self-destructive nature.

Modern society exhibits some vestiges of rituals (that is, "ritualism"), despite a conscious attitude that disparages their existence and relevance. A contemporary example of ritualistic behavior is revealed by men who served in the Vietnam War. There are verified reports of Americans cutting off the ears of the slain enemy. This is another form of coup counting. Urban youth gangs provide another example of contemporary ritualistic behavior: that is, "break dancing." Break dancing did not originate as an art form but arose as a spontaneous ritual alternative to hostile competition and "warfare" among youth gangs in New York City. Other vestigial ritual behavior patterns appear in competitive athletics. For instance, football players break out in spontaneous victory dances in the end zone after a touchdown is made and have engaged in "head butting" and other rituals after particularly dramatic plays (that is, a modern war dance).

Another important place to look for ritualistic behavior is in the art and science of negotiation. Painstaking care is taken in choosing the shape of a negotiating table, in the placement of individuals around the table, in the protocol before, during, and after formal negotiation, et cetera. Close analysis of the negotiation process reveals that what is said (and written) and how it is said, or not, are significantly governed by ritual.

Neumann says of ritualism: "Ritual becomes independent of man. It is performed without any analogous psychic process taking place in the indi-

---

[37] Being "above" the instincts has always been viewed as a mark of the highest form of civilized being.

vidual, and it becomes a 'happening in itself.'. . . ." He goes on to say that "the ritualism which celebrates the archetypal image independently of the individual, causes us in the West to stand amazed before the richness of eternal image now deposited in ritual . . . but we are equally overwhelmed by the fact that Western man is not seized, not formed by this image."[38]

This could also explain, in part, our "numinous" fascination with nuclear arsenals, per se, without being able to relate in personal (as opposed to "intellectual") terms to the megadeath that they represent.

This ritualism is unconscious archaic ritual that has lost most of the archetypal power. Ritualism does not carry the psychic power necessary to contain the instinct to war. At the same time, however, ritualism points to an innate striving by the human psyche to reconnect with powerful transformative rituals that were enacted at some point in human history to minimize the instinct for war. Some present-day attempts (for example, break dancing) are successful, but most (for example, cutting off the ears of the slain enemy) are not. The latter act could be deemed a "successful" ritual if the cutting off of an ear of an opponent were in lieu of killing him. However, the identical act could represent a "war trophy," a symbol of a man's power and prowess as a warrior hero, thus giving impetus to the instinct to make war and to kill—as was the case in Vietnam. The decisive factor in determining whether this identical act would stem the instinct to kill or further it would be the presence or absence of ritualized rules of behavior. I suggest, moreover, that to the extent to which these instincts can be transformed into ritualized behavior, psychic energy can be shifted

---

[38] Erich Neumann. "On the Psychological Meaning of Ritual," *Quadrant* (Winter 1976): 22–23.

As Admiral Noel Gayler points out, "Although communications have been restored at a high level, arms control negotiations are still inadequate. . . . After thirteen years of negotiations about cuts, the number of strategic warheads on both sides has tripled." "The Way Out: A General Nuclear Settlement. *Yale Law and Policy Review*, 5, no. 1 (June–July 1982): 134. Until the signing of the INF Treaty in December 1987, our "ritual" of disarmament talks has not worked in its primary objective.

Psychodynamically, we may be at a potential turning point with the advent of the first nuclear weapons *reduction* treaty negotiated by the Reagan administration and the Mikhail Gorbachev administration in 1987. However, it is crucial to realize that such a turning point would be reflected not by the actual treaty itself (treaties can always be undone, witness Salt II), but rather by a greater capacity for, and commitment to, subordinating political (power) gain to the higher principle of "moral consciousness." More on the latter in Chapter 7.

away from the dominant influence of the warrior hero to greater influence by the archetype of peace.[39]

I propose that ritual can be used as a powerful tool in preventing warfare in the modern age by channelling and releasing energy generated by the archetype of war. Archaic ritualism needs to be converted into conscious ritual in order to reconnect with the archetypal power necessary to contain war-inducing energy. This could be accomplished through researching and then reformalizing archaic behaviors into new ritual systems. These new ritual systems could then be tested and evaluated on the basis of the strength of archetypal holding power they have or do not have in containing and channeling the aggressive energies released through warfare.

Some persons with whom I have discussed this idea think it too far-fetched and radical. It simply could not be done! However, what is proposed here is not much different from what all troops (American and Soviet, among others) presently go through in their respective basic training: that is, simulated combat conditions with live ammunition, including simulated blood and gore. This proposition may seem farfetched to others because psychologically the *purpose* of the exercise would be changed— to dissipate warrior energy rather than build it up, which is the present function of the basic training exercises. The idea of warfare as a "natural" inherent aspect of the masculine psyche and of the patriarchal collective psyche of Western civilization is so ingrained that to propose the same behavior in the name of *dissipating* warrior energy may seem preposterous.

An example: in American combat in Vietnam a well-planned violent assault on a mock village with very credible human dummies that bled— gore would be essential—might have been extremely effective in dissipating the energies that led to the My Lai massacre. Such a "ritual" might have prevented this atrocity that appears to have resulted from an eruption of the collective unconscious more than from any other reason.[40]

---

[39] The archetype of peace is discussed in Chapter 9.

[40] It is not suggested that this approach could be used on a routine basis under battlefield conditions. At best it could be used under extraordinary circumstances, My Lai being one such possibility. I am attempting here to present a psychological scenario to make a point about psychodynamic process and the potential of ritual to control instinctual energy that can—and in the case of acute stress during times of war and other conditions which could lead to war, does—overwhelm the ego. However, this dynamic applies not only in the case of the military battlefield. To quote Roger Molander, former nuclear strategist for the White House National

To be effective as a preventive measure in managing and channeling the aggressive energies between the Soviet Union and the United States, both sides would have to participate in war rituals. This would call for a joint research effort to develop appropriate rituals and the conditions under which they would take place.[41]

Security Council, "The last place I expected to find adults losing control of themselves was in the White House rooms with nuclear war planners. But there the tantrums were—directed at officials of other countries, at briefing books, at staff, at other high U.S. officials, at almost anything you can think of. I had hoped that the White House's nuclear war business was in the hands of people who were rational and calm under pressure." "How I Learned to Start Worrying and Hate the Bomb," *Washington Post, Outlook*, March 21, 1982, pp. D1, D5.

With regard to My Lai, Charlie Company had been in Vietnam just three months, went immediately into combat, had virtually never physically seen the enemy, who was continually harassing it, culminating in a land mine explosion that killed or wounded one third of the entire company. This led to a psychic frenzy on the part of the men, who felt that they were "the hunted," impotent and without recourse like defenseless animals, resulting in intense psychic and emotional tension within the company. Had the company commander been trained to identify and deal with such a situation, he might have recognized the psychological and emotional explosion building up in this company and possibly could have used a ritual exercise to siphon off the frenzied fear and rage experienced by the men of his company. This might have taken the form of setting up mock figures of the enemy (straw dummies), preferably with fake or animal blood contained within them, and a "staged" attack on the enemy with bayonets and knives (more brutal than just shooting at them) to release their pent-up rage at the impotence of their situation. In the absence of such a ritual exercise, the massacre itself took place as an eruption from the "group self" (group psyche) of the company, and the villagers of My Lai ended up serving as "the dummies." This principle can be applied on a macro scale between the two superpowers.

Also see Sue Mansfield, *The Gestalts of War*, for an analysis of the underlying psychological factors involved in the My Lai massacre.

[41] Archetypally, this notion can be said to exist already in the Soviet national psyche. Chingiz Aitmatov's modern Russian fairy tale of *The Day Lasts More than a Thousand Years* portrays a *joint* Soviet-American space project and a modern scapegoat ritual involving the sacrifice of an American and a Soviet cosmonaut. The fact that this novel was first published by an official Soviet organ, *Novyi Mir*, gives it psychological standing in the Soviet national psyche. (See my Chapter 2, note 7, for explication of this modern fairy tale.)

In her essay "The Scapegoat Complex" (*Quadrant* 12 [2] [Fall 1979], Sylvia Massell (Perera) points out that, archetypally speaking, there are *two* necessary scapegoat rituals: a banishment into the desert of "the evil one" and a holocaust: that is, a *voluntary* sacrifice. The banishment of the American and Soviet cosmonauts meets the one requirement, and the sacrifice of the traditional enmity between the two superpowers in order to establish a joint space military defense against the intruder planet meets the other.

Athletic competitions such as the Olympic games provide a functional arena for the discharge of pent-up collective energy. American football is the closest thing to ritualized warfare in competitive sports. The fact that no other country plays American-style football may be an expression of a comparatively higher level of aggression in American culture.

Olympic style, multinational competition is of particular value, because, along with proxy wars and intense economic competition, competitors can functionally sublimate high levels of intense unconscious as well as conscious aggression between nations. Because of the national character of the competition and the emotional investment on the part of the public at large of each of the competing nations, they afford a unique opportunity for the dissipation of aggressive instinct in the larger collective.

Major General William R. Kraft, Jr., USA (Ret.), formerly chief of staff of the U.S. Army in Europe and commander of the Third Armored Division, reported that during the period of occupation of Berlin in postwar Germany, tensions rapidly rose between occupying American and Soviet forces. Spontaneously, the American and Soviet troops engaged in volleyball games at the military liaison mission. The regular contests that ensued between the two sides played a significant role in lowering tensions, which were often at the flash point. A significant amount of the "fight" under which both armies smarted was played out and functionally discharged.[z]

Interestingly, in the preface to his book, Chingiz Aitmatov noted, "There is one strange paradox in this world: in Ancient Greece, wars ceased during the Olympiad; but today the Olympiad has become, for some countries, an excuse for Cold War" (p. xix).

It is significant that both superpowers chose to boycott the 1980 International Olympics as a protest of each other's behavior in the world scene. It was as if each were saying to the other, "Since you broke the [unwritten] rules governing the pursuit of power ambitions, I'm not going to play anymore." Ironically, it is the very type of behavior that each chose in order to disengage that is needed to help avoid the kinds of situations that each was protesting.

We should reexamine for a moment the Soviet invasion of Afghanistan and the American invasion of Grenada, as well as the Falklands (Malvinas) war between Great Britain and Argentina in the context of ritualistic behavior. Similarly, these wars[42] in Angola and Nicaragua (between the

---

[42]They are referred to euphemistically by the United States and the Soviet Union as "regional conflicts."

Sandinistas and the Contras) might be seen as proxy wars between the Soviet Union and the United States. Although significantly different in scope and result, these invasions or proxy wars may be viewed as being *unconscious* acts on the part of each country to dissipate war-inducing energy (that is, ritual warfare) that otherwise might have built up to the point of precipitating a major military confrontation between the superpowers.[43] Because each of these military actions has been seen primarily in political, not psychological, terms by the superpowers, the long-term value of unconscious ritualized warfare is limited at best, and highly dangerous at worst.

Vamik D. Volkan, in disparaging the use of "action as ritual," observes:

> War games and the like indicate that peaceful rituals have given way to something more malignant. In the end, war breaks out directly between the major opposing groups, or, in a displaced way, indirectly between smaller nations or ethnic groups that are the puppets of larger ones.[aa]

Yes, but . . .

War games reflect more than pathology—they reflect a natural archetypal energy, what Volkan refers to earlier in his article (p. 188) as "derivatives of aggression," which need to be kept under control. (Do we envision a world without acted-out aggression between nations if enough "peaceful rituals" are observed?) Volkan appears to equate "peace(ful)" with "benign" and with the absence of aggression.[44]

It is true that benign rituals have progressively given way to more malignant behaviors. However, benign rituals have lost their archetypal power to control and transform aggressive instinct because they are unconscious acts of ritual*ism* (not rituals per se) and thereby have lost the vital element of playfulness that Volkan rightly asserts is essential to keep derivatives of aggression under control (p. 188). Thus, many such rituals have lost their archetypal power to constrain aggressive instinct *because* the rituals themselves are too distanced from, and devoid of, aggressive energy. But what would happen if conscious, jointly defined rituals that were sufficiently "playful" and expressive of aggressive drive were developed between the Soviet Union and the United States? Could it be that the proxy wars and fights between smaller nations and ethnic groups might diminish? Might it not be that their mutual commitment to avoid war between themselves as manifested through their joint rituals would

---

[43] See note 3 of Chapter 6.
[44] See my definition of *peace* in Chapter 9.

forge between these committed enemies a powerful bond for survival that is even more powerful than their enmity? Might it not be that conscious rituals, because of their jointly determined and highly defined and policed procedures, could bring about a higher level of ego control and provide more real separation between the antagonists than some more indirect benign rituals? Might such a drama be in the making between the Soviet Union and the United States in the Persian Gulf, Angola, and elsewhere? (See Chapter 7.)

The two superpowers seem to have sensed this danger at some limited level with respect to the not so "little" Iran-Iraq war. Although each had limited the amount and kinds of armaments supplied, until the Iran-Contra scandal of 1987, neither had cut off shipments of war materiel to the antagonists (the United States to Iran and Iraq and Russia to Iraq). At the same time, both sides have held regular meetings with each other to keep communication channels open to avoid miscalculation and to keep the scope of the war from drawing the superpowers into direct conflict.[45]

In the long run, the security of the world will be much enhanced through a realization of and focus on the unconscious forces that move men and nations toward conflict in the first place rather than solely on mechanisms to deal with the destructive result of our unconsciousness.

---

[45] Deeper implications for the superpowers regarding the Iran-Iraq war are discussed in Chapter 7.

⑦ Primary Cooperation

THE TRANSCENDENT FUNCTION

Carl Jung formulated the psychodynamic concept of the "transcendent function."[a] This notion holds that the psychic tension resulting from the competition or clash of opposites (drives, emotions, ideas or ideologies, et cetera) can produce a creative (transcendent) third position or reality. This "third," or transcendent, position is not the sum of, or a rational compromise of, the two opposites that have given rise to it, but is a synergism. This synergism represents a new psychic quantum, which may not resemble at all either of the opposites that were the source of the tension giving rise to its birth. This fact suggests that the new third represents a psychic potential that has lain dormant in the individual self, in the relationship between individuals, or in the collective unconscious itself. It is at the level of the collective unconscious that the transcendent function emerges with regard to the psychodynamics of relations between nations.[1]

That this new psychic quantum represents a potential inherent in the self (be it of a single nation or the relational dynamic between nations) has profound implications for international relations, especially between enemy nations with radically opposing ideologies such as is the case between the Soviet Union and the United States. It suggests that there is usually a transcendent psychic potential *inherent in the conflict itself,* which, if realized, can transform even the most impossible dilemma and seeming stalemate. One way of understanding this psychodynamic phenomenon is to consider that the conflict, in part, exists for purposes of giving birth to a new psychic quantum: for example, the birth of a new era in national or international consciousness.[2]

It is the case, more often than not, that the new consciousness that emerges as a result of the transcendent function does not fit any preexisting rational framework originally connected to the problem or conflict.

---

[1] See my Introduction for a discussion of the "collective unconscious."

[2] An obvious example would be the birth of the new political idea of republican government in 1776.

For example, given the intensity and absoluteness of the respective hostile stances between the two superpowers (translated in practical terms into more than fifty thousand nuclear warheads), who would have thought that the way out of the deterrence standoff/threat/dilemma would be "cooperation" between the two enemy nations? "Mutually assured destruction" (MAD), the literal antithesis of "cooperation," both in spirit and in fact, was the cornerstone of what later became modern-day deterrence policy. I am suggesting that cooperation, as defined in this chapter, is the new psychic quantum produced by the transcendent function in Soviet-American conflict.

The implication might seem to be that if we have only enough conflict of sufficient intensity, the transcendent function will emerge with the solution. Far from the case, unfortunately. Such a simplistic approach will nearly always lead to disaster (as in the Middle East conflict).

The transcendent function emerges as a result of the *struggle* (as opposed to *clash*) between opposites. This kind of struggle usually is heavily influenced by moral consciousness. In individual and collective psychology, it results from an ego struggle to prevent total identification with one or the other opposite position involved in the conflict—often not out of choice, but out of necessity to prevent a disaster perceived or felt to be more destructive or morally untenable than the conflict itself. The transcendent function usually emerges when there is a stalemate, and there is no seeming solution to the tension and conflict, *provided* that the parties to the conflict do not give in to the urge to destroy one another and remain consciously engaged in the struggle for a way out of the impasse. These conditions have been amply represented in the conflict between the Soviet Union and the United States.

It bears repeating that the new third position is not a rational result of deductive process. It does represent a quantum leap in conscious reality. The outcome will likely not look like any logical or behavioral truth that the parties to the conflict have known and therefore will require an alertness and openness to a new way of perceiving and thinking.

PRIMARY COOPERATION AS A TRANSCENDENT
DYNAMIC IN SOVIET-AMERICAN RELATIONS

The advent of nuclear weaponry and missile technology has had the primary effect of eliminating world war as an acceptable means for settling disputes on the part of those nations capable of engaging in it. There is

Drawing by Tom Kleh. Copyright © 1985 by Tom Kleh. Used by permission.

little doubt anymore that world war carries the unacceptable risk of escalating into nuclear holocaust. Indeed, there is growing recognition that *any* war, no matter how small, carries the gravest of dangers—namely, the involvement of the superpowers and a resultant nuclear confrontation with unacceptable consequences for all.[3]

We are in the midst of a process where there is a virtual universal perception and a new *conscious* realization that war itself, not other groups and nations, has become the greater threat to the survival of life. This fact represents an event in the evolution of civilization on the order of man's shift to agriculture from hunting and gathering, and the discovery of the wheel. We are in the grips of a still-unfolding evolutionary process of historic proportions, and the United States and the Soviet Union apparently are its primary instruments.

However, this evolutionary shift, and the resultant struggle by the su-

---

[3] An important exception is that of fanatics who not only do not subscribe to this implicit value system, but use the threat of nuclear holocaust toward their own ends. More about this exception later.

perpowers and their allies to avoid nuclear annihilation, has brought with it a host of new problems, the major one being what do we do with our instinct to make war? And what is the nature of civilization without world war? How do we manage the dilemma of a peace whose almost exclusive technology of deterrence to date carries with it the threat and the capacity to bring about the very extinction of life it is designed to protect? What are the other implications of this evolutionary turn in the road?

Cooperation, based on moral consciousness, is rapidly displacing deterrence as the primary technology of peace for the superpowers. Deterrence is the agent that is forcing cooperation between the Soviet Union and the United States. It has generated a new class of problems for which the only solution is the cooperation of the two enemy superpowers. Historically, cooperation has always taken place in the name of survival. It has involved intergroup cooperation against other groups and nations perceived as competitors or enemies.

The "cooperation" alluded to in this context involves two enemy states cooperating against their mutual enemy, war. This represents a new, transcendent psychodynamic that has never existed before in man's history.

Either the two countries cooperate in the prevention and containment of war *and* their deterrence technologies as well, or they risk mutual national suicide and the gravest of sins—the killing of life itself. This is the reality of the present and the future. It cannot be undone, any more than the atom bomb can be undone.

Moreover, these facts and conditions, at least for today and into the foreseeable future, apply *only* to the Soviet Union and the United States. They alone have the capacity to destroy life on this planet.[4] Never before in human history have two countries found themselves facing the awesome fact that what they do can decide not only the fate of their peoples and the world at large, but of life itself. I stress this point because it is the moral shadow that hangs over all of the deterrence policy and planning between the two countries and therefore is an ever-increasing force per-

---

[4] It might be argued that France, Britain, and China (as well as Israel, the Union of South Africa [?], India, and others) also have the capacity to destroy life on this planet. Although each may possess (and this is not certain) a sufficient number of warheads and megatonnage quantitatively to bring about a nuclear winter, it is unlikely that any or all of them could deliver and detonate a large number of warheads (or, conceivably, any!) against the wishes and the defensive technologies of the Soviet Union and the United States. Thus, my assertion that the Soviet Union and the United States alone among nations have the capacity to destroy life as we know it.

meating their perceptions of the conflict between them. Not of their choosing, the Soviet Union and the United States find themselves in an unholy marriage having become the *joint* guardians of the future of mankind and of life itself. Like it or not, we have become partners, as much as, if not more than, we are enemies—indeed *because* we are enemies— and we find ourselves in the extraordinary position of having to protect each other in order to protect ourselves. Psychologically, this is not only a profound turn in events, its represents a new psychic principle governing relationships between nations.

Détente was a conscious instrument of policy aimed at changing Soviet policies and behaviors.[5] Forced cooperation—I shall call it "primary cooperation"—is not as much a decision of policy as it is a realization of the limits of power politics and the policies and strategies that ensue therefrom. It reflects a realization that neither side can win, that they can only lose. And I would argue that this realization applies to the totality of the superpower relationships, not just the military aspect. However, this fact has not yet fully crossed over into the threshold of superpower consciousness (although there is increasing evidence that General Secretary Gorbachev may have such a broad vision).

All of this already has brought about radical changes in thinking and behavior on the part of both superpowers. In the years before and after World War II up to the 1970s, it would have been unheard of for two enemies to exchange technical data on the size and movement of ground and naval forces and to invite enemy observers on site at their military maneuvers. To provide each other with numbers, telemetry, location, firepower, protective defenses, cost factors, photographs, and the like on

---

[5] Seweryn Bialer observes: "Our expectations of detente were very simple. We thought that by developing economic ties with the Soviet Union, by having arms limitation agreements, by creating a web of cultural exchanges and economic and technical relationships with the Soviets, we could moderate Soviet international behavior and make the Soviet Union less interested in invasions.

"The Soviet Union had . . . a different concept of detente. [It] expected that the achievement of military parity with the United States . . . should be accompanied by *political* parity with the United States. The Soviet leaders thus expected to be treated . . . as equals. . . . While the Soviet Union agreed to a freeze of its expansion in Europe, it also expected that it could expand, by military means if necessary, in the grey areas of the world.

"There was also a discrepancy between the development of American perceptions and will and of Soviet perceptions and will." In Nish Jamgotch, Jr., *Sectors of Mutual Benefit in U.S.–Soviet Relations*. (Durham, N.C.: Duke University Press, 1985), p. 159.

their respective weapons systems, et cetera, would have been considered treason, if not madness. Yet all of these behaviors are routine today.[6]

Moreover, the two enemy superpowers increasingly are spending more time on avoiding conflict between themselves and their client states or groups. In the interest of avoiding military confrontation between themselves, they have held regular, unofficial meetings concerning such conflicts as the Iran-Iraq war and the war in Angola, along with other areas of conflict in the world, to set and maintain for their respective clients boundaries of support not intolerable to the other superpower. There are tacit agreements establishing limits on levels of military support and types of military technology that each makes available to its client states and groups.

An example would be the exclusion of most types of offensive weaponry in the Middle East, the exclusion of offensive weaponry such as tanks and helicopters by the United States to the antigovernment forces fighting in Afghanistan, and the Soviet exclusion of attack aircraft and tanks from the materiel provided the Sandinista government in Nicaragua.

Of particular, but not much heralded, note are the Confidence- and Security-Building Measures, developed in two stages over an eleven year period, under the 1975 Helsinki Accords. These confidence- and security-building measures have been considered a stepchild operating in the shadow of the more glamorous arms-reduction treaty process. However, I would argue that the confidence- and security-building measures process holds the greater long-term potential for sustaining the peace. In addition, that process reflects an emergent consciousness of a new kind concerning the nature of war and the requirements for managing the peace.

The second phase of this process was completed in September 1986 at a conference in Stockholm. The Soviet Union, the United States, the Warsaw Pact and NATO countries, among others, are signatories to the critically important final document. These confidence- and security-building measures (CBMs, as they are called) are important not only for their specific provisions, but they represent the first major development since the formalization of "conflict resolution" as a discipline, toward what I call a new "peace technology."

The provisions of the Conference on Security and Co-Operation in Eu-

---

[6] For an excellent summary of the history of Soviet-American cooperation in the development of mechanisms and technology for protecting themselves from nuclear annihilation through misunderstanding, miscalculation, miscommunication, or third-party forces, see Jamgotch, chapter 2.

rope (otherwise known as the Stockholm Conference) require signatory nations to provide advance notification of all military activity involving thirteen thousand troops or at least three hundred battle tanks and require the invitation of up to two observers from nonparticipating nations when the number of troops involved exceeds seventeen thousand or, in the case of amphibious or parachute assault, five thousand troops.[b] In order to allow the observers to confirm that the notified activity is non-threatening in character, the host State will:

• at the commencement of the observation programme give a briefing on the purpose, the basic situation, the phases of the activity and possible changes as compared with the notification and provide the observers with a map of the area of the military activity . . . and an observation programme with a daily schedule as well as a sketch indicating the basic situation;

• in the course of the observation programme give the observers daily briefings with the help of maps on the various phases of the military activity and their development and inform the observers about their positions geographically;

• provide opportunities to observe directly forces of the States engaged in the military activity so that the observers get an impression of the flow of the activity; . . . the observers will be given the opportunity to observe major combat units of the participating formations of a divisional or equivalent level and, whenever possible, to visit some units and communicate with commanders and troops. . . .[c]

In addition, any signatory nation may demand, once in a given year, a mandatory inspection of the territory of another when it suspects that compliance with agreed confidence- and security-building measures is in doubt.[7]

Under the provisions of the Helsinki Accords of 1975, the Soviet Union and the United States have been committed to, and have essentially complied with, the provision of advance notification of maneuvers. The invita-

---

[7] With regard to inspections, including mandatory inspections, the formal document also provides, "Any possible dispute as to the validity of the reasons for a request will not prevent or delay the conduct of the inspection" (p. 21), and "The reply to the request will be given in the shortest possible period of time, but within not more than twenty-four hours. *Within thirty-six hours after the issuance of the request, the inspection team will be permitted to enter the territory of the receiving State*" (p. 23). (My emphasis.)

tion of observers from the other side was voluntary and essentially not complied with by the Soviet Union and the Warsaw Pact countries between 1975 and 1986.

However, it was at the Stockholm conference, which took place between January 1984 and September 1986, that the Soviet Union and the United States agreed to modify the Accords to provide for *mandatory* observations of maneuvers on each other's territory and *mandatory* territorial inspections, all of which would become binding on all signatories as of January 1, 1987. The Reuters News Service reported on January 6, 1987, that, in compliance with the Agreement, the Warsaw Pact had invited Western observers to nine large-scale maneuvers that year, more than in all the previous ten years. From January 1987, when the program began, through December 1988, Warsaw Bloc countries have notified NATO of forty-six exercises and hosted observer teams at fifteen of them. Likewise, NATO notified Warsaw Pact of thirty-five exercises, seventeen of which were observed by teams from Warsaw Pact countries, both camps therefore being in full compliance with the Stockholm Agreement. There were nine inspections each on both sides, suggesting that consistent with past political behavior, when one side implies suspicion of an activity by the other, there is a kind of tit-for-tat behavior. To date there have been two protests, both in 1988, with the Warsaw Pact in each case accusing the Federal Republic of Germany of not living up to the letter of the agreement. (There appears to have been no follow-on to these protests, suggesting that they were not of too serious a nature.)[d]

These agreements represent astonishing progress on the part of the United States and the Soviet Union in developing a technology to monitor and contain deterrence as well as to prevent war. They reflect, also, a level of containment (but not necessarily conscious integration) of shadow projection unprecedented in the superpower relationship.[8] They repre-

---

[8]The difference between containment and integration of shadow elements is that the former involves only behavioral constraint in the name of a higher goal; for example, arms-reduction treaties. Perceptions and attitudes toward the other remain essentially unchanged—the evil empire is still the evil empire and the repository of all evil—ours as well as theirs. (Former President Reagan's disavowal of the Soviet Union as the "evil empire" in the wake of the 1988 Moscow summit does represent some significant shadow integration on his part. However, Mr. Reagan's psychological growth did not carry over to other critical elements within his administration; namely, Vice President Bush and Secretary of Defense Carlucci.)

In the case of shadow integration the Soviets would recognize consciously that, at best, their invasion of Afghanistan was fundamentally no different morally from

sent the first formal recognition that ultimately man's future is dependent on the psychology of his behavior more than on his ingenuity in developing the physics of war.

The Document of the Stockholm Conference states that these provisions are aimed at reducing the dangers of armed conflict and of misunderstanding or miscalculation of military activities—in and of themselves historic and extremely valuable agreements. However, I would submit that an unconscious aim of these provisions is to force a progressive noncombatant relationship between hostile and enemy nations, particularly their military and intelligence personnel, and to further the development of cooperation as a primary tool in a new peace technology that is beginning to emerge. It is important to note here that this represents a significant psychodynamic shift. Typically, transformation must take place before cooperation can take place. In this instance, primary cooperation is the change agent that has begun to transform the hostile relationship between the superpowers. It is also changing the nature and dynamics of power relationships between all nations, including the ways in which power is perceived.

The advent of nuclear weaponry and missile technology has turned on its head reality as we have known it. In the present context and into the future, while *any* of the world's countries or fanatical groups may disrupt the peace, it now requires *both* the United States and the Soviet Union to maintain it. Thus, to avoid nuclear confrontation, the superpowers will have to cooperate with each other to prevent war between themselves, and to do that they will have to prevent or contain all war and conflicts that can precipitate war between them.

Containing all war does not mean the elimination of all war—which does not appear to be possible in the foreseeable future. However, it does mean that the two superpowers will have to become progressively more conscious in controlling the scope and nature of the proxy wars that are fought between them, as in Afghanistan and Nicaragua. Doing this will require progressive consciousness-raising as to the reasons for and value

---

the American invasion of Cuba or Grenada. Americans would recognize consciously that the manipulation of the overthrow of the Allende regime in Chile and covert military support for the Contras in Nicaragua is fundamentally no more moral than Soviet actions in Angola and Afghanistan. (Before the start of the withdrawal of Soviet troops, one might assert that the presence of Soviet troops in Afghanistan was more immoral than American behavior in Nicaragua, where no American troops were sent. Notwithstanding, that does not make American behavior moral.)

of a given proxy war, in addition to controlling the scope and nature of actual hostilities. As hostilities mount and the risk of a wider involvement of the two superpowers increases, each side will be forced to reexamine and redefine the value of a given proxy war.

For example, in 1986 the United States introduced Stinger ground-to-air missiles in the Afghanistan war, placing Soviet helicopters in greater jeopardy. There was also an incremental escalation in 1987 of Soviet intrusions into Pakistani air space and bombing of supply routes and staging areas in Pakistan. It is debatable (notwithstanding the Soviet decision to withdraw from Afghanistan) as to whether the introduction of the Stinger missiles actually increased *real* pressure on the Soviets to withdraw from Afghanistan, or whether it made it more difficult for them to withdraw because of Soviet reluctance to be militarily humiliated. In any event, it is likely that these decisions increasingly will force a deeper level of consciousness about the implications and value of power confrontation and will further heighten contact between the superpowers in an effort to contain their respective power drives.

Relatedly, it seems apparent in the wake of the post-Reykjavik shock of 1986[9] that the Soviet Union and the United States are learning that although neither country wishes to live with the nuclear threat, neither is it feasible to live without it. Notwithstanding their unanimous approval of the INF Treaty entered into by the United States and the Soviet Union in December 1987, our NATO allies fear the removal of the American nuclear umbrella over Western Europe.[10] In addition, how could the super-

---

[9] A summit meeting between President Ronald Reagan and General Secretary Mikhail Gorbachev in Reykjavik, Iceland, on October 11–12, 1986, at which historic proposals for drastic nuclear weapons reductions were agreed to by both sides only to become stalemated on the United States refusal of the Soviet demand to compromise its SDI program. (Unofficial reports revealed that even total elimination of strategic nuclear weapons was momentarily agreed to.) The "shock" had to do with the realization—for the first time by both sides—that there was a real desire and readiness to eliminate nuclear weapons in the absolute sense. In pursuing that desire, each realized that real elimination of nuclear weapons posed its own problems. This has become translated into a focus on "minimum sufficiency," the *minimum* number of nuclear weapons each side must maintain to meet its own perceived national security needs.

[10] On March 28, 1987, Prime Minister Jacques Chirac of France expressed his concern regarding American negotiations with the Soviet Union to eliminate intermediate-range missiles from Europe. He was quoted in the *Washington Post* as stating, "An agreement on medium-range missiles must not undercut the overall balance of nuclear forces. . . ." The *Post* went on to state that Chirac would convey to President Reagan the strong private misgivings of the French, Brit-

powers, without nuclear weapons, confront another country or group possessing nuclear weapons or devices?[11]

In sum, the problem with which we have thought we have been dealing since the Cuban Missile Crisis has changed under our very noses. Although the ballistics-missile and deterrence technology have changed the meaning of *war, peace, survival, winning, losing,* and *enemy,* the Soviet Union and the United States still behave as if they are dealing with a problem that is primarily technological and logistical.[12] With the two exceptions of the United States–Soviet Hotline and the Confidence- and Security-Building Measures,[13] our solutions still are almost exclusively weapons-oriented. For example, take SDI. Even if it worked with better than 90 percent effectiveness, which no one, including the Reagan admin-

---

ish, and, to a lesser extent, West German officials concerning the impact of proposed INF agreements on the Atlantic Alliance. (The *Washington Post,* March 29, 1987, p. A-1.)

This attitude not only represented (as of April 1987) that of the majority of governments in the Western Alliance, but also reflected the concerns of a large number of American officials of all political persuasions, both in and out of government, including former President Richard M. Nixon, former Secretary of State Henry A. Kissinger, and even Edward L. Rowny, special adviser on arms control to then President Reagan and Secretary of State George P. Shultz, both of whom were the chief architects and proponents of the plan to eliminate intermediate range missiles from Europe and Asia. (The *Washington Post,* April 29, 1987, p. A-1.)

[11] Additionally, it is the threat of nuclear weapons that is forcing cooperation between the superpowers. Take that threat away and the relationship likely will regress to a more primitive and perhaps even more destructive level. Conventional political and military wisdom at the time held that the elimination of certain nuclear weapons will almost surely mean an eventual buildup of conventional forces in Europe and a possible destabilization of the European peace maintained since the end of World War II. In addition, the treaty removing INF missiles from Europe does not eliminate tactical nuclear weapons nor the strategic arsenals of the two superpowers.

[12] In his annual military report, released on January 10, 1987, then Secretary of Defense Caspar Weinberger asserted that high-tech weaponry and new tactics are the only way to compete successfully against Soviet advantages in numbers and perennially high defense funding. (The *Washington Post,* January 11, 1987, p. A5).

[13] Including the 1972 Incidents at Sea Agreement, which was a forerunner to the more formalized CBMs consummated in the Stockholm Agreement of 1986. The Incidents at Sea Agreement establishes standard procedures and signals to be employed by the navies of both countries in avoiding incidents at sea. The recognition that such incidents could escalate into military confrontation was the impetus for the Agreement, which has worked effectively on both sides.

istration, claimed, its putative protection would last only as long the next round of technological warfare, which the Soviets no doubt would pursue regardless of cost.

Deterrence technology, in and of itself, will no longer work independent of cooperation technology. Although the world has been fortunate—lucky—that it has worked these past forty years, the odds are that, uncontained, deterrence eventually will be our undoing. It has generated the amassing of more than fifty thousand warheads in the respective nuclear arsenals of the superpowers in the name of keeping the peace. And this threat from deterrence would not be eliminated in its essentials even if all of the proposals for missile cuts put forward at Reykjavik were to be implemented.[14] The more pressing problem is that, to date, the superpowers haven't had an alternative to deterrence.

Nuclear deterrence and pseudospeciation together have brought the world to the crossroads.[15] We have gone about as far as we can go with our mentality of attempting to solve conflicts with our enemies almost exclusively through military and technological supremacy. Over the last ten to fifteen years we have been learning, gradually, that deterrence can be our undoing as well as having been our salvation for over forty years. We have yet to grasp the full reality of pseudospeciation and its implications.[16]

Man's psychological predisposition toward pseudospeciation serves as a perpetual generator of energy that feeds the archetype of war. In other words, *the instinct to aggression + pseudospeciation = the psychic conditions that feed the archetype of war.* Moreover, pseudospeciation constellates the most primitive paranoia in the human psyche and subtly, but definitely, activates man's instinct to aggression. Whatever constructive gains we have been able to achieve by way of conflict resolution, disarmament treaties, and the like, pseudospeciation lurks ever-present, ready to undermine and rend it all asunder. Man *will* have his enemies—pseudospeciation will see to that.

The critical question before us is: Now that civilization has reached a

---

[14] Even a 90 percent reduction in the present level of all nuclear warheads would leave more than five thousand warheads. Evenly divided, that would leave each side with twenty-five hundred warheads—still more than enough to destroy life as we know it.

[15] "Pseudospeciation" is a psychological phenomenon wherein a given social, cultural, or ethnic group perceives itself as if it and other groups of people were a separate species unto itself, some other "species" being perceived as undesirable, and often seen as hostile and a threat.

[16] See Chapter 8 for a more extensive discussion of "pseudospeciation."

point where the destructive element of its developmental spiral[17] threatens to eradicate permanently any possibility of future growth, what can be done about man's inherent tendency toward pseudospeciation, which threatens the annihilation of the species itself? We will have to find a way to transcend the ingrained, but not genetic, psychodynamic predisposition toward pseudospeciation and better manage our instinct to aggression. To do that, I propose, we will have to develop a whole new technology—a peace technology.[18]

As a central component of a new peace technology, I propose that the United States and the Soviet Union move toward engaging in joint war games directly with each other. Such war games would occur under jointly determined, ritualized rules that would optimize the discharge of aggressive energy while controlling and minimizing the destructiveness of the games and the loss of life. No territorial or other material gain would be involved. All war games would end with appropriate rituals for reestablishing the psychic balance and for assuring that neither side left the experience unduly humiliated. This last point is crucial.

The containment of the archetype of war by the United States and the Soviet Union has not come without a psychological price. Over the past forty years an enormous amount of aggressive energy has been dammed up in the collective unconscious. Newton's law of the conservation of energy holds that energy, as such, cannot be destroyed; it can only be transformed or channeled. This is no less true in man's psychological nature than it is of the physical world. Ironically, while deterrence has been effective over the past forty years in containing world war, it simultaneously has increased tension in the collective unconscious for war. If the nations of the world, the superpowers in particular, do not find *ongoing and controlled* outlets for the psychic energy dammed up in the collective unconscious, eventually it will break through with a vengeance none of us or our progeny may survive.

It is clear that the psychological momentum for nuclear arms cuts begun at Reykjavik in October 1986, coupled with the social and political revolution taking place in the Soviet Union, has markedly reduced tensions between the United States and the Soviet Union and in the rest of the world. Whether this reduction in tension will be sustained remains to be seen. The momentum for further radical cuts in nuclear weapons by

---

[17] Which up until the mid-1980s included war as a major tool in the evolution of culture.

[18] See Chapter 9 for a discussion of "peace technology."

the superpowers stalled pending the change in administration after the American elections of November 1988. There is also the question of whether or not Mr. Gorbachev can sustain and deliver on his political revolution.

It is the thesis of this book that the deeper psychological derivatives of conflict must be addressed along with prevalent political issues if long-term permanent change in world order is to happen. There is danger that we can be lulled into a complacency based on the existing psychological atmosphere in the wake of the INF treaty of 1987.[19]

We have stretched deterrence as far as it will go; a science of ritual warfare is indispensable to contain and prevent world war (and thus nuclear holocaust) into the future. Ritual warfare could—has already begun to, I would argue—compensate for the paradox of pent-up energy in the national psyches of the superpowers that will continue to result from their increasing capacity to restrain the instinct to aggression (that is, resulting from the absence of direct warfare between them), and as a result of pseudospeciation. Although other forms of cooperation (for example, a joint Soviet-American exploration of Mars) and competition (for example, Olympic competition) between the superpowers are essential for creating positive transformative models of competitive cooperation and for releasing some degree of psychic tension between them, ultimately actual war games are essential for displacing the powerful aggressive instinct that persistently threatens to precipitate killing on a large scale.

Primitive man may have been able to contain at a symbolic level the urge to kill his enemies. Symbolic containment alone will not suffice for deritualized civilized man—Western man in particular—because of his lust for power (absent in primitive, ritually connected man). Civilized man's identification with his power drive has been not only a major source of conflict in the world, but it has been also a primary source of his insatiable materialism, which has deified acquisition of property and control over nature (and countries) and brought about the atrophy of his ritual life.[e]

To be able to develop a science of ritual warfare, the Soviet Union and the United States will have to develop a formal technology of cooperation. Both of these will be central components of what I have broadly termed "peace technology."

---

[19]The INF treaty in fact eliminates less than 5 percent of the nuclear arsenals of the superpowers. Present weapons plans and appropriations of both the Soviet Union and the United States, unchanged, will wipe out those reductions within the next two to three years.

What does ritual warfare have to do with present-day conflict between the superpowers? The war games conducted by NATO and Warsaw Pact countries could be viewed as a kind of sham warfare.[20] Although at a conscious level these war games are conducted for the purpose of training *for* war, unconsciously they may also serve as a psychological means of containing the archetype of war in a manner similar to that of primitive tribes.

We have already discussed in the previous chapter the power of ritual to contain what would otherwise be unbridled primitive aggression resulting in the loss of scores of lives, if not whole social groups. *Psychologically,* that is the express purpose of ritual warfare—to serve as a means of dissipating the energies that build from the instinct for aggression while minimizing the loss of life and preserving the cohesion of the groups and societies involved.

At the same time, ritual warfare serves another subtle, but crucial, psychological function—to bring instinctual aggression under control of the ego. What is harnessed by the ego and called forth at will, *with the aid of ritual,* can also be put back into psychic containment through an ego decision. That is exactly what happens in modern-day war games. Men are worked up to fever pitch and go about their mock warfare with all seriousness and intent. But the object of war game is to train for war, not to kill. In military preparedness, the Soviet and American ego is harnessed to contain, as well as to express, the instinct to war.[21] The crucial question is: Are we sufficiently mature psychologically to have war games with an enemy?

This is not as farfetched as it may sound at first reading. In fact, the basic psychological groundwork for such a possibility already has been laid; ironically, both sides have moved unconsciously in that direction. During routine American naval maneuvers, the Soviet navy regularly "shadows" the American navy. Likewise, American naval captains use these Soviet submarines and ships as so-called "targets of opportunity"

---

[20] In the case of sham warfare among primitive groups, some forms would involve "fights" between enemies and some would involve parallel "fights" where each side would engage in ritualized sham fights within its own group in full view of the other enemy tribe or group. NATO and Warsaw Pact maneuvers would fall into this second, "parallel," category.

[21] In the parlance of conventional warfare, it takes one hell of a lot of ego control to wait "until you see the whites of their eyes" before firing!

that are hypothetically "attacked" and "sunk" during war games, so that each simultaneously is target for the other. Such naval maneuvers often constitute naval battles without shots being fired.[22] Similar shadowing of the aircraft of the two nations takes place as well.

In fact, during joint U.S. naval maneuvers with the South Korean Navy in the Sea of Japan, on March 21, 1984, a Soviet Victor 1 nuclear-powered submarine was forced to surface in the midst of the U.S. naval task force because it had been hit by the aircraft carrier USS *Kitty Hawk,* and severely damaged. The U.S. aircraft carrier and the Soviet submarine had been tracking each other during the naval exercises, and it was thought that the sub was running too close to the surface, causing the collision. There have been so many such incidents that the United States and the Soviet Union concluded the Incidents at Sea Agreement to establish standardized universal rules and communication signals for conduct of ships at sea.

Moreover, on January 8, 1986, for the first time, ships of the Seventh Fleet of the U.S. Navy and the navy of the People's Liberation Army of the People's Republic of China jointly conducted an "exercise in passing" in the South China Sea.[23] The ships involved were the USS *Oldendorf,* a destroyer, and the USS *Jack Williams,* a guided-missile frigate. The Chinese ships involved were a Luda class destroyer and a Fuquing class oiler. The activities involved in the exercise included the exchange of various communication symbols (flag hoist, flashing lights, electronic), maneuvering and station keeping, and simulated underway replenishment and personnel training. The exercise was jointly approved by the United States departments of Defense and State, and more are planned. This exercise is of particular significance, because it is the first *conscious* military exercise

---

[22] Source: Interview with Rear Admiral Eugene J. Carroll, Jr., USN (Ret.), on August 12, 1985. Admiral Carroll is the former commander of Task Force 60 of the U.S. Sixth Fleet in the Mediterranean, first naval officer to serve as director of U.S. military operations for all U.S. forces in Europe and the Middle East, and former assistant deputy chief of naval operations for plans, policy and operations, in which capacity he was engaged in U.S. naval planning for conventional and nuclear war. He is presently deputy director of the Center for Defense Information in Washington, D.C.

[23] A "passing exercise" is composed of two to eight ships normally involved for approximately one day. The ships conduct mutual training activities that are normally not possible in formations of single ships of similar types.

Source: Telephone interview with the U.S. Navy Office of Information, Commander-in-Chief, Pacific Fleet.

engaged in by the United States with a country perceived officially as an adversary, and one that only a few years ago was perceived as an enemy.

The most dramatic and instructive example of modern-day ritual warfare has involved the United States and Libya. In February 1986, the United States began holding several weeks of naval maneuvers in the Mediterranean Sea, off the coast of Libya. The conscious purpose of these highly visible maneuvers was to signal Libya's leader, Colonel Muammar Qaddafi, that his alleged support of international terrorists could be highly costly. During these naval maneuvers, American warplanes from two aircraft carriers made several "intercepts" of Libyan warplanes, some of them reportedly having approached within two hundred yards of American fighters. In one day alone—February 12, 1986—there were more than twenty-five encounters reported between Libyan and American aircraft. The *Washington Post* reported on February 13, "While the Pentagon did not say so, its assertion that no hostile encounters occurred indicates the Libyan pilots let themselves be shouldered away before nearing either carrier's battle groups."[f]

The implication is that both the United States and Libya consciously determined to carry out military maneuvers "against" each other, but without overt hostile action—that is, they made a subconscious decision to engage in de facto ritual warfare.

These naval maneuvers were ordered after considerable debate within the Reagan administration over whether the United States should bomb strategic targets within Libya in retaliation for terrorist attacks in Rome and Vienna on December 29, 1985, which the United States alleged were directed and supported by Libya (and for which other countries, including Israel, blamed Syria). It is noteworthy that this first round of military exercises was *in lieu of* the proposed bombing of Libya—the precise psychological and archetypal aim of ritual warfare: the avoidance of overt hostile action leading to killing on a large scale.

It is clear that, initially, each nation saw itself as making only a political statement to the other, and surely neither recognized that they were engaged in de facto ritual warfare.

The military exercises (de facto ritual warfare) between the two countries continued for approximately six weeks without overt hostilities until March 22, when the Libyans fired ground-to-air missiles at American planes and the United States responded by destroying an on-ground radar site, sinking two Libyan ships and damaging a third with an estimated loss of thirty Libyan lives. It is an important detail that the American naval commander knew with virtual certainty, as did the Libyans who launched them, that the Soviet-supplied heat-seeking SAM missiles were fired at too great a range from the American aircraft to be able to hit them.[24] Thus it might be said that while the Libyans were "playing by the rules" of this de facto ritual war (unwritten and unstated though they were), the United States decided not to.

I would propose that the de facto ritual warfare did work, as such, for a five-and-a-half-week period from February 13 until March 22, 1986.

When ritual warfare is engaged in unconsciously, rules are not defined, and it is difficult to maintain boundaries. In any case, ritual warfare on a sustained basis of several weeks continuously would be difficult to contain under any circumstances, as events proved with the American bombing of Libya on April 14, 1986. In the case of conscious ritual warfare, it would be better to have several short-term engagements of much limited duration (one to two weeks maximum).

Whatever the conscious motivation for such activities on the part of the governments involved, this example represents a de facto war game between enemy states. The fact that the Reagan administration had been looking for reasons to justify military confrontation with Libya does not change the psychological (as opposed to the political) function of the activity. The same would be true between the Soviet Union and the United States.

Psychodynamically, the Soviet Union and the United States *unconsciously* are moving toward the implementation of ritual warfare as a substitute for direct hostilities with one another and to contain the archetype of war.[25] The ultimate question is whether or not they can accept such behavior on a *conscious* level. Psychologically, the above-cited American naval exercise with the People's Republic of China is the first small step in this direction. The most important factor here is not the extent nor the direct impact of this limited example in containing war. Rather, it is what the national psyches of enemy states were and are reaching for.

Again, it is recognized that the professed aim of the joint American-Chinese military maneuvers (and subsequent formal and secret defense agreements between the two nations) is a political one aimed at "contain-

---

[24] The *Washington Post* quoted Donald A. Hicks, undersecretary of defense for research, as stating that it was no surprise to him that the six SAMs fired at Navy planes missed. The missiles were at their "outer range," he said. (April 4, 1986, p. A12.)

[25] I include "sham wars" in the concept of ritual warfare as it is used in this context.

ing" Soviet military domination of the Pacific. However, notwithstanding conscious motives, there are at the same time powerful unconscious drives that have a radically different agenda—probably in this case, the beginning of the development of ritual warfare between hostile and enemy states on a formal and structured basis.

With regard to consciousness-raising, once there has been a first step, no matter how small, a threshold is crossed and there will almost certainly follow a second . . . and a third . . . , et cetera. This is particularly so when there is a psychic mandate in the collective unconscious to move the antagonists toward cooperation as a means of survival.[26] Rituals that are consciously engaged in have the greatest potential power for containing archetypal energies such as the archetype of war.

To begin to implement on a conscious level the kind of concept that is proposed here, it would be necessary to begin with a very limited objective that held extreme threat and the same or nearly the same degree of self-interest, import, and immediacy for both superpowers. Such a beginning would have to involve a *joint* Soviet-American military or paramilitary force. This would have to be the case because it is apparent that at this point in the superpower relationship, there is not sufficient consciousness nor maturity to enter into joint war games voluntarily. Therefore, the first conscious war game between the two nations will have to be forced upon them by necessity.

This in fact happened on a small scale in the summer of 1987 when the United States, at the request of Kuwait, in the Persian Gulf, put a number of Kuwaiti oil tankers under the United States flag as part of a scheme for guaranteeing the safe passage of Kuwaiti oil through the Persian Gulf. (And, by way of example, it would enhance the safety of the shipping and oil of all other countries in the Persian Gulf.) The United States action was in direct response to, and military confrontation of, Iran's increased hostile naval actions on oil tankers in the Persian Gulf.

On an unconscious level, the United States and Iran were engaging in de facto ritual warfare in a manner not unlike its action with Libya in 1985. In this instance, Iran was less overtly provocative militarily than was Libya, and as of September 1987, one tanker (the *Bridgeton*) had hit a (suspected) Iranian mine (suffering minor damage) and the United States fired at an Iranian aircraft one air-to-air missile, which fell short of its target.

---

[26] Similarly, the INF Treaty signed by the two countries on December 8, 1987, eliminating an entire class of weapons, creates a psychic precedent as well as a political and military precedent.

At the same time, the Soviet Union, at the invitation of Kuwait, deployed five naval ships in the Gulf to protect merchant shipping from hostile action by Iran. Thus, the Soviet Union and the United States, out of their respective interests, found themselves militarily on the same side for mostly the same reasons: guaranteeing the free passage of ships in the Persian Gulf, containing Iran militarily, and forcing an end to the Iran-Iraq War.

Moreover, contacts between the two governments intensified to assure no incidents took place between their two navies in the Persian Gulf, since they themselves in all likelihood used each other as "targets of opportunity" as part of their own war games, and the two governments intensified their joint planning to find a way of forcing Iran and Iraq to a cease-fire. Most important, given my thesis of primary cooperation as a new kind of peace technology, their policy of forcing an end to the Iran-Iraq war came not primarily out of having taken sides in the war, but because the war had taken on too great a risk of provoking military confrontation between the United States and the Soviet Union.

A PRACTICAL EXAMPLE OF A DEVISED RITUAL WAR GAME BETWEEN THE SOVIET UNION AND THE UNITED STATES

The one area that seems to pose an equal degree of threat to both superpowers is nuclear terrorism. Although the imminence of the threat of terrorism (of any kind) seems to have been felt more in the West (particularly in the United States) than in the East, *nuclear* terrorism poses a very unique and special kind of threat. *Any* act of nuclear terrorism poses the immediate threat that either or both superpowers may perceive the other as being implicated in the act. This would hold true even if the terrorist act took place in a third country not formally aligned with either superpower (for example, Sweden, India, Sri Lanka, or Togo), and even if no direct demand or threat were made to either superpower government. No matter what the circumstances, an act of nuclear (or chemical) terrorism[27] would immediately raise the specter of confrontation between the

---

[27] Chemical terrorism, particularly by third-party nations or terrorist organizations who could deliver such a blow with a guided missile, looms as an increasing menace toward the end of the 1980s. However, the ensuing political complications created between the superpowers generally would not be as immediate and encompassing as an act of nuclear terrorism.

Reprinted by permission. Tribune Media Services.

two superpowers and the danger of a nuclear exchange between them. In short, nuclear terrorism threatens to take the decision of whether to launch nuclear missiles out of the hands of both superpowers.

Furthermore, no amount of "cooperation" between the two governments under such a situation would eliminate the inherent danger posed by the terrorist act or a similar act by a third country. No amount of exchange of information about political and/or ideological position, number and whereabouts of terrorists involved, types of arms possessed, et cetera, could fully dispel suspicions that "the other side" might be colluding with the terrorists. Not only would such information be suspect, but under extreme circumstances, either government might use such information as a justification for unilateral military action against the terrorists, irrespective of national boundaries (for example, the 1985 *Achille Lauro* affair).[28] This could lead to miscalculations that might precipitate hostilities between the superpowers.

---

[28] In the case of the *Achille Lauro* affair, where Palestinian terrorists commandeered an Italian cruise ship and killed one American citizen, United States warplanes intercepted an Egyptian civilian airliner carrying the alleged leader of the terrorist group over international waters and forced it to land on Italian soil,

Notwithstanding the fact that acts of terrorism seem to have been fewer in the Soviet Union, there is a growing concern in that country as well as in the United States, about *nuclear* terrorism. Along with this growing concern in the Soviet Union is the recognition that the safest protection from being manipulated into nuclear confrontation with the United States by a third party or parties is a joint approach to the problem. An April 1984 article by G. Shakhnazarov, president of the Soviet Political Science Association and first vice-president of the International Political Science Association, published in the Soviet publication *Century and Peace* states: "Potential participants in the conflict are forced to reckon with the security of the opposite side as with its own. This formal interconnection demands the understanding and recognition of the fact that only collective security is possible in the nuclear era" (p. 10). The article goes on to discuss a scenario where a nuclear bomb could be exploded in the United States by a third party and the U.S. mistakenly might retaliate against the Soviet Union.[g]

Indeed, the concern about nuclear terrorism by both superpowers has been so great that in 1985 the Standing Consultative Commission (SCC) in Geneva reached agreement for formal American and Soviet consultations related to nuclear terrorism. The SCC was established in 1972 as a result of the SALT I Treaty and comprises American and Soviet teams of approximately fifteen working-level officers, a commissioner who is a diplomat, and a deputy commissioner of military rank. The original mandate of the SCC was to provide information that either side considered necessary for compliance with the SALT I Treaty. Although this function is voluntary and there was much American skepticism concerning Soviet willingness to provide information, the SCC, in fact, has worked extremely well over the years and its functions have expanded. Significantly, it takes a joint decision by *both* commissioners to make findings public.[h]

The SCC has served as a model for the design of the proposed two Nuclear Risk Reduction Centers (NRRCs), as agreed to by Mr. Reagan and Mr. Gorbachev at the September 1985 Geneva summit. The detailed structure of the two centers was negotiated bewteen 1985 and May 4, 1987, at which time a draft agreement on the NRRCs was reached. They were originally conceived to monitor events such as nuclear terrorism or third-party nuclear threats that could lead to crises between the superpowers and to prevent those parties or accidental nuclear-weapons use

where the Palestinian was arrested (and subsequently released by the Italian government). Egypt protested to the United States its violation of Egyptian sovereignty as a result of having its airliner commandeered by the United States Navy.

from triggering nuclear war between the superpowers.[i] The formal agreement to establish the centers was signed on September 15, 1987, by Soviet Foreign Minister Eduard Shevardnadze and Secretary of State George Shultz in Washington, D.C. The Soviets will operate one center on the soil of the United States, and the latter country will operate a center on the soil of the Soviet Union. The function of the two NRRCs that was formally agreed to fell significantly short of the initial proposals put forth by Senators Sam Nunn (D-Ga.) and John Warner (R-Va.) because of resistance by conservative elements within the Reagan administration and because of the radical nature of the proposal itself.[29]

The primary function of these centers will be to keep a twenty-four-hour watch on events that could lead to nuclear incidents and to prevent miscalculation between the superpowers. In its initial stages, the principal function would be crisis prevention, not crisis management. The centers will connect with the respective crisis management mechanism of each country: for example, the crisis-management team headed by the U.S. vice president, which would manage any given crisis. The centers appear to have been given a major responsibility for monitoring the destruction of intermediate range ballistic missiles under the INF Treaty.

The original conception of the Nuclear Risk Reduction Centers envisioned a *joint* Soviet-American command structure similar to that of the SCC. The NRRCs were to have played a more central and direct role in monitoring and coordinating the management of crises involving nuclear (or chemical) terrorism by third-party groups or nations. However, the concept of joint Soviet-American staffing or command of a center or centers apparently was too radical an idea for either the Reagan or Gorbachev administration at that time. The Department of Defense objected strenuously to the notion of a joint Soviet-American command because of fears of Soviet spying and unveiling of some of the more sophisticated technological secrets of the United States. It is not known what the initial Soviet position was on this score, but it is likely that their intelligence and military agencies raised objections similar to those raised by their American counterparts.

---

[29]The Weinberger Defense Department, which persistently reflected traditional conservative paranoia regarding the possibilities of cooperative agreements with the Soviet Union, effectively lobbied to have Richard Perle, then assistant secretary of defense, appointed as the leader of the team designated to negotiate the NRRC agreement with the Soviets. This act effectively doomed for the short-term agreement on the more comprehensive model of the NRRCs envisioned by Senators Nunn and Warner and supported by the State Department.

It is part of the plan that as operational experience and trust grow in conjunction with these centers, their role and functions will expand, possibly including joint planning for responding to incidents involving the use or threatened use of nuclear weapons by terrorists and others. At present the original conception of joint Soviet-American manning of each center seems more than either side could buy. As the Congressional Research Service pointed out: "The basic dilemma . . . is that the U.S.–Soviet relationship is largely competitive, not cooperative. Thus, there is inherent tension in measures (such as nuclear risk reduction centers) that seek to ameliorate that competition."[j] Notwithstanding the truth of the above quotation, the principle of "primary cooperation" formulated here will significantly overrule this heretofore defining characteristic in the Soviet-American relationship.[30]

Although the two Nuclear Risk Reduction Centers will undoubtedly reduce significantly the threat of nuclear terrorism, in the absence of joint Soviet-American manning and command of these centers, each country will have to rely on information provided by other as well as from its own sources. Although the two centers will be in virtually constant communication with each other, and there will be a number of "fail-safe" mechanisms built into the system, without joint staffing and command, a question will linger as to the trustworthiness of the other and the possibility of utilizing the system for the political and military advantage of the other country. Notwithstanding the unprecedented atmosphere of lessened tensions between the two superpowers, one incident involving nuclear terrorism could restore the status quo ante.

During periods of extreme crisis, with the threat of imminent or actual explosion of a nuclear device by terrorists or a third nation or group, even the smallest margin of error is too great and risks an inadvertent nuclear exchange between the superpowers.[k]

Indeed, two out of three Arms Control and Crisis Management (ACCM) crisis-simulation games conducted by the Center for Strategic and International Studies (CSIS) in 1986 ended with imminent hostilities between

---

[30] Indeed, there is increasing evidence to this effect. On July 12, 1988, Marshal Sergei Akhromayev, chief of staff of the Soviet armed forces, and Admiral William J. Crowe, Jr., chairman of the Joint Chiefs of Staff, announced their intention to create a "joint military group" to study ways to avoid dangerous military incidents between the superpowers (*Washington Post,* July 12, 1988, p. A17).

Meetings between Crowe and other top American military officials and Akhromeyev and his top-level delegation of Soviet Army, Navy, Air Force, and Marine officers took place the next day in the secure "tank" in the Pentagon where the Joint Chiefs of Staff meet.

the United States and the Soviet Union.[1] The scenario of Game 2, set in January 1987, posits "dramatic gains in strength and popular support for the Contras in Nicaragua during 1986, leading the U.S. administration to believe that a quick victory is possible during the year. Over the preceding year, the United States substantially increases materiel and advisory assistance; begins gradual military and naval buildup in the Caribbean basin, particularly Honduras; recognizes a contra government-in-exile; and proclaims a military blockade of Nicaragua.

"Unable to challenge U.S. military strength directly, the Soviet Union attempts to raise the cost of a U.S. victory by stepping up guerrilla actions in Honduras, Guatemala, and El Salvador, and by increasing both advisory strength in Nicaragua and sophisticated military shipments of surface-to-air missiles (SAMs) and Hind attack helicopters" (pp. 8–9).

The scenario of Game 3 posits, "As the players walk into the [National Security] Council room, they are told that a U.S. civilian aircraft en route from Munich to Rome has been hijacked to Sigonella air base in Sicily. The four hijackers, of German and Palestinian origin, identify themselves as the 'April 15 Commando' and announce that they are retaliating for the U.S. raid on Libya. They insist that the U.S. cease its ongoing exercises near the Gulf of Sidra and demand additional fuel to fly to an undisclosed location.

"The hijackers claim that explosives have been concealed in the cargo area of the plane and that they possess an electronic detonating device. They warn that the plane will be destroyed in the event of a rescue attempt.

"Unbeknownst to the hijackers or the NSC team, the explosives on board have been seeded with cobalt 60 and have been preset to detonate at 12:15 P.M. that afternoon. Both hostages and hijackers are being irradiated while the plane sits on the tarmac. . . .

"While condemning the nuclear terrorism incident, the Soviet Union takes the position that 'warlike' acts against Syria will not be tolerated. The Soviets move their Mediterranean task force close to Syrian shores, implying that they will interpose their forces in the event of a U.S. retaliation" (pp. 10–11).

In the conduct of these crisis simulations, the NRRCs were used hardly at all, and when they were used, it was almost exclusively for processing information between the United States and the Soviet Union.

In Game 2, when the NRRC twice urged the NSC to support the Soviet offer to freeze its escalation of pressure in Southwest Asia in exchange for a United States freeze of its escalation in Nicaragua, the president recalled the NRRC for consultations and subsequently replaced the head of the NRRC.[m] It is also noteworthy that Game 2 ended with the United States about to bomb Nicaragua with conventional bombs, the imminence of open hostilities with the Soviet Union, and the risk of nuclear confrontation.

In the context of the games, the NRRCs were utilized or looked to for assistance a number of times by both sides, the Soviet side somewhat more than the American. Their effectiveness was limited. As represented in the war-games scenarios, the NRRC was used as a communication conduit, not for crisis management, as it had originally been envisioned.

A careful analysis of these games reveals that a significant, if not the primary, defect in the crisis-management structure was the virtually total absence of direct interface and any kind of *joint* consultation and coordination between the Soviet Union and the United States concerning these hypothetical crises. Communications and "negotiations" were handled through technological means, with little direct human contact. This fact alone would exacerbate paranoid projection to an extreme. Moreover, it was clearly obvious that once the crisis had begun, meaningful joint crisis management between the two superpowers was virtually impossible because of the rapid escalation and pressure of events. The study concluded:

> Ironically, the aspect of crisis management to which most analysts pay closest attention—direct superpower interactions—occupied a relatively small portion of each crisis game. Short of very visible Soviet maneuvers that the players perceived as provocative, the NSC teams often tended to ignore, avoid, or suppress creative, long-range strategic thinking about dealing with Soviet leaders until well after the crisis was under way. Moreover, players exhibited profound inhibitions about initiating military operations that would engage them in a cycle of escalation. Yet, once Soviet involvement became too pronounced to ignore, NSC team actions tended to be wildly escalatory—global in impact, but without any sophisticated underlying strategic rationale.[31]

It seems clear, as the two ACCM game simulations reveal, that in the nuclear age, where crises erupt and become full-blown in a matter of hours and must be concluded within a matter of hours or days, commencing the

---

[31] Kupperman, p. 34. It is noteworthy that the game teams comprised Congressmen, former members of the National Security Council, former presidential national security advisors, a former director of the Central Intelligence Agency, a former chairman of the Joint Chiefs of Staff, high-ranking personnel of the departments of State and Defense, and other individuals who have been or will be involved in managing actual situations like those simulated in the ACCM games.

process of protracted planning and negotiation with the Soviets in the context of the crisis will not work in most cases. An NRRC concept with joint staffing and joint command offers the possibility of joint planning *before the fact* to (1) identify present and probable future crisis situations that both superpowers would find inimical to their national security interests (for example, terrorist attacks on nuclear power plants or situations like Game 3 mentioned above) and develop joint scenarios and relevant follow-through procedures and mechanisms to anticipate and to act in concert to bring those crises to a swift conclusion; (2) develop systems that will enable both sides to determine with much higher reliability the role of the other, if any, in the crisis at hand; (3) develop and jointly train crisis-intervention teams that would significantly reduce the potential for third parties to manipulate conflict between the two superpowers; (4) provide a mechanism for ongoing dialogue between crisis-management personnel of the two superpowers regarding existing and potential crises, which would have the effect of developing a more refined crisis-management capability on both sides.

This fourth point is crucial. Crises of the type described call for cool heads and a capacity to perceive the real desires of the other superpower to avoid confrontation leading to nuclear escalation. Aside from the SCC, which is a consultative mechanism, not an ongoing quasi-staff relationship, the United States and the Soviet Union have no mechanism that involves an integrated staff working with each other on a day-to-day basis. Yet it is precisely this kind of relationship that is indispensable to building the trust necessary for managing third party-induced crises between the two superpowers. The mutual interest of the two superpowers in such a crises cannot be lost. In the end, it will not be a computer that determines a course of action in the midst of a crisis—it will be a human being. The kinds of crises likely to be encountered in the present time and into the twenty-first century increasingly will have to involve a coordinated response between the two superpowers.

One wonders what the outcome of Game 3 would have been if the first report of the hijacking had come from a joint Soviet–American-commanded NRRC. No doubt the Soviet co-commander in the room with his American counterpart (or in a separate adjacent room) would be sending back a very different kind of picture and information to the Kremlin than would the Soviet ambassador to Syria or the Soviet foreign minister, neither of whom would have face-to-face contact with the emotional import of the drama unfolding from the American perspective. (Of course, the same would be true in reverse.)

As some studies have pointed out, there is the clear risk that either side may try to take advantage of the other in the context of a jointly manned NRRC center. Some of these are valid concerns; some are the product of paranoid projections. However, a possibly overriding principle may be that the context of a jointly staffed and commanded NRRC or NRRCs over the long term will force the superpowers to explore in much greater depth on an ongoing basis the risks to their mutual national-security interests from various crises, particularly nuclear terrorism, thus bridging the splits that result in paranoid projection and the heightening of crisis situations. This is a most important point, for it is the very separateness and disconnectedness of their deliberations about each other that heighten paranoid projection. It is unlikely that improved technological communications in "real time" alone will sufficiently alter the tendency toward paranoid projection. Perceptual splitting of the magnitude that has existed between the Soviet Union and the United States requires a unified field in which to bring those perceptual splits together. The more each superpower is aware of the activities *and the thinking and feelings* of the other on an ongoing basis, the less likely it is that either would be manipulated into conflict with the other by a third party. A day-to-day working relationship between Soviet and American personnel at the NRRC or NRRCs would do much to bridge those splits. Sometimes it is the sweat on the brow, the fear in the eyes, the quiver in the voice, the pained look on the face that convinces an adversary of the genuineness of the other's representations.[32]

Some of the other findings of the CSIS study provide insight into the paranoid process between the superpowers:

1. As each game evolved, the central problem that confronted the players was that their self-perception of caution was interpreted by the Soviet players

---

[32] It is also important not to overlook the natural dynamic of interpersonal bonding, which requires ongoing interpersonal contact.

In his speech of June 3, 1988, to the Royal Institute of International Affairs at the Guildhall in London, in the wake of the Moscow summit, then President Reagan observed: "To those of us familiar with the post-war era, all of this is cause for shaking the head in wonder. Imagine, the president of the United States and the general secretary of the Soviet Union walking together in Red Square, talking about a growing personal friendship and meeting together average citizens, realizing how much our people have in common. It was a special moment in a week of special moments. My *personal impression* of Mr. Gorbachev is that he is a serious man, seeking serious reform. I pray that the hand of the Lord will be on the Soviet people, the people *whose faces Nancy and I saw everywhere we went . . . those faces that we will never forget.*" (As reported in the *Washington Post*, June 4, 1988, p. A18. Emphasis added.)

either as passivity or, at the other extreme, as a deliberate lack of communication in anticipation of further aggressive activity.

2. . . . a transformation had . . . occurred in the perception of major players. Earlier, the players had avoided assigning to the Soviets a master plan or implying a high degree of Soviet involvement in the triggering events. Later, after feeling that the Soviets were deliberately violating the implied rules of the game, they would project onto the Soviets an insidious master design for which there was little evidence.

It is probable that neither understood the same rules, since none had been worked out between them.

3. . . . At no time was there any evidence of Soviet involvement in the radiological terrorist incident [in Game 3], which sparked the crisis in the first place. Nevertheless, the shifting perspective on Soviet policy of the NSC team was summed up in one member's view that "we are extremely naive if we think that the Soviets are not behind this in some way, shape, or form, and [they] have been from the very beginning."[n]

The CSIS study, as well as the history of the relationship between the superpowers, strongly suggests that the extremely sudden advent and escalation of modern-day crises, the extreme risk of nuclear confrontation between the two superpowers by third parties or by miscalculation, the absence of joint long-term planning for anticipating and managing such crises, and the tendency to rely on technological, non-face-to-face communication between the two superpowers during times of crisis point to the conclusion that the two centers inevitably will have to have restored the full scope of functions originally envisioned for them and be jointly manned with coequal Soviet and American commanders.[33] In such a structure, presumably all action decisions will require a joint decision by the Soviet and American commanders. It is also likely that as the centers prove their worth, the scope and function of their operation will be augmented to include direct participation in planned responses to the use or threatened use of nuclear (or chemical) weapons by terrorists and others.

In my opinion, joint Soviet-American political-military war games in narrow fields such as antiterrorism will become a fact in the decade of the 1990s.[34] CSIS, in its studies, has come to recognize the need to reduce the

---

[33] It is hoped, without a precipitating crisis such as the one described by Dr. Shakhnazarov. (See page 114 above.)

[34] One vignette pointing in that direction: In early August 1988, then Defense Secretary Carlucci, during meetings in the Soviet Union with his Soviet counterpart and other high-level Soviet military officials, reviewed a series of field exer-

tendency toward abstracting the conflict and to broaden and deepen input on crisis management by emphasizing the importance of "domestic and allied considerations as a brake on effective crisis management." It goes on to advocate the involvement of members of Congress and senior members of European governments in joint exercises.° It will not be too long before we see the involvement on both sides of Soviet and American officials dealing with scenarios that involve nuclear (or chemical or biological) terrorism and other third-party-induced conflict that threaten the stability of the superpower relationship.

I propose that as an integral part of a mutual terrorist control effort, the Soviet Union and the United States develop a joint military or paramilitary strike force (JSF) consisting of equal numbers of Soviet and U.S. personnel, jointly trained and under the joint command of a Soviet and an American officer of equal rank. Both officers would be fluent in English and Russian. This would enhance the ability of the JSF to function as a truly integrated unit as well as the caliber of the JSF as a whole, and would reduce paranoid suspicions within the JSF, since both officers would understand commands given to their respective troops. Each command officer would be responsible to his own government and *any* action taken by the JSF would require a joint decision by the co-commanders of the Nuclear Risk Reduction Centers. The specific and limited purpose of the JSF would be to forestall any act of nuclear terrorism or such threat from a third party or nation.

While the proposed Nuclear Risk Reduction Centers have crucial merit in their own right, once they begin to operate under joint Soviet-American command, they would also be a first step toward meeting the necessary requirements for developing between the Soviet Union and the United States a conscious "war game" that would be governed by jointly deter-

---

cises at the Taman division garrison southwest of Moscow. The *Washington Post*, on August 3, 1988, reported: "Standing on the roof of a small house overlooking a lake, a field and a forest in the distance, Carlucci and [Soviet Defense Minister General Dimitri] Yazov watched as one officer explained how the Soviet forces would 'take the road' near the forest.

"Over the next 20 minutes, tanks rolled and fired, rockets screamed through the air, artillery guns rang out. Carlucci and Yazov seemed to enjoy the whole 'operation.' Later, after inspecting a series of Soviet tanks, armed personnel carriers and artillery pieces, they rode to another site and watched another mock operation, this time featuring some hand-to-hand kung fu battles amid the rocket blasts.

"Carlucci pronounced it all 'very impressive'" (p. A12).

mined rules. By "conscious" war game, I mean consciously chosen, not forced, cooperation.[35]

It is recognized that the line between non-nuclear and nuclear terrorism may be very thin during times of crisis. It is not clear at this time what the full specific parameters of the mandate of the JSF would be. However, whatever they might be, they would still be *jointly determined* and under *joint* command, thus providing for essential checks and balances. The specific nature and design of the proposed JSF would require extensive study jointly undertaken by the Soviet Union and the United States.

The operation of the Nuclear Risk Reduction Centers, and most particularly the joint American-Soviet strike force(s), would meet the general requirements outlined above for a beginning approach to ritualizing the impulse to make war. The NRRCs, as a first step in that direction, offer the dual advantage of beginning to manage the instinct to war between the superpowers while at the same time providing a necessary measure of protection against an accidental nuclear exchange between the superpowers. It would unite them against their common enemy, war. If the proposed JSFs come into being, they will have demonstrated the feasibility of joint military maneuvers between the two superpowers and will have laid the groundwork for joint "war games" on a broader scale.

It is clear that the deliberate implementation of joint war games would require a level of understanding and trust between the two superpowers that may seem almost out of reach today. However, in an interview on January 17, 1986, with Ambassador James E. Goodby, U.S. representative to the Conference on Disarmament in Europe from 1984 to 1985, I proposed the idea of a joint Soviet-American strike force to intervene, as necessary, in the case of actual or threatened nuclear terrorism. Ambassador Goodby expressed his belief that such a proposal was both feasible and desirable.

It seems clear that it will not suffice for the superpowers to be dragged along to a "cooperation" that neither government sees clearly nor wishes to fully commit to. In any case, the window of opportunity for developing a peace technology that would sustain and further the kind of primary co-

---

[35] If that "choice" were to come in the wake of a forcing event (for example, the explosion of a terrorist nuclear device), then the choice will have been more forced. However, such forced situations are the increments that raise consciousness and ultimately give rise to a greater capacity for free choice before the fact, as it were.

operation between the two superpowers outlined here will not last too long, for the forces that impel us to our nuclear holocaust simultaneously are powerful and relentless. It would behoove the two governments to be mindful of that most troublesome characteristic of human nature—we are creatures of habit and strongly resist change. Historically, governments, as well as individuals, have learned their most important lessons through tragedy.

⑧ Paranoia between Groups and Nations

Paranoia has long been a recognized and given aspect of relationships between groups and nations. As a dynamic between groups and nations, it is largely a by-product of "pseudospeciation"—a psychodynamic process wherein a given human group has a sense of sociocultural separateness as if it were a distinct biological species, and in which that group, or nation, considers itself more or less the true and good human species, and others, and especially *some* others, are considered to be less than human and bad or evil.[1] It would behoove us to take a step back and to ask the question: What end does pseudospeciation serve?

---

[1] Erik Erikson further defines this term, which was originally coined by Konrad Lorenz, as follows: "Man has evolved (by whatever kind of evolution or whatever adaptive reasons) in pseudospecies, i.e. tribes, clans, classes, etc., which behave as if they were separate species, created at the beginning of time by supernatural intent. . . . [Not only did each group develop] *a distinct sense of identity*, but also

In psychoevolutionary terms, pseudospeciation has been essential for producing the cultural differentiation and conflict essential for the evolution of civilization.[2] This means that the development of civilization has been dependent upon pseudospeciation and thus upon paranoid process, which is inherently constructive as well as destructive.

Pseudospeciation has been the sine qua non of the human condition in man's recent history (that is, within the last few tens of thousands of years).[a] Humans have always lived in psychosocial groups. The instinct to bond in groups is one of the most powerful and primitive of all human instincts. Pseudospeciation, however, is a psychic instinct, not a biological one. The difference is that the biological adaptation is present to adapt for the survival of life of the species and the psychic adaptation aims at directing the nature and direction of the evolution of the life form itself. Psychosocially (but *not* genetically) speaking,[3] in the case of man, nature's way seems to be division of the species into smaller groups for diversification for specialization. Hence the advent and evolution of cultures and of civilizations.

Pseudospeciation, then, although aimed at enhancing survivability of the larger unit *Homo sapiens*, may, because of the paranoia it produces, at this juncture in history end up working against its survival as much, if not more, than enhancing it. Of course, in the special case of species *Homo sapiens*, humans have the unique ability to reflect upon, understand, and to manipulate their relationships, albeit not always with great success.

Modern-day humans, as was the case with primitive humans, cannot survive outside a psychosocial group. Bonding in psychosocial groups means differentiation, and differentiation, by definition, sets up the condition for aggression. As Konrad Lorenz puts it, "The principle of the bond formed by having something in common which has to be defended against outsiders remains the same, from cichlids[4] defending a common

---

a conviction of harboring *the* human identity". In Vamik D. Volkan, "The Need to Have Enemies and Allies: A Developmental Approach," *Political Psychology*, 6, (2) (June 1985): 224–245. Also see Erik Erikson, "Reflections on Ethos and War," in the *Yale Review*, 73, [4] [July 1984]: 481.)

The quintessential example of this dynamic was Hitler's branding of Jews, gypsies, homosexuals, the handicapped, and other minorities as subhuman (pseudospecies) and evil.

[2] See Chapter 6 for a discussion on how cultural differentiation and conflict between groups has been essential in the evolution of civilization.

[3] Hence the use of the prefix "pseudo."

[4] Spiny-finned freshwater fishes.

territory or brood, right up to scientists defending a common ideology. In all these cases, aggression is necessary to enhance the bond."[5]

Thus, aggression, by definition, is a necessary primitive and inherent aspect of group formation. Above and beyond commonly held values and beliefs, the aggressive element of a group's bond provides cohesive libido, which gives the group constancy and strength. It is a bond *against*.

Because sustaining aggressive libido requires the presence of an "other" perceived as hostile, the integrity and strength of a group is dependent upon a group self-image that sees itself in opposition to an enemy. Self-value and -validation derives, in part, from devaluing others. This in turn leads to a tendency to perceive the world in terms of in-groups and out-groups, the former being the source of that which is good and valued, the latter being the source of that which is bad and devalued.

In short, humans, men in particular, have an inherent need to identify some people as allies and others as enemies. The integrity of the self is, in part, based upon a perception of others as being different from ourselves and thus potential enemies. Oftentimes that perception is distorted, and what we are perceiving in the other are our own traits that we find most objectionable and that we correspondingly project onto others.[6] Man, through his psychosocial group affiliations, has a need for enemies.

At the same time, we can, and do, perceive others as different from ourselves without perceiving them as enemies. These individuals and groups do not carry a hook for the qualities about ourselves we do not like. Indeed, some may carry a positive hook onto which we may hang idealized projections: for example, a Ronald Reagan, who until the 1987 Iran-Contra affair could do no wrong in the eyes of the American electorate.

Freud conceptualized instincts in pairs of erotic/unifying instincts and aggressive/destructive instincts and held that both types are involved, in concert or in opposition, in all phenomena of life, including war.[b]

Pinderhughes discusses what he calls "the ubiquity of paired behavioral phenomena and the universality in mental processes of paired categorization and stereotyping, with idealization of one member of the pair and

---

[5]K. Lorenz, *On Aggression*, (New York: Harcourt, Brace, and World, 1966), p. 188. Although bonding, as Lorenz says, sets up the condition for aggression between groups, obviously it does not always lead to aggression between all groups. There are many groups that have benign or positive relations with other groups and their members. But each of these, in all likelihood, has a hostile attitude toward, or hostile relationships with, *some* other group or groups.

[6]See Chapter 3.

devaluation of the other member of the pair." He implies that paired behavioral response is an inherent characteristic of human nature, and that what he terms "D-bonding," based on differentiative-aggressive physiology and behaviors, is just as prevalent as "A-bonding," based on affiliative-affectionate physiology and behaviors. He hypothesizes that to resolve ambivalence, differential bonding takes place in a paired process of A- and D-bonding simultaneously. Thus, when one affiliates with one group, one simultaneously (and often unconsciously) discriminates against and rejects another. (Thus, if Pinderhughes is right—and I think he is—it is important to be aware of where the D-bonding goes when alliances are made and undone, for it must go somewhere. This is particularly important at this juncture in Soviet-American relations when A-bonding between the two is in ascendancy.)

This appears to be the case between nations as well as between groups. A good example of this dynamic was Russia's enmity toward the United States prior to its being invaded by Nazi Germany in 1941, and its official and unofficial admiration for the United States after the Nazi invasion. Obviously there were reasons of political expediency such as the Lend-Lease program, for Russia's change of heart toward the United States. But it is suggested here that the intrusion of a new enemy into the Russian psyche (as well as its geography) resulted in a withdrawal of considerable aggressive energy (not just a change in political strategy) from projection onto the United States which was redirected toward the new enemy, Nazi Germany. At the end of World War II the common enemy—Hitler and Naziism—was removed for both the United States and the Soviet Union, both of whom then fixated on each other as enemies. This dynamic implies a relatively fixed amount of A- and D-bonding libido. This carries far-reaching implications that will not be explored in depth here because of the extensiveness and complexity of the issue.

A-bonding is associated with introjective processes and D-bonding is associated with projective processes.[c] It appears, because of a stronger valence associated with the aggressive libido that is associated with D-bonding, that, generally speaking, differentiative-aggressive bonding carries more power in relations between nations than does affiliative bonding, which is why we are so fixated on, and spend such a disproportionate share of our material and psychic resources on, the hostile relationships we have with our perceived enemies.[7]

---

[7] In interpersonal relationships, as opposed to relations between nations, this generalization does not appear to hold true.

Prior to the advent of agriculture and the development of the village about ten thousand years ago, the basis for group formation largely was physiological characteristics. With the emergence of agriculture, common social factors such as differences in types and styles of skills, taste in foods, religious beliefs and practices, and trade became increasingly prevalent, along with physiological differences, as bases for psychosocial group formation. Pinderhughes points out that thinking itself involves transitory attachment to one mental impression after another, so that differential bonding takes place not only around people and things, but on the basis of thoughts and ideologies as well.[d]

Given the fact that man's documented history over the past ten thousand years of his existence involved slaughtering neighboring groups or being slaughtered by them, it should not come as a surprise that we all carry a certain degree of paranoia as individuals and groups.[8] When addressing the historical period prior to the seventeenth century, a more proper term would be *xenophobia*, "fear and hatred of strangers or foreigners or of anything that is strange or foreign."[e] Today, we use the term

---

[8] An almost random thumbing through of the Old Testament will yield ample evidence of the practice of one group slaughtering another. In Old Testament times, this practice was not carried out exclusively in the name of land acquisition for subsistence or other "legitimate" reasons. It often carried the connotation of being a holy endeavor to eradicate a group because of its heathen religious practices.

The ruthlessness of this practice was so total that even King Saul, first king of the Hebrews, was driven mad for not observing the literal word of God to destroy every living thing in the land of Amalek—men, women, children, camels, oxen, and sheep, et cetera. Saul, though he did have slaughtered all of the Amalekites, and almost all of their animals, made the mistake of saving some of their finest animals for sacrifice to his God, who, it turned out, was not appreciative of the gesture (I Samuel 15).

Xenophobic paranoia resulting from pseudospeciation is not just an ancient phenomenon. In the well-publicized December 1986, Howard Beach, New York, situation, where a group of white teenagers attacked three blacks whose car broke down and who sought help in a local pizza parlor, the boy who incited the melee by telling his friends at a party that "There were some niggers in the pizza parlor. . . . Let's go back and kill them," it turns out, had a recent former girl friend who was black and who described him as one of the nicest kids she had ever met. Group affiliation, even on an ad hoc basis such as a party, can constellate the most primitive psychic instincts in man, including the instinct for pseudospeciation which can momentarily overwhelm a contrary rational standpoint.

And, of course, we are all familiar with the dynamic of pseudospeciation as it has carried tens of thousands to their deaths over the centuries, continuing into the present, in the Middle East conflict.

paranoia, "a tendency on the part of an individual or group toward excessive or irrational suspiciousness and distrustfulness of others."[f]

We tend to ignore the fact that for the last ten thousand (and probably fifty thousand to one hundred thousand) years of man's existence, his literal survival frequently depended upon the acuity of his xenophobia (paranoia). And if the human organism is biologically and psychologically adaptive, then paranoia must be deeply imprinted in man's brain[9] and resides as a powerful and adaptive innate psychic instinct in all of us, individually and collectively.[10]

It is suggested that paranoia, individually and collectively, is not only an abnormal condition as in paranoid psychosis, but that it is also a natural (normal) and adaptive characteristic of man's psychological heritage. Moreover, because warfare and carnage have been inextricable from those pro-

---

[9] As a clinical psychologist and psychoanalyst, I cannot avoid the obvious clinical observation that paranoia in general and xenophobic-like paranoia in particular is more prevalent in contemporary men than in women in the American population at large. Although my observations are limited to this culture—the only one I know clinically—it is likely, for archetypal reasons, to hold true on a universal scale.

[10] Pinderhughes ("Differential Bonding," p. 171) asserts that mental representations (imprints) of "social, psychological, and somatic processes" are linked physically in the brain.

Based on extensive research involving 34 countries, he concluded also that discrimination and the paranoid process are universal. (Cited in Volkan, "The Need To Have Enemies and Allies," p. 225.)

Even the most liberal of us today, were we to experience a life-threatening attack by a Black, an Asian, or an individual of any color or ethnic affiliation other than our own, might find our liberal standpoint sorely shaken, if not totally dissipated, to be replaced by a paranoia against everyone identified with that group, whether they attacked us or not. The degree of paranoia would be a function of the degree of emotional maturity of the individual and the difference between ourselves and the threatening individual or group, especially along the lines of color. For whites, the darker the color difference, the greater the paranoia. An obvious example of this psychological trait was the internment of Japanese-Americans at the outbreak of World War II while German-Americans and Italian-Americans generally were not prevented from the pursuit of their lives.

Another example along ethnic (as opposed to racial) lines was German anti-Semitism. It is not accidental or insignificant that German anti-Semitic propaganda as well as present-day anti-Semitic propaganda tries to make a case for the Jewish people being a distinct race: that is, a pseudospecies. Were Jews to be perceived as a race, as opposed to an ethnic group, then "normal" primal xenophobic hostility based on biological speciation could be invoked, since all races instinctively perceive other races as potential enemies more readily than they do different ethnic groups within the same race.

cesses that encourage intergroup cooperation and favor the advancement of civilization(s), paranoia is deeply rooted in, and inseparable from, man's creative as well as his warring nature.

It behooves us to remember that innate fear of foreign aggression can, and, more often than not does, influence the behavior of any group, even though we tend to deny such fears. The *less* the danger of *imminent* attack by adversarially perceived foreign elements, the greater the tendency toward paranoia. Thus, the longer the peace between adversaries, the greater the paranoia between them—lacking mutually focused efforts to transcend it.[11] The Cold War exemplifies this principle.

W. W. Meissner in his landmark work, *The Paranoid Process*, picks up on the concept of paranoia as a primary adaptive mechanism of normal human development. He writes:

> The same [paranoid defense] mechanisms demonstrate, even in their most distorted forms, an adaptive function which serves to preserve object-relations and defend the self from narcissistic injury. This adaptive aspect of the paranoid mechanisms extends beyond the reach of psycho-pathology to the level of normal and culturally induced adaptive patterns of action and interaction. The same mechanisms can be socially and culturally reinforcing and supportive in one context, or can be distortive and maladaptive in another. Any theory of the genesis of paranoia must keep both aspects in perspective, and must bring those forces into focus which determine when the identical mechanisms are either adaptive or pathological.[g]

This adaptive function of the paranoid process applies no less on a collective level between groups and nations than it does in individual psychology. Paranoid mechanisms are manifested in broad segments of the general population and can be seen in the general clinical states of envy, jealousy, prejudice, et cetera. In fact, if one takes the trouble to look, one can observe without too much difficulty that society in general, as well as individuals, can sustain a high degree of tolerance for such behaviors without regarding or reacting to them as forms of pathology.

The paranoid process appears to be essential for enhancing the cohesion and solidarity within a group through rigidly held belief systems. While strengthening the group—often in necessary and healthy ways—it

---

[11]The relationship between the People's Republic of China and the United States might appear to be an exception. However, it does not appear to follow this rule, because both parties have displaced their paranoia toward each other onto the Soviet Union and China does not pose a threat to American military supremacy and thus does not "qualify" as a prime candidate for American paranoia.

simultaneously stimulates rejection and devaluation of competing ideologies. The facts be damned! Historically, this has been precisely the case between the Soviet Union and the United States, with the members of each group (nation) perplexed as to why the other group does not recognize the "obvious" error of its ways. (If we're right, they have to be wrong, and vice versa.)

Each tolerates its own paranoid pathology and rationalizes it into the fabric of its national ideology, seeing its own paranoid ideation and fantasies projected onto the enemy. Thus, for the United States, only the Soviets are paranoid and vice versa.

A unique difference between paranoia experienced on an interpersonal level and paranoia experienced within and between nations is that in the latter case, power and relationships based on power are the core (but not exclusive) considerations.

THE UNIQUE DETERMINANTS OF RUSSIAN PARANOIA COMPARED WITH OTHER NATIONS

Primary factors in precipitating a paranoid orientation are life-threatening trauma and social and cultural isolation, all of which lead to a depressive response. A paranoid pattern would emerge as a means of restoring and preserving a sense of safety, self-esteem, and self-worth. This is no less true at the collective level in the community of nations than it is on an individual level.

My earlier definition of paranoia includes the words *excessive* and *irrational* (suspicion). It is suggested that a significant degree of what is excessive and irrational in the suspiciousness of the Soviet Union and the United States toward each other has come from the innate fear each carries of the other as foreigner[12] along with the dynamics inherent in shadow projection. It is this "excessive" and "irrational" component that makes the most mischief in the attitude that each nation holds toward the other and therefore bears closer examination.

It is important that what is excessive and irrational in any given situation is relative and will depend on the perceiver and the perceived,

---

[12] One might argue that Russians are no more foreign than any other European cultural group. However, there appears to be general consensus in the West that, by virtually any measure, "Russians" constitute a dramatically unique group distinct from any other in Europe. I have heard many Russians argue vehemently against this view, but never a non-Russian European.

largely as a result of their personal experiences. It is never an objective or equal quantity.

Until 1987, when General Secretary Gorbachev's policy of *perestroika* had begun to take root, when attending conferences on the Soviet Union or on Soviet-American conflict, inevitably one would hear clinical laments about "Soviet paranoia" from Americans who deal with Russians on a regular basis. The implication is that the Soviets are excessively paranoid and as a result have been virtually impossible to deal with. The tone was often patronizing and reflected exasperation.

However, closer examination of Russian history poses the question as to how "excessive" Russian paranoia really is. The Russians are quite open about, as every professional in the foreign policy, intelligence, and defense establishment knows, the trauma the Russians still feel having lost twenty million souls (more than all the rest of the combatants combined) and having been left with a wrecked country at the end of World War II. Most are also aware that the Soviets sustained horrendous losses in World War I. What apparently is not so well known is that the Russian nation has sustained by foreign invasion some of the worst devastation of its land, its people, and the very fabric of its social cohesion, of any civilized nation in history. A short overview of this aspect of Russian history would be instructive.

In the tenth century, Russia consisted of a series of principalities and city-states connected to Byzantium. Between the tenth and eleventh century it also began to relate to western Europe.

By the thirteenth century, the Mongol invasion became a major threat to Russian society. In fact, it was in response to that threat that the various Russian princes of the independent principalities united under the leadership of the prince of Kiev to resist the Mongols. This event constituted the first unification of Russia as a national entity. However, their armies were successively defeated, Russian cities, including Kiev, burned to the ground, and the local populations decimated. Indeed, the sweep of the Mongol invasion was so great that in 1238, the forces of Genghis Khan crossed the Volga River, destroyed Kiev, enveloped most of what is modern-day Russia, threatened and defeated the knights of northern Europe, and reached within sixty miles north of Venice, at which time their advance was halted only by the death of the khan.

However, the Mongol armies remained and set up a kingdom around what is now Volgograd. At this point in its history, at the very moment when it was beginning to take its position along with the other civilized countries of Europe, Russia was taken out of the orbit of Europe for all practical purposes, with the exception of some trade with Sweden around Novgorod.

In the next 250 years, with the exception of the trade center at Novgorod, only twelve or fourteen people traveled to Russia from western Europe! Russia, for all practical purposes, ceased to exist as a national entity and its people retreated back into the forests away from the proximity of the Mongols. As a result, some of the most powerful events of human history that determined the very nature of Western civilization—for example, the Renaissance, Reformation, and Counter-Reformation—did not touch Russia. She was more or less reduced to a tribal society without national cohesion until the Orthodox church began to bring about societal cohesion around the end of the fifteenth century.[h]

In addition to its impact on the evolution of Russian society for centuries to come, the Mongol invasion left scars on the Russian national psyche unprecedented in the experience of any other country extant today.[13] Those scars and the ones to come later, particularly during the twentieth century, have led to a profound Russian mistrust of foreigners—that is, Russian "paranoia"—that takes its roots in objective history and is embedded in the very fabric of the Russian psyche, and that seems *psychologically* unavoidable.[14]

Meissner (pp. 133–134) emphasizes the potentially devastating importance of social isolation in the development of a paranoid response. It is well known that the human personality cannot sustain normal functioning except in a matrix of social interaction. Relatedness is essential for developing and maintaining personal definition and meaning, and thus is derived from, and dependent upon, meaningful interaction with other individuals and upon the general cultural matrix. When the social situation is fragmented, as was the case with Russia for over three hundred years, the result is a depressed and backward society with low self-esteem, a national inferiority complex, and an absence of a sense of security and na-

---

[13]The systematic devastation and dismemberment of Cambodian society by the Khmer Rouge in the wake of the Vietnam War might be considered an exception to this statement. However, the political impact on the world scene of Cambodia as a nation does not compare to that of the Soviet Union, nor to the protracted fragmentation of Russian society over a period of centuries.

[14]In 1919, the United States sent troops into Russia, as part of an expeditionary force, along with France, Great Britain, and Japan, to fight in support of the so-called "White Russians" against the Bolsheviks and others who ultimately were victorious.

tional identity, all of which give rise to a paranoid process.[15] Another frequent consequence is a vulnerability to "idiosyncratic belief systems, and the workings of the paranoid process . . . [which] begin[s] to verge toward the pathological."[i] This would account for the primitive nature of Soviet paranoia historically—due to the early stage of Russia's development as a modern society.[16]

This becomes a particular problem when subjective and emotional needs have such strong valence that they overwhelm the validity of objective data and/or the objective data is not clear and discernible. The more this is the case, the more rigid the paranoid construction, until it shifts from "construction" to "paranoid defense," where the *function* of the de-

---

[15] One could raise the question as to whether China should not be as paranoid as Russia, given China's noted isolation from the rest of the world over the centuries. China, with its Eastern philosophical orientation, which stresses and values an introverted attitude to life against an extraverted one, chose its "isolation," which it has valued highly. "Relatedness" took place (and still does) within Chinese society on an intense, but very introverted basis.

Russia, on the other hand, had its isolation imposed from the outside by foreigners. Where the Chinese have always prided themselves for their capacity to "embrace" and absorb enemy invaders, all of whom were changed by Chinese culture more than they changed it, Russian society was torn to pieces by foreign invaders. In the case of the Mongols, they enforced a three-hundred-year isolation on the Russian people, which severed it from its cultural connections to Western civilization with consequences that are still apparent in Russian society today.

Meissner defines the "paranoid process" as "that cognitive process by which incoming impressions are organized into a pattern of meaning which is primarily validated by reference to subjective needs rather than objective evidence or consensual agreement" (*The Paranoid Process,* p. 116). The paranoid construction is a basic inherent mechanism, which all of us engage in to greater or lesser degree, for apprehending, processing, and integrating information.

[16] Although Russian society and its level of paranoid functioning have developed to a higher state by the mid-1980s, one sees vestiges of that primitive paranoia bubbling to the surface, even under Gorbachev, as in the Soviet claim that the presence of the AIDS virus in the Soviet Union was due to the CIA, which developed the virus in a biological warfare laboratory to subvert Soviet society. Source: "Surviving Together," *ISAR*, Washington, D.C. (Fall 1987), p. 37.

Although under Gorbachev, the Soviet Union has acknowledged that its invasion of Czechoslovakia was "unfortunate" and that there are similarities between the "Prague Spring" and the reforms Gorbachev is instituting, much of the old paranoid line remains as of August 1988. The *Washington Post*, on August 22, 1988, reported that *Tass* "denounced the western press for using such 'terrifying terms' as 'invasion,' 'occupation' and 'suppression' to describe the 'entry' of Warsaw Pact troops into Prague" (p. A19), which, of course, is exactly what it was.

fense, which is feeling-based, is to keep out conflicting data or to distort the data that do come through so as to support the existing structure.[17]

Obviously this is not just a phenomenon experienced exclusively with the Soviet Union. The United States can engage in as great a degree of distortion through its own paranoid defense. However, because feeling is at the core of a paranoid defense, as opposed to a paranoid process, typological factors would tend to predispose the Soviet Union, with its introverted feeling orientation, to a more rigid paranoid defense than that of the United States, with its more extraverted thinking orientation.[18] Also, unlike Russia, America has had the paranoid process in its culture mitigated by a pluralistic society, intense dialogue at all levels of society, an open press, a vocal public opinion, a highly functional institutionalized system of checks and balances in government, and accountability of government at all levels to the people at large. As Mr. Gorbachev is recognizing, a one-party system is an optimal structure for paranoia, as well as other problems.

Although there were, and are, clearly pathological elements in the Russian paranoid defense, this defense also was indispensable to the restitution of her national identity. It is clinically and politically observable that, under Gorbachev, Russia seems to be moving away from a primary position of paranoid defense to the developmentally and politically healthier position of paranoid process. (See my note 17, above.) It is noteworthy that when internal security and identity are lacking, the individual or nation must rely more on external supports for a sense of self-worth.[j] In the case of the Soviet Union these "external supports" primarily take the form of a quest for international status as a superpower. However, that status has been conferred by the international community almost exclusively on the basis of Russia's nuclear arsenal and huge military apparatus, without which the Soviet Union probably would be viewed as a second-rate coun-

---

[17] In a paranoid process, the cognitive component of the self is subject to change in viewpoint and can admit and integrate data that conflict with its basic self-image as long as the self feels cohesive and not too threatened.

The distinguishing factor between a paranoid *process* and a paranoid *defense* is that, in the case of the latter, the paranoid process is no longer powerful enough to protect the emotional core of the self from feeling dangerously vulnerable to attack, fragmentation, and/or annihilation and death. The emotional core of the self then feels itself in a desperate life/death struggle and must keep out all threatening data. Examples of the latter are Albania, Iran under Khomeini, the Union of South Africa, and Japan before 1945.

[18] See the section on Psychological Types in Chapter 3 for an explication of these typological differences.

try (at best), compared to other European nations, still struggling to consolidate itself as a modern twentieth-century nation. Thus, the "meaningful relatedness" sought by the Soviet Union through superpower status remains yet elusive and has been a source of chronic wounding to Soviet self-esteem.

It appears that Mr. Gorbachev is the first leader of his country who recognizes that the Russian national psyche will remain wounded and not achieve the relatedness in the community of nations and the respect as a world power that Russia craves until its aspirations are matched by real achievements domestically and internationally, and not through immature narcissistic demands, political bluffing, and paranoid demands that she be granted what she wants.

It is true that much of the superpower status of the United States is also conferred on the basis of its nuclear arsenal and, though smaller in manpower, quite substantial military machine. However, unlike the Soviet Union, the United States is and has been recognized as a world power for nearly a hundred years on the basis of its technological, economic, social, and political achievements and potential. In essence, it has earned that status.

In considering the problem of Soviet paranoia, it is important to remember that barely seventy years ago the Soviet Union, as a modern state, was born out of the agony of its history of invasion and national, social, and economic decimation and in the midst of overwhelming military humiliation in World War I. Whatever one may think about the injustices of the Soviet system, historically there can be no question that it was the pain of privation and human desperation on a universal scale that gave rise to the Revolution of 1917.

The revolution that gave birth to the United States, on the other hand, was born out of a *sense* of political and economic injustice, and was more focused on political ideals rather than on great personal and national privation and suffering. Further, unlike the United States,[19] the Soviet Union had had fewer than twenty-three years of national existence—hardly enough time to consolidate itself as a new state—before it was again devastated by the Nazi hordes in one of the most brutally destructive and traumatic wars of modern history.

---

[19] Although the United States technically was not a recognized national entity, by 1776 most of the thirteen colonies had been in existence for fifty years or more, they were geographically separate from the mother nation, England, and were engaged at various levels in forming the compact that later led to the Declaration of Independence and formal nationhood.

This profound and chronic suffering and loss gave rise to a sense of wounded injustice, of a deprivation[20] that could not be justified by any logic—and thus, to an overwhelming rage. That rage gave rise to the repressive and depriving system of Soviet Communism itself in the name of exercising a control over the fortunes of the Russian people that never again would permit the kind of suffering it had known throughout its history.[21]

Because the Communist system is utopian in its ideal—its premise being a guarantee of attainable human welfare and dignity—in the face of failed promise, the mechanisms of denial and projection were inevitable as a primary means for preserving the integrity of its own philosophy, and the self-image and self-esteem of the Soviet Union as a nation. These paranoid defense mechanisms would then displace blame for that failed promise onto other nations and even impersonal forces such as the system of capitalism, which came to be seen as the primary source of injustice and evil in the world. The United States—as a great and powerful nation that had attained national cohesion, strength, pride, and self-respect, as well as status as a world power, the material standard for which Russia had yearned for hundreds of years—was psychodynamically a natural prime target.

As Meissner points out, "The envious person begins to feel not only that he has a right to the possession or state of well-being that he desires, but that other person's possessing it is a form of injustice that has been worked upon himself."[k] "The envious person does not accept or resign himself to the loss or deprivation that he feels. . . . The feelings of resentment and injured deprivation can easily take a blaming course—a bridge over into a paranoid position."[l] At a pathological level, all behavior of the other—that is, the United States—is interpreted in a manner that supports the notion that it is the primary, if not only, source of any deprivation that might be felt. On the other hand, the United States, in its deter-

---

[20] Certainly its own internal despotism was no small contributing factor to Russian paranoia, from Tsar Ivan the Terrible, to the Stalinist purges of the 1930s and 1940s through the excesses of Beria up to the premiership of Khruschev in 1953.

[21] How many of us, in a wounded rage at some point in our childhood, swore an oath that when we became parents we would never permit our children to suffer the kind of emotional or material privation we suffered as children—only to realize to our dismay in later years that, indeed, we had brought about the very feelings in our children that we had sworn we would avoid?

The lesson to be learned is that *anything* done in the name of wounded rage is likely to be blind and dogmatic, laced with paranoia, and to lead to behavior that will cause the very emotions and feelings we so intensely wish to avoid.

mination to prevent the Soviet Union from becoming a world power, reinforces this aspect of Soviet paranoia and contributes to masking its more pathological elements.

This paranoid process within the Soviet psyche also serves an adaptive function, however. Without the defenses of denial and projection to provide ideological cohesion, the system may have been perceived by the Soviets themselves as having failed and could have faced collapse, with the country and its people once again thrust into the chaos of anarchy and revolution.

There has been a tendency in American foreign policy and the arms negotiation process to make simplistic comparisons of Soviet and American paranoia—with the Soviets almost always being found to be impossibly paranoid. It may well be that Soviet paranoia over the years has been evident in intransigent negotiating stances and in suspicious refusals to cooperate with on-site inspections, and to provide accurate data necessary for monitoring treaty compliance and the like. However, even if we assume that the Soviet scorecard has been considerably worse than that of the United States, such simplistic appraisals of Soviet paranoia are more hurtful than helpful to the process of improving the relationship between the two superpowers, because they assume that all paranoia is pathological and they do not distinguish between what is adaptive and what is pathological in the paranoid process.[22]

THE PARANOID PROCESS IN THE RELATIONSHIP BETWEEN THE UNITED STATES AND THE SOVIET UNION

The Soviet Union and the United States have the third and fourth largest populations of any countries in the world and have the largest and broadest amalgamation of ethnic groups composing their national populations. However, the similarities stop there.

---

[22] From a clinical perspective, the issue is no different between nation "patients" and individual and couple patients. One only exacerbates paranoid defense by name-calling, blaming, rational arguments, and power confrontation. To heal and get beyond paranoid defense one has to reach empathically beneath the defense itself to the wounds that have given rise to it. Some of the wounds in the Russian psyche that have given rise to her paranoid defense have been described above. The importance of empathy (clinically speaking) in the Soviet-American relationship—and I do mean for both parties—will be discussed in Chapter 9.

In the case of the United States, the ruling group itself consisted of "outsiders." The thirteen colonies spent nearly a century consolidating themselves as quasi-independent states, developing relationships with other colonies, and laying the foundation of the compact that was to become the United States of America, culminating in the Declaration of Independence in 1776 and, later, the Articles of Confederation. It could be said that the impetus for the creation of the United States as a nation was exogenous—a nation created by outside nonindigenous peoples. Most important, the oppressor was an outsider (or perhaps better put, "outlander")—England—separated by thousands of miles of ocean and unable readily to reach the shores of its own colonies.

There was only one ethnic group to subdue and bring under control of the ruling group—the American Indian. Their numbers were small, and they consisted of even smaller separate tribal units, most unallied and some with long-standing hostile relations with other tribal groups. They never posed a serious threat to the emerging American nation.

Moreover, the subsequent ethnic makeup of the United States, with the single exception of Black Americans, representing 12.1 percent of the population, is composed of ethnic individuals, all of whom chose to enter this country and all of whom this country chose to accept. The coming of immigrants was compatible with the nature of the ruling group, themselves descendants of immigrants, notwithstanding ethnic differences.

In this sense, America represents a new kind of national entity—a nation built by immigrants, drawn from the various pseudospecies of the world. In essence it represents the fact of man's psychophysiology having come full circle to species *Homo sapiens*—a national entity that can embrace the pseudospecies of the world to its bosom, albeit not without difficulties, rather than exclude them.

The Soviet Union, on the other hand, comprises twenty-three distinct nationalities, fifteen formerly independent republics with preexisting national identities, speaking 112 officially recognized languages with five different alphabets, virtually none of whom chose to give up their national identities for association in the Soviet state. The white ruling class of Slavs constitutes 52.4 percent of the total population and is projected to be statistically in the minority by the end of the 1980s.[m]

Group cohesion requires support for the values of the group. Since personal values are important cohesive elements of national self-identity as well as individual personality, there is considerable pressure from within for allegiance to the nation state. The perception of a threatening enemy, notwithstanding its destructive potential, can have a powerfully enhancing impact on group cohesion. The greater the perceived threat by an enemy, the more the group (nation) will value the tenets of the group and the more its members will invest in it and everything it stands for. This is certainly a powerful dynamic in the political process.[23]

However, a major problem in this regard is that there is a very fine line between "patriotism"—love of one's country—and "chauvinism": excessive or blind love of one's country. The former leads to a healthy and vibrant national self-image; the latter often leads to paranoia and paranoid relations with other nations. Most national leaders, particularly the leaders of the Soviet Union and the United States, confuse the two and very often end up using chauvinism in the guise of patriotism for maintaining power within, and for directing national resources toward the desired ends of the leadership. Meissner points out that Stalin used this tactic to the hilt, mobilizing the Russian economy on the backs and stomachs of its people, and for getting away with one of the most despotic and murderous periods of domestic violation of any nation rivaling, if not exceeding, the excesses of the Nazi state.[n]

In American domestic politics we had the period of "the red scare" in the fifties, and the more recent example of the Reagan administration's justifying on the basis of the Soviet "threat" not only its unprecedented buildup of nuclear arms, but domestic cutbacks and attempts to justify violations of historical and fundamental civil liberties around the issue of secrecy. In the foreign policy sphere, the Reagan administration (and, with the single exception of the Carter administration, all other administrations since Roosevelt) justified, in the name of preventing the spread of communism, its support for murderous regimes in Argentina, Chile, and the Union of South Africa, and elsewhere, some committing excesses seemingly beyond those of the Soviets.

From its revolution in 1917 through World War II and the decade of the 1940s, of necessity, the Soviet Union primarily was focused inwardly on

---

[23]The United States, as perceived enemy, over the years has deflected a great deal of inner tension within Soviet society on the part of a number of nationalities (for example, Tatars and Muslims) and former national entities (for example, Armenia) that did not voluntarily choose affiliation with the Union of Soviet Socialist Republics. In August of 1987 there was a demonstration in Moscow by Tatars wanting more respect and autonomy as an ethnic group. As Mr. Gorbachev implements his policies of *perestroika* and *glasnost, and* as tensions between the United States and the Soviet Union have decreased, there has been increasing unrest among various minority groups within the Soviet Union. In other words, as external threat is perceived as being diminished, internal instability will become more prevalent within the Soviet Union.

consolidating its nation status and forging allegiance from its disparate and sometimes resistant ethnic groups and its military and political conquests in Eastern Europe at the end of World War II.

Paranoid mechanisms are always involved in the development of more complex levels of social involvement.° As the Soviet Union moved out of its period of internal paranoid isolation in the post–World War II era to more complex involvements in the community of nations, the nature and degree of its paranoid process shifted and became more hostile to the United States as Russia set out to achieve status as a world power. Its initial moves to assert its power in Europe through the retention of control over the countries of Eastern Europe stimulated heightened paranoia on the part of the United States and Western Europe as a whole.

A major complicating factor has been the fact that in the post–World War II era, paranoid process has been pressed into service by both sides as a political tool, distorting what is and is not pathological.

The two prevalent components for the Soviet Union and the United States in their respective paranoias are these: for the United States, threatened loss of power and world supremacy, which by definition conflicts with its fundamental chauvinistic, ideological, and heroic self-image and which is therefore never admitted overtly as a real fear. To admit that it fears the loss of power and world status in the absolute sense (not just as a result of Soviet "aggression")[24] would be to threaten its self-image as the most powerful nation in the world. The United States sees itself as preeminent not only in fact but by right, since its ideological heritage promotes the principles of personal freedom and democratic process, which are seen as "good" in the absolute sense.

To date, the denial by the United States of its need for world power supremacy and its tendencies toward enlightened and unenlightened imperialism and hegemony are consistent with its ideological self-image. However, it is crucial to realize that this denial is in part a dangerous paranoid defense that perceives virtually everything it does that violates its own ideals and laws exclusively in terms of "policies" necessary to contain Soviet aggression, not as violations (necessary and justifiable though

---

[24] Historically, in American propaganda and rhetoric, the phrase *Soviet aggression* has become almost synonymous with the country's identity. Its psychological as well as political purpose has been to deny any legitimate claim Russia might have to world power status. Such a claim, by definition, would be "aggression" and thus, by definition, illegitimate.

Similarly, but less consistently, Soviet propaganda has used the phrase *capitalist imperialism* as synonymous with the identity of the United States.

some might be) of its own ideals and laws.[25] In its extreme, it can lead to lawlessness.[26]

Two recent examples of this kind of paranoid defense at a governmental level are the Iran-Contra affair where the Reagan administration violated its own policies and probably the law—The Arms Control Act, and/or the Omnibus Diplomatic Security and Anti-Terrorism Act of 1986 and the Boland Amendment prohibiting the use of United States funds to purchase weapons for the Nicaraguan Contras—and claimed that rather than trading arms for hostages, it was only trying to influence moderate elements in Iran who might succeed the Ayatollah Khomeini. Another was the invasion of Grenada, which was initially justified in the name of saving the lives of American medical students on the island, and a denial of the determination of the Reagan administration not to permit the creation of another Marxist government in the Western Hemisphere.

For the Soviet Union, the primary component in their paranoia toward the United States is a sense of national inferiority and a jealous and envious craving for legitimate world power, for which it has received some acknowledgment based on the potential threat from its nuclear arsenal. It is important to recognize that from the Soviet perspective, its claim and need for world power is legitimate and an inherent part of its emerging national selfhood. The United States, in its paranoid stance, fears loss of

---

[25] In an interview on "The MacNeil, Lehrer Newshour," in response to a question concerning the role of the CIA in supplying arms to the Contras in Nicaragua, Constantine Menges, until earlier in 1986 on the staff of the National Security Council, with specific responsibility for Latin American affairs, said: "The communist government of Nicaragua has lied for seven years to its own people and to the American people about what it is and what it's doing. I don't know what ID cards were really found on the plane or what they may have forged. It's hard to know. If there were such ID cards actually on the individuals [Eugene Hasenfus, who subsequently confessed to working for the CIA, and the pilot of the plane, one "Cooper"], they may have been obtained in a variety of ways that have nothing to do with the U.S. government. I don't think the step from little ID cards, which can easily be made by almost anybody, to U.S. Government auspices makes any sense at all. I believe the U.S. government when it said there is no connection." Notwithstanding Mr. Menges's claims, there is abundant evidence to suggest otherwise. ("The MacNeil, Lehrer Newshour," October 8, 1986, transcript #2878, p. 6.)

[26] Lieutenant Colonel Oliver North of the Iran-Contra Affair comes to mind. Former Vice President George Bush, during his 1988 presidential campaign stated that he felt that Lieutenant Colonel North should be found not guilty and that he would not rule out a presidential pardon for North, should North be found guilty and should he, Mr. Bush, be elected president.

power in the face of Soviet quest for power. The advent of nuclear parity by the Soviet Union represented the first time in American history that its military power had been neutralized.[27]

Russia's paranoid attitude stems from its history and contains both pathological and adaptive elements. To the extent that its paranoid process has been adaptive, the goal of its adaptive paranoia has been to assist the Soviet Union to evolve into a successful nation state, viable politically and economically within the community of nations, and, above all else, to rise above its history of privation, anarchy, and national humiliation.

The adaptive aspect of Soviet paranoia can be seen, particularly with regard to the West and the United States, in Stalin's amazingly successful, albeit ruthless, mobilization of the Russian economy and heavy industry (before and after World War II) as a direct result of real and paranoid fears of attack by the West.[28] It gave impetus to the development of a cohesive national self-image over against the capitalist West, with an increasing sense of purpose and self-respect. Its ability to hold its own militarily and especially to neutralize the superiority of the United States in nuclear and strategic and tactical missile weaponry, provided a source of enormous pride, self-esteem, and respect, albeit much of it given grudgingly, within the world community. Until the advent of Gorbachev's policy of *glasnost,* Soviet leaders have skillfully and successfully redirected interethnic tensions within their own republics toward the United States as the primary enemy.

At the same time, in its paranoid competition for world status and power it has had to alter its policies, tactics, politics and even its very perceptions of itself and of other nations in order to compete in the international political arena.[29] Its commitment to compete with the West irre-

---

[27] The ideological stance of the People's Republic of China has been as hostile to American ideology as that of the Soviet Union. Yet China and the United States have been rapidly becoming allies, including military allies, at the expense of the Soviet Union. This is because China poses nowhere near the potential threat to American military, economic, technological, and foreign-policy power interests that the Soviet Union does. Thus, it does not tend to stir up American paranoia.

[28] Although the pathological aspect of Stalin's paranoia became apparent with disastrous consequences when Stalin ignored the warnings by Western leaders of Hitler's imminent invasion of Russia in June 1940.

[29] There was much ado about the sartorial state of Premier Bulganin and General Secretary Khruschev in their first few trips to the West in the 1950s. They came with baggy clothes that one reporter said looked as if they had been got out of the Salvation Army and that reflected the backwardness of Soviet society. Khruschev's wife, hair covered with a kerchief, was derisively described as look-

vocably committed Russia to a dialogue with other nations, opening it to criticism and feedback that virtually never touched it during its period of closed paranoia under Stalin. However, in the post-Stalin era, this dialogue with Western nations brought about increasing self-reflection and evaluation of its own system and policies, ultimately increasing political accountability internationally and, as of the mid-1980s, domestically.

Under Stalin, Russia was totalitarian, despotic, and tyrannical. Russia today under Gorbachev is totalitarian, but not tyrannical, and is showing dramatic signs of liberalization and the emergence of radical democratic reform, including the areas of individual freedoms and respect for basic human rights valued so highly by Western democracies.

However, at the same time, pre-Gorbachev, the advent of Russia as a potential world power with an antithetical ideological framework has evoked a high level of hostility from the United States, deflecting much of Russia's paranoid process onto the United States, thus pathologizing dynamics in Russia's paranoid process that might have been adaptive. This contributed to a major diversion of Russian psychic and material resources from its evolution to a higher plane of development domestically.

If the trend toward liberalization and democratization in the Soviet Union continues, the ultimate question may be whether the United States, in its own self-interest but contrary to the dictates of its own paranoia, can work with and facilitate that trend in Soviet society today. The problem is that while constructive political change is so difficult to bring about, it is so easy for the paranoid process to derail it and maintain the paranoid status quo. In this sense, the United States is in a position, perhaps even more so than internal conservative Russian resistance, to abort the changes in Soviet society vigorously pursued by Mr. Gorbachev.

Central to the paranoid process in an individual is the perceived threat to personal autonomy. This leads to an obsession with control and domination. Individuals who are caught in such a paranoid web cannot give in to another person on any issue of consequence without feeling that they have been thrust into a position of total or near-total surrender of autonomy and independence.[p] From my perceptions in studying American and Soviet behavior over the past few years, these dynamics apply on the collective level between the two superpowers no less than they do with any given individual.

American attempts to get the Soviets to admit to their shortcomings

---

ing like a peasant woman. By the time of Khruschev's trip to the United States, he was dressed more stylishly by Western standards.

(while denying its own) and their distortions and propaganda—to admit to their own paranoid position—will only reinforce the paranoid process on the part of both the Soviet Union and the United States. At the same time, the United States tends to be oblivious to its naive need to get the Soviets to admit their "sins" to preserve the stability of its own paranoid view of the Soviets as evil, repressive, anti–human rights, seeking world domination, et cetera—a view that not only perceives real shortcomings of the Soviet system and policies, but one that projects onto them short-comings and power-oriented excesses of the United States as well. In a pathologically paranoid framework, only one party—the other—is seen as sick, judged so by the self-presumed healthy party. This furthers split-ting,[30] paranoid projection, and the heightening of tensions and hostility.

There is a crucial difference between reinforcing desired *behavior* on the part of the Soviets—for example, freeing of Sakharov and other dissi-dents—and insisting at the same time that Russia openly admit the error of its ways. The former permits Soviet values to change from within to meet their own evolving internal needs, *one* of which might be the reduc-tion of American hostility over Soviet human rights violations.[31] The latter openly attacks their values and self-image, and thus the self-esteem of the Soviet Union itself, threatening internal psychic cohesion and directly playing into the most primitive levels of the Soviet paranoid process. The result inevitably will be heightened defensive behavior, including para-noid defenses such as denial of irresponsible and inhumane acts for which they are responsible, increased paranoid projection onto the United States, leaving the United States in an "I told you so" position, which will be reflected in arms negotiations and elsewhere in American foreign and defense policy strategy.

It is possible to influence a change in Soviet behavior—negatively as well as positively. But to expect the Soviets to acknowledge, openly or tacitly, that they have been the source of evil in the world or, more

---

[30] See note 4 of Chapter 4 for a definition of *splitting*.

[31] An example of this was then President Reagan's June 12, 1987, speech at the Brandenburg Gate (site of the Berlin Wall), West Berlin, where, in dramatic high style, he challenged: "Mr. Gorbachev, open up this gate! Mr. Gorbachev, tear down this wall!" This approach is cynical at best and irresponsible at worst be-cause, as every politician, including Mr. Reagan, knew, the most effective way to bring about political change is through quiet diplomacy, not public embarrass-ment. It is recognized that another possible reason for Mr. Reagan's speech was to placate with anti-Communist rhetoric the conservative base of his support in the Republican Party. However, such rhetoric would tend to reinforce Republican conservative paranoia as well.

simply, that their system is corrupt, unjust, power-hungry, et cetera—as was the case throughout most of the Reagan administration—is naive at best. More important, it serves as further proof to the Soviets that the primary interest of the United States is to humiliate the Soviet Union and keep it as a permanent hook for American projections of the defects and evils inherent in the capitalist system. Indeed, during a press conference following the December 1987 summit between Mr. Gorbachev and Mr. Reagan in Washington, D.C., Mr. Gorbachev said that during talks with Mr. Reagan, "I told the president that you are not the prosecutor and I am not the accused. We have to strike a balance here; otherwise you will get nothing out of us."[q]

Apparently Mr. Reagan heeded those words as well as his own enlightenment through personal contact with Mr. Gorbachev and Soviet citizens when he retracted this view of the Soviet Union in the wake of the Moscow summit of June 1988. It is noteworthy and of concern that, with the exception of then Secretary of State George Schultz, no other key figures in the Reagan administration echoed Mr. Reagan's changed sentiments regarding the Soviet Union.

In this regard, Professor George Kennan made the following observations:

> The problems that they [the Soviets] pose for U.S. policymakers will continue to depend on what we are attempting to achieve as we conduct our relations with them. If we hope to force a change in their system of government that they could scarcely be expected to survive as governmental leaders, or if we represent any reasonable political or military concessions they might make at the negotiating table as something forced on them by the spectacle of our growing military strength, then we will find no lack of evidence that they are highly obstreperous, difficult, unreasonable people to deal with. If, on the other hand, we were prepared to recognize the Soviet thirst for prestige, and if the aim of American diplomacy was to be restricted to the search for accommodations, then success would be not at all beyond the limits of possibility.[r]

In the context of paranoid process, political rhetoric is no longer free (if it ever was), even when the other side "understands." It is naive for the United States to take credit for producing enough political, economic, and military pressure on the Soviet Union to force structural changes of its society and system.[32] Soviet society changes because of its own internal

---

[32] In a speech before the World Affairs Council of Northern California on June 29, 1988, then Vice President Bush warned, "The Cold War is not over" and said that it would be a mistake to relax the pace of American military buildup.

The *Washington Post* reported on June 30, 1988: "He said that it was too soon

needs, just as American society does. (We in the United States don't appoint Supreme Court justices because this or that country criticizes the American stance on racial issues or civil rights.)

It is true that "linkage," such as the Jackson-Vanick Amendment, in the past apparently has levered limited changes in Soviet behavior: for example, temporary increases in the number of Soviet Jews permitted to emigrate. However, these and other expedient changes in Soviet behavior—in the case of Jackson-Vanick to gain trade advantages with the United States—were opportunistic political shifts that in no way reflected the kinds of structural changes taking place in the Soviet Union under Mr. Gorbachev.

Revising and liberalizing the criminal code of the Soviet Union, promulgating new laws that protect individuals against the notorious practice of psychiatric abuse of dissidents by the political system, the various liberalizations regarding free speech under the policy of *glasnost,* experiments with a multicandidate electoral process, and other components of the policy of democratization bespeak structural changes in the political system itself that will have permanent impact on Soviet society and its system of government. These are undertaken primarily for internal political and domestic reasons, not in response to linkage.

Current structural changes in the Soviet Union will not be speeded by American pressure. Nor will they be reinforced by an American cynicism that does not acknowledge that the Soviet policies of *perestroika* and *glasnost* are Soviet in origin, not primarily the result of military and economic pressures put on their system by the United States. This was reflected in a September 1987 article in *Tass,* which stated, "The U.S. president, while claiming [in his speech to the United Nations] to be interested in changes happening in the Soviet Union, gave his own interpretation of *glasnost,* limiting it to a list of demands on the Soviet Union. . . . There was not even a hint of any kind of readiness for a change in thinking and politics from the American side."[s]

---

to know if the change[(s) resulting from *glasnost* and *perestroika*] would be real or lasting and that the United States cannot afford to relax.

"'We can't know that now,' Bush said, 'but we can know that the promise of *glasnost,* of *perestroika,* didn't take place in a vacuum but in the context of reinvigorated American strength" (p. A14).

His vice presidential running mate, Senator Dan Quayle (R-Ind.), said: "*Perestroika* is nothing more than refined Stalinism. . . . It's not changing the system" (The *Washington Post,* September 6, 1988, p. A16).

It is important that Americans learn to open their perception to seeing the changes that are taking place in the Soviet Union in Soviet terms, rather than measuring the extent to which Soviet society compares to the American image of what they should be (that is, like us). Americans want Soviet ideology to be changed first before they can be "believed." In fact, all ideologies emerge out of circumstance rather than purely as the result of intellectual process. The conceptual germ may be present, but it is the living circumstance that gives it form and calls it forth. This was true of the American Revolution as well as of the Soviet Revolution of 1917 and the Soviet revolution of the 1980s.

Soviet reforms could be slowed by Ameican rhetoric that could heighten Soviet paranoia, siphoning off energy and resources for change. What is needed is genuine dialogue—without demanding concrete results—in place of rhetoric. The dilemma is that rhetoric is an ingrained dynamic of both political systems and politicians fear, with some reason, their ability to get and retain power without it.

It is all too often forgotten, to the extent that it is recognized at all by government officials, that "denial" is not only a political ploy, consciously employed. It also is a powerful psychological defense mechanism that comes into play *unconsciously* with great frequency on the part of politicians and diplomats on both sides. This is an important fact, because the attribution of consciousness where it does not exist inevitably leads to heightened paranoia on both sides and can grossly exacerbate relations between the two superpowers. Additionally, the perpetrators of the denial oftentimes come to believe the content of their own "ploy."[33] This is psychologically and politically dangerous. A psychological defense such as

---

[33] Constantine Menges, former National Security Council staff member in charge of Latin American affairs, in response to a question from Jim Lehrer as to why Mr. Menges believes [everything] the United States government says officially concerning policies and covert action in Nicaragua, responded: "Because I know that the United States government tells the truth in international politics." ("MacNeil, Lehrer Newshour," October 8, 1986, transcript #2878, p. 6.)

Given that the United States government, when forced by exposure in the press, has admitted such activities as a formal "disinformation" program operated by the CIA against Libya, the mining of Nicaraguan harbors by the CIA, the trading of arms to Iran for hostages by operatives of the National Security Council, and other "programs," *all* of which were lied about initially by official government spokesmen, including the president, it is hoped that no one else in such a high position in the United States government shares Mr. Menges's viewpoint and his hold on reality.

denial must be treated altogether differently from a conscious political ploy if paranoia is not to be pathologized and exacerbated.

Robert Shapiro points out that the paranoid actively scans his environment "to pick up bits of information or data which will lend credence to his inner system." This behavior results in denial and perceptual and interpretive distortion, confirming the inner view of the world of the individual or nation. Many of the inner mental perceptual and analytical tools are used primarily in the service of reality distortion. This is crucial, since awareness and understanding of reality do not rest on simple perceptions alone, but involve a value judgment.[1]

How one collects and uses and processes analytical data is of critical importance at this juncture in Soviet-American relations. Two analysts can use the identical data to make opposing cases regarding a given action or policy. The stunning changes in Soviet policy and behavior under Gorbachev, domestically and internationally, point to fundamental shifts in the Soviet system itself. Even if, as many in the United States assert, the release from internal exile of Andrei Sakharov in 1986 was a propaganda ploy to improve the Soviet image regarding human rights, it would not have been necessary for Mr. Gorbachev himself to call Sakharov, with no less than shattering implications for domestic policies, let alone to offer Soviet facilities for an uncensored interview of the dissident by Western media or a subsequent interview of Sakharov in the official Soviet newspaper, *Izvestia*, in January 1987.

Similarly, on January 9, 1987, the Communist Party newspaper *Pravda* announced the dismissal of a senior KGB officer for engineering the illegal arrest of a local reporter. Viktor Chebrikov, chief of the KGB in the Ukraine *and* a member of the ruling Politburo as well as chairman of the Committee for State Security (KGB), in his letter to *Pravda*, stated that he personally would "take additional measures to ensure the strict observance of law" by the KGB.

By his action, and by the official positions he took, Mr. Chebrikov acknowledged for the Soviet government the historic and notorious excesses of the KGB in the area of civil rights, Soviet ruthlessness toward human rights activists, and outright violations of Soviet law. Moreover, because the case that the Soviet government chose to demonstrate a major policy shift was the framing by the KGB of a Soviet "interpretive reporter," symbolically it chose to put focus on the very issue that has always been taboo—the role of the press in Soviet society. Such unprecedented public disclosure and acknowledgement of a need to abide by Soviet laws would be unnecessary unless the Soviet government itself, at the highest levels, was signaling a major shift in policy toward government by law and the observance of basic human rights—that is, moving from totalitarianism of the elite toward accountability based on universal law.[34]

The point is that even if those who are deeply suspicious of Soviet motives are right and that they do not signal major changes in Soviet policy and reflect only short-lived expedient behaviors toward the end of getting the West to lower its guard, that fact would be demonstrated no sooner than if the United States acted as if they do represent serious policy changes. If they represent real policy shifts, then the trend will continue even if the United States does not respond dramatically by such measures as lifting the embargo on allowing the sale of computer technology to the Soviet Union.

On the other hand, if the United States were to respond only with cynicism—that is, accusing the Soviet Union of engaging in propaganda ploys without real commitment—it could have the effect of heightening Soviet paranoia and thus contribute to bringing about a self-fulfilling prophecy. Pavel T. Podlesny, senior scholar of the Institute for U.S.A. and Canadian Studies of the Soviet Academy of Sciences, observed that

> hostile and insulting rhetoric, fanning military feelings, opens up the possibility and admissibility of a nuclear war . . . [and] engenders mistrust concerning the other side's true intentions; it clouds the real existence of spheres for mutual cooperation, and it makes a return to normal interstate relations more complicated and painful.[1]

The word *painful* is important here. It *is* painful to be subjected to disbelief, cynicism, and ridicule as one bares one's weaknesses in an attempt at reforming and changing them. There is little to be gained by this attitude on the American side, but something to be lost. Senator Dale Bumpers (D-Ark.) recognized this when he stated:

> For 70 years this nation has waited for the old Bolsheviks to die off and a new leader to emerge. . . . Now that one has, one that has already taken major steps to deal with socialist oppressions as well as socialist inertia, his ability to continue reforms that we believe fundamental to a new and realistic arrangement between us depends in no small way on our responses. [If President

---

[34] Contrary to the belief of many Americans, including individuals in high positions in government, such rights are, and have been, guaranteed in the Soviet Constitution. The problem has been that Soviet governments have not lived up to the guarantees of their own constitution.

Reagan continues his] tack [of negotiating only on his own terms], Gorbachev may survive, but only after the initiatives he's now taking have been halted and reversed.[v]

Soviet and American paranoid constructions look different from each other's perspectives because their inner systems and national self-concepts are different. In addition, other cultural and psychological differences influence the nature of their respective paranoid processes. For years, Soviet citizens in interviews with representatives of the Western media (when obtainable) have expressed a desire for more, not less, government control to bring about an improvement of the quality of Russian life. In the Russian way of thinking, given its system of central planning and control, particularly with regard to the production of consumer goods, the only way to improve the situation is to have more and better control. Hence much of the internal opposition to Mr. Gorbachev's policy of *perestroika*— that is, restructuring of the Soviet system. However, the idea of more government control plays into American paranoia about the nature of Soviet system as totalitarian and repressive and the vision of a downtrodden oppressed Russian people eager to throw off the yoke of their oppressive system.[35]

---

[35]At a symposium entitled "How We View Each Other: The Psychological Dimension of Relations between the Soviet Union and the United States," on April 3–4, 1987, sponsored by the C. G. Jung Foundation of New York, Robert Kaiser, associate editor of the *Washington Post*, who was its Soviet correspondent for the period 1971–1974, during which time he resided in Moscow, observed that Americans assume that all that we consider repressive in Soviet society is imposed by government control. Although this is true in limited instances (for example, foreign travel, granting of visas to Jews), by and large the concern with conformity comes out of cultural values that are reflected in, not always imposed by, government policy.

In Soviet society there is a right way to do everything. In a society where conformity and adherence to group values are the higher value (over nonconformity and individuality), conformity is the defining norm and essential for group cohesion, whereas in American society the opposite is true. Thus "normal" behavior of Soviets will appear to be paranoid to the United States and the concept of personal freedom, in the American sense, has never been meaningful to the Russians. Therefore, our criticism and attacks on their values seem patronizing at best and gratuitous and paranoid at worst. We attack them for adhering to their own basic values.

Pavel Podlesny put it, "And it is necessary to familiarize oneself with each other's specific, national interests including historical, political, cultural, and other traditions, all this being conducive to creating a climate of confidence in relations among states" (in Meissner, *The Paranoid Process*, p. 175). Of course, this would apply equally with regard to the Soviets.

Likewise, the total absence of censorship of the American press, with its routine sensationalism, affirms the Soviet view of American society as decadent and insensitive to human suffering. In a discussion in 1984 with the head of the Washington office of *Izvestia*, I was asked why our nightly TV newscasts aired only news about killings, rape, fires, and other violent aspects of American society. I asked him why he thought that was so. (And, for the most part, I do agree with his description of what is aired on the late evening news.) He said that it reflected the decadence of American society as a whole, particularly the fact that TV stations sought to make a profit on human misery and such sensationalism. To him, clearly the more moral and ethical stance would be to censor such news.

Psychologically, the United States expresses its paranoia in an extraverted way that has come out as aggressive attacks on Soviet actions and negotiating stances. The Soviet Union has expressed its paranoia in an introverted way, making it less accessible—the infamous "Russian silence" or "Nyet!"—often without revealing their real feelings behind the official position taken.[36]

Thus, from the Soviet perspective, Soviet behavior would seem not very paranoid and American behavior would appear to be quite paranoid and "obvious." From the American perspective, the opposite would be true—American behavior would appear to be nonparanoid and Soviet behavior would appear to be optimally paranoid—"obvious" because of their morose intransigence and silence. In fact both operate on the basis of paranoid process—the Soviet paranoid system more primitive in its construct and dynamics than the American, which is more sophisticated, and therefore less obvious.

The paranoid structure of the United States is dubbed more sophisticated because it has had a longer period of evolution, growth, working through, and integration. An extraverted paranoid structure generally experiences greater reality testing than an introverted paranoid structure because of the inherent nature of the two typologies. This would be all the more true in the case of Extraverted *Thinking* typology (the United States) over against an Introverted *Feeling* typology (the Soviet Union).

It is important to recognize that these two paranoid systems also form a whole,[37] since one feeds the paranoid dynamic of the other. Were either to change, the other, almost by definition, would change—either for worse or for better.

---

[36] See the section on Psychological Types, in Chapter 3.

[37] Stein (1982) uses the term *adversary symbiosis*. In Volkan, "Psychoanalytic Inquiry," p. 189.

The question is: What can be done? At a minimum, it is vital that those dealing with foreign policy have a better understanding of the functions as well as the dynamics of paranoid process, most particularly its adaptive role in supporting and preserving the development and integrity of the selfhood of nations as well as of individuals. If this one concept alone were understood better by foreign policy professionals and politicians, the face and nature of foreign policy and superpower politics would change dramatically over time. Being able to see the necessarily adaptive function of a given political position taken on the part of one's adversary can reduce the paranoid reaction on the other side, since it could recognize that the given position is more self-serving to the adversary/enemy than necessarily hostile to itself. This in turn would minimize those paranoid reactions of the other side which could further incite paranoia between both.

An example of this would be the long-standing Soviet policy of suppressing, especially internally, information that might tend to embarrass the regime—events such as failures in weapons tests and the space program, internal dissent, social problems such as the incidence of alcoholism in the Soviet Union, as well as major disasters like the Chernobyl nuclear accident. This policy seems to be in the process of radical modification under Gorbachev, especially in the wake of the Chernobyl incident, and is being supplanted by the policies of *glasnost* and *perestroika*.

When the United States attempts to take advantage of repressive and primitive aspects of Soviet society, it brings about a coalescence of most elements of Soviet government and society against a common foe, "the enemy," deflecting domestic attention away from real issues. A perfect example was the gloating attitude (there is no other word for it, in my opinion) of the United States government (including the Congress) and most of the American press, over the Chernobyl nuclear disaster.[38] From the So-

---

[38] Because of the rudeness of some of the congressional committee members and the sensationalism of the accident itself focused on by the media, the more important event in Soviet-American relations was missed: that is, the virtually unprecedented appearance before a congressional committee of an official of the Soviet government (First Secretary Vitaly Churkin of the Soviet embassy) to explain the situation. The attacks on Mr. Churkin and the lack of follow-through in pursuing a level of dialogue on the issue reinforced Soviet paranoia that the United States did not genuinely want improved relations with the Soviet Union and sought only to embarrass it.

This unfortunate encounter also points out the pent-up frustration that attends

viet perspective, offers by the United States government of humanitarian aid must have seemed not only disingenuous, but tainted with duplicity.[39] As a result, an opportunity to bring about some healing in a sick and paranoid relationship was lost to a reinforcement of the paranoid pathology that has been a primary bond between the two superpowers.

Additionally, further research on understanding the adaptive and non-pathological roles of the paranoid process in superpower politics could make possible the identification and development of mechanisms that would aid in the withdrawal of hostile projections, facilitate communication, and provide for a whole new body of "therapeutic" techniques that would enable the reinterpretation and treatment of conflict situations.

The cornerstone of the nonpathological paranoid process is the need for the individual or nation to preserve internal cohesion and self-identity, without which, he or it would disintegrate. Central in this dynamic is the need for self-esteem—to see oneself as good and to see evil as external to oneself. This leads to rigid categorical thinking—that is, the world is seen in absolutes of good and bad, black and white—and intolerance for ambiguity. Crucial in this dynamic is the need for a *plausible* object onto which to project the negative aspects of the self. This means that all objects of paranoia, by definition,[40] contain a sufficiently objective hook for that projection—that in the eyes of the projector of the paranoia, the "other" carries sufficient objective characteristics that fit the paranoid structure. Otherwise, the paranoid projection(s) would not "stick." This is true of the paranoid projections of both the United States and the Soviet Union. (See Chapter 3.)

The implications of this fact are far-reaching. What if the object of the paranoid projection took away that "sufficiently objective hook" so that the paranoid projection couldn't stick? In other words, what if one or the other took away the "bad" characteristic(s) that the other was used to

---

a paranoid relationship. One has to have some sympathy for Congressmen, long frustrated over Soviet evasiveness and denial, having difficulty restraining themselves once they had a "live" Soviet in the chair.

[39] It is ironic, as noted by the Washington, D.C., public radio station WETA, in its program "All Things Considered," three days following the announcement of the Chernobyl accident, that the reaction of the government of the State of Pennsylvania and of the United States government, during the initial three to four days of the Three-Mile Island nuclear accident in spring of 1979 was similar in a number of particular respects to that of the Soviet government concerning Chernobyl.

[40] Excepting situations of outright paranoid psychosis.

using for its hook? We are in the midst of beginning to get a look at that dynamic.

A case in point: The United States has long chided the Soviet Union for its paranoid stance regarding continuous on-site inspection of Soviet missile production, assembly, and maintenance plants in conjunction with arms-reduction talks. The Reagan administration in particular had been obsessed with Soviet cheating and treaty violations. On several occasions during the Intermediate Nuclear Forces (INF) Reduction Treaty and other arms-reduction negotiations, the United States claimed that the Soviet position regarding on-site inspection was a major stumbling block to concluding a treaty. However, when the Soviets did an about-face and agreed to virtually all of the United States demands for on-site inspection, including the right of either side to send a team of inspectors on short notice to the site of a suspected treaty violation in the other's territory, the United States found itself caught up short and left with its own paranoid position. American intelligence and defense agencies vigorously objected to Soviet inspection of "sensitive" Western military facilities. As a result, the United States changed its stance—over Soviet objections—and the INF Treaty reflects a curtailed "demand" inspections system when treaty violations are suspected.[41]

How much of the American stance on on-site inspections regarding the INF treaty is valid on national security grounds and how much is paranoid defense is difficult to discern.

If General Secretary Gorbachev is successful in his campaign to free dissidents, to loosen up on cultural repression, and to introduce multiple candidates and the secret ballot into the electoral process of choosing party members for positions within the Communist Party and positions in other parts of national and local government—all of which constitutes

---

[41]Nonetheless, the inspections provisions in conjunction with the INF Treaty are nothing short of revolutionary. They list twelve sites in five West European countries where Soviet inspectors will conduct inspections, and approximately seventy locations in the Soviet Union and Eastern Europe where American inspectors will operate (the *Washington Post,* December 10, 1987, p. A29).

The *Washington Post* reported on July 23, 1988, "The Soviet Union has developed a detailed plan for verifying constraints on nuclear-armed cruise missiles that would allow U.S. and Soviet inspectors unprecedented access to each other's bomber bases, strategic naval ports and military ships, Moscow's top arms control specialists said. . . .

"But . . . the Reagan administration has thus far blocked the plan because of Navy and Air Force resistance to the proposed Soviet inspections, and they [Soviet Foreign Ministry and military officials] called on Reagan to 'make a political decision' in the next six weeks to overrule the military" (p. A1).

a form of removing the "sufficiently objective hook" for American paranoia—the United States will either resort to paranoid attacks on these new policies, branding them insufficient propaganda efforts, or it will be forced to change its view of the Soviet Union and of itself and let go of some of its paranoid attitudes. It also will be confronted increasingly with its own paranoid process and its own negative shadow as Soviet hooks for paranoid projection are withdrawn. At that point it will either integrate shadow elements in a healthy way or it will seek a new nation or hook or issue/hook for its shadow projections.[42]

This sounds not too difficult at first blush. But when one considers that the size of the American defense budget (and the attendant jobs associated with it) in part has been in direct relationship to the level of American paranoia about the Soviet Union, the picture changes considerably. Thus, in this instance, assuming that objective justification exists for it, letting go of some American paranoia toward the Soviet Union will pit the United States against its own obsession with maintaining power supremacy, most readily symbolized by its preeminence as a military and economic power.

The Reagan administration (ironically excepting the president himself), true to its own record, for the most part, opted for the route of continuing paranoid attacks on Gorbachev's new policies while taking political advantage of them (for example, the 1987 INF Treaty). The primary source of these attacks emanated from the defense establishment and those conservatives who believe that there is *no* alternative in the superpower relationship short of maximum defense readiness—absolute and permanent military superiority, not parity. In his annual military report released on January 10, 1987, Secretary of Defense Caspar Weinberger asserted that high-tech weaponry and new tactics are the only way to compete successfully against Soviet advantages in numbers and perennially high defense funding.[w] Frank Gaffney, Richard Perle's replacement as assistant secretary of defense, was quoted as remarking regarding the decision to conclude the INF Treaty: "The blood is in the water; the treaty makers are in a feeding frenzy."[x] At the same time, this intransigence was probably no small matter in the resignation of Weinberger as secretary of defense in 1987.[43]

---

[42] "Issue/hooks" might be the international drug problem, environmental issues, "unfair" trade practices of other nations, et cetera.

[43] However, Carlucci's replacement of Weinberger did not seem to alter the outlook of the Defense Department—indeed, it may have hardened it. Columnist Lou Cannon reported in the *Washington Post* on June 13, 1988: "One note of cau-

These are perilous times *because* significant change appears to be taking place within the Soviet system. If they are thwarted by American paranoia, the result can be an even more repressive and belligerent Soviet system. It would behoove future administrations to understand this dynamic and to go out of their way to avoid agitating Soviet paranoia. The best way to do that would be to officially, publicly, *and benignly* acknowledge those positive changes that do take place. If that is not possible, the best alternative would be silence.

CREATIVE TENSION IN THE PARANOID PROCESS

The natural coalescence of social groups and systems automatically constellates the paranoid process, which itself becomes indispensable to the cohesion and evolution of those groups and systems. Jung pointed out that all growth is a function of the tension of opposites. The paranoid process often is essential for maintaining a creative tension between opposing social groups and, within acceptable bounds, is a core and indispensable factor in the creative evolution of social systems. The civil rights movement of the 1960s is an excellent example of this dynamic. The creative tension of that era not only led to battered heads and the jailing of thousands, it also led to enormous growth of Black pride and self-esteem as well as the enactment of laws to protect and further the rights of all minorities and raised to a new plateau the consciousness of our nation concerning civil rights. It is questionable as to how many of the positive results of that movement would have taken place without the paranoid element.

When I refer to a "creative tension" in the paranoid process, I am referring to a situation where the paranoid mechanisms of the one side (usually

---

tion was sounded last week in Tokyo, where [then] Defense Secretary Carlucci said that changes in U.S. defense policy should await 'tangible changes' in the Soviet Union. . . .

"'Summitry is no substitute for security,' said Carlucci. He contended that western assistance to help Gorbachev modernize the Soviet economy could be a mistake that would make the Soviets more militarily formidable in the 1990s than they are now.

"'He is not, so to speak, changing the fundamental structure of society, he is just trying to make the system more efficient,' Carlucci said . . ." (p. A2).

Coming out of a power stance, there is a fundamental assumption that the Soviet Union's getting out of its underdeveloped state and becoming a real superpower is inherently bad for the United States. At the same time, we chastise the Soviet Union for being who they are. This is a classical paranoid position.

the disempowered faction) is met with the paranoid mechanisms of the other, *coupled with a partially benevolent and enlightened paternalistic response.* This is clearly evident in the Kennedy administration's tapping of the phone and other violations of the civil rights of Dr. Martin Luther King and his followers along with official support for the goals of Dr. King and his civil rights movement. It may be seen also in the constrained response (as compared with that of Richard Nixon) of the Johnson administration to the rioting and other social upheaval of 1968 and 1969. It can also be seen in contemporary times with China's attempts to contain (to avoid repressing) the "prodemocracy" movement in its major cities in December 1986 and January 1987. It could also be seen in the desperate, but failed, attempt of the Polish government in 1981 to contain (save?) the Solidarity Movement.[44]

However, when the "partially benevolent paternalistic" component is missing, or when paranoid defense is predominant on the part of the group in power, the results are fascistic repression, as was the case with the Nazi regime and, in the 1970s and 1980s, with the various right-wing repressive governments in South Korea, the Union of South Africa, Latin America, and elsewhere. When the paranoid process is particularly prevalent among a very large disempowered group and the group in power is either equally paranoid or particularly weak, revolution can be the result. This can be seen historically in the Russian and French revolutions and, in more recent times, the peaceful revolution in Rhodesia (now Zimbabwe).

We are now witnessing in the Union of South Africa the rapid and seemingly inevitable evolution of the world's next violent revolution. Although the group in power is far from weak, the combination of the huge outgroup population of the country coupled with increasing international pressures on the government appear to be sufficient in time to counterbalance the military power of the government. At the present time the nature of political paranoia in South Africa is such that the group in power appears to be in the grip of its own paranoid defense, leaving little room for political compromise.

It is of the utmost importance to realize and acknowledge that states of

---

[44]The Polish government at the time offered one concession after the other to Solidarity and pleaded with it to not back the government into a corner with demands for full enfranchisement. It appeared at the time that Lech Walesa tried desperately to get Solidarity to agree to the impressive gains that it had wrought. But the movement, caught in its own repressed emotions suddenly let free and the headiness of momentary success, was not containable by anyone.

paranoia and paranoid projection occur as a natural and sometimes necessary phenomenon in the psychological development of individuals and nations. They are not always predominantly pathological. In the case of nations, what distinguishes "normal" from "abnormal" paranoid states is degree and deviation from the international "norm" and capacity for tolerating paranoid states (both as subject and object) as process, *without identifying with the process itself*.

Growing evidence suggests a much higher capacity for benign toleration of paranoid states than had heretofore been thought possible. Conscious awareness of the nature and dynamics of paranoid states and the fact that they are developmentally much more prevalent and necessary than had been thought can make them more possible to deal with, contain, and resolve. If nothing else, awareness will prevent the dismissal of all paranoid behavior between the Soviet Union and the United States as pathological. By differentiating "normal" paranoia from the pathological in the relations between the two superpowers, it will be possible to distinguish what aspects of their respective self-esteem each is trying to preserve and can provide an entirely different perspective for conflict resolution. Aiding the other in preserving its self-esteem (even if just by inaction), in this context, can enhance the self-esteem and self-cohesion of both.[45]

For example, given that the kind of failure experienced at Reykjavik would heighten the inherent paranoia on the part of both countries, if the two superpowers had an awareness of this dynamic they would have sat down together before leaving Reykjavik and worked out a joint plan for

---

[45] Another case in point is the state of Israel. Historically, given the diaspora over the centuries, later followed by the Holocaust, Jewish culture as a whole carries a large paranoid element. In addition, as described in this chapter, *any* new nation that comes into existence as a result of struggle and over against the wishes of powerful enemy states will experience a sustained period of active paranoid defense as an intrinsic part of its normal development as a nation-state. (The length of this period seems to vary among nation-states, depending on other characteristics, such as wealth, political allies, and military power. However, a minimum period would appear to be between fifty and sixty years from the founding of the nation.)

It is vital as we move into the decade of the nineties that the Bush administration distinguish between nonpathological and pathological elements in Israeli attitudes and policies as it endeavors to move Israel toward political accommodation with the Arab populations in Israeli-occupied territory. This distinction alone, and the manner in which those different paranoid elements in the Israeli national psyche are treated, could spell the success or failure of peace mediation efforts in the Middle East.

preventing paranoid splitting in making public presentations about their failure to reach agreement on arms reduction. It might be argued that such a proposition requires a sufficiently nonparanoid state of being from within which to implement it and that it would be impossible for them to do so at this point in their relationship. Perhaps so. But if we institutionalized the presence of jointly trained Soviet and American observers at all negotiations between the two superpowers whose job it would be to work together to monitor the negotiation process from a psychological or group dynamics standpoint with a particular eye to paranoid projection and splitting, the outcome might be quite different. Their mutual job would be to make the negotiational *process* (not the outcome)[46] a success. To perform their function adequately, they should have no role in negotiating substantive issues, per se, although they would have to be knowledgeable of, and competent in, the substantive area under discussion.

To undertake some of the approaches outlined above, both the United States and the Soviet Union would have to recognize the primacy of their *relationship* above any single issue (for example, regional conflicts), save national survival itself. Since, in the thermonuclear age, national survival has become virtually synonymous with the survival of the other, the interdependency of the relationship between the two superpowers rapidly is becoming recognized by both as primary. This recognition has been the missing prerequisite necessary to enable the next stage in the resolution of Soviet-American conflict. Meissner expresses the view that "humans are basically paranoid, especially in our group-related behavior. Generally we use our intelligence in support of our various paranoias and only rarely, under great stress do we use our intellect to curb and control our pathogenic projections and false beliefs."[y] I believe that this is exactly the "rare" place to which nuclear weapons and the missile have brought us. Therein there is an unprecedented opportunity to facilitate profound change into the relationship between the Soviet Union and the United States.

---

[46] A successful outcome might be to recognize, without blame, that one or both parties were not ready or able to agree on the given issue. It might even result in one side assisting the other in reaching a point where it could resolve its own obstacles or reservations to agreement.

⑨ Conclusion: The Entelechy[1] of Transformation

We need a new way of thinking. It is impossible to solve the burning problems of today, let alone of the coming century, if one is to be guided by views characteristic of past centuries, past decades, or, in any case, of times prior to the emergence of nuclear weapons and the recent upsurge in the scientific and technological revolution.
—Excerpt from a speech by General Secretary Gorbachev given in Moscow on July 14, 1986

The time urgently demands a new understanding of the present stage in the development of civilization, of international relations, of the world. The world is full of contradictions, it is complex, but it is objectively united by bonds of interdependence. International relations are such that, with all the differences and clashes of interest, one can no longer live according to the millennia-old traditions of fist law. Civilization has demonstrated an unprecedented strength of the human mind and human labour and, at the same time, its own fragility its vulnerability to the forces released by the human genius but placed at the service of destruction. All that dictates the need for and makes urgent a radical break with many customary attitudes to foreign policy, a break with traditional political thinking, traditional views on problems of war and peace, on defense, on the security of individual states and international security.
—Excerpt from a speech by General Secretary Gorbachev given in Vladivostok on July 28, 1986[a]

---

[1] *Entelechy* is taken from the Greek *entelechia*, and means "the full realization of form-giving cause or energy, esp. as contrasted with mere potential existence; the form that actuates this realization." *Webster's Third New International Dictionary, Unabridged* (Chicago: Donnelley 1966), p. 756.

This book attempts to show that the world has indeed moved into a condition where "the millennia-old traditions of fist law" are no longer compatible with the continuance of life. Indeed, the very psychic principles and laws under which civilization has operated over the millennia have changed and demand a radical change in human perception and thinking.

Deterrence itself grew out of an increasing recognition that nuclear weaponry and the guided missile made world war in general, and war between the superpowers in particular, untenable. Over the past decade there has been a growing recognition that deterrence itself, with its huge arsenal of nuclear weapons and layered technologies, though they have been successful over the past forty-four years in keeping the peace, pose the threat of accidentally triggering nuclear annihilation at some point in the future.

The latest "technology" spawned by the United States (under the Reagan administration) is one dubbed "competitive strategies," which aims at keeping the Soviet Union in economic stagnation. It justifies on economic grounds the development of technologically supersophisticated weapons systems such as Stealth aircraft and various missile and other weapons systems, to force the Soviet Union to allocate a high proportion of their gross national product to the development of weapons sytems and technologies to counter those developed by the United States. Presumably, an economically weak and unstable Soviet Union makes for a strong and secure United States (and the rest of the free world), never mind that to bring about Soviet economic vulnerability we would be giving the Soviets an imperative to develop ever more sophisticated weapons systems, thus dramatically increasing the risk of war.

The point is worth belaboring in the context of the larger point of this book. Former Secretary of Defense Caspar Weinberger, in his 1986 annual military report, stated, "I have directed the deputy secretary [of Defense] to oversee the institutionalization of competitive strategies through the Defense Department [rather than to try to match] the Soviets tank for tank, ship for ship or aircraft for aircraft." The *Washington Post* quoted Weinberger:

> To cope with the ATB [advanced technology bomber, or Stealth bomber] the Soviets will be forced to make an enormous investment in new defensive systems over a span of many years, while their existing enormous investment becomes rapidly obsolete. The ATB will not only dramatically degrade existing Soviet air defenses, but also those of Moscow's Warsaw Pact allies and Third World client states.

At the same time, Moscow will not be able to scrap its existing air defense systems because the B1B [bomber] and the advanced cruise missile launched from our B52s [bombers] will maintain the effectiveness of our conventional penetrating bomber force well into the 1990s.

Should the Soviets attempt to restore these defenses, considerable resources will have to be diverted from other programs. . . . We must continue to adopt the competitive strategy approach in our weapons development, in our operational planning and in our military doctrine.

This is really the only way we can overcome Soviet numerical advantages and deal with the other military advantages their political system gives them.[b]

As a solution to the problem of the threat of nuclear suicide resulting from Soviet-American conflict, the "logic" of deliberately provoking an enemy to develop more sophisticated weapons systems, in the name of preventing nuclear war, by psychological standards, would qualify as a paranoid delusion. Never mind that a policy of "competitive strategies" coupled with SDI threatens to bankrup the United States as well as the Soviet Union.[2] Such a policy also does not recognize that the Soviet Union, on the basis of its standard of living and the fact that it has never known a higher living standard, psychologically is in a much better position than the United States to endure the economic sacrifices of such a strategy.

It is not that the United States can get out of the business of military deterrence. The United States (and the Soviet Union) into the foreseeable future will have to maintain and develop formidable military systems *as part of* an overall approach to peace. But to survive we will have to develop our thinking to go beyond the narrow, if not fatal, concept of defeating the enemy and keeping the enemy from defeating us.

The United States and the Soviet Union share the mutual problem of surviving their deterrence arsenals. We are not unlike the cancer victim who gets chemotherapy to arrest or to kill his or her cancer and then must take additional treatments to prevent his or her demise from the side effects of the chemotherapy.

This book tries to show that we have lacked both the thinking and the commitment of resources to develop an effective containment of deterrence—a "peace technology"—and that it is time that the role of psychology be recognized as being of no less importance than those of physics, engineering, and military science in maintaining the peace.

---

[2] As is well known, in the 1980s the United States has managed to transform itself from the world's largest creditor into the world's largest debtor.

Many of the proposals put forth here may appear to some to be naive, irrational, overidealistic, too radical, unfeasible, et cetera. But deterrence has brought about the necessity of operating on a new and radically different set of psychic principles that will govern the future survival of humanity. I do not know specifically what Mr. Gorbachev had in mind when he said that we need a "radical break with many customary attitudes to foreign policy, a break with traditional political thinking, traditional views on problems of war and peace." Indeed, he may not have known, either, what he had in mind specifically. He would not have to know to be right.

WAR GAMES

Clearly the most radical proposal made here is for direct war games between the Soviet Union and the United States. In all probability, such a direct event will not take place in the immediate future. The important point is that unconscious, de facto war games are already taking place between the superpowers.

This book challenges the belief that war is purely the instrument of rational process and that it can be undecided as well as it can be undertaken.[3] Our current struggle with the threat from deterrence speaks to the fact that there is something quite powerful in the background (that is, the archetype of war and the tendency toward pseudospeciation) that impels nations toward warfare.

Since all forms of energy are dynamic and never static, psychic energy, like any other energy, must have somewhere to go. As we become more effective at stemming direct warfare between the superpowers, the psychic energy that gives rise to the impulse to make war must have somewhere to go, lest it catch us from behind the trip us into war. To date, the primary "somewhere elses" have been through disarmament negotiations, proxy wars, and other *unconscious* forms of ritual (sham) warfare such as those described in Chapters 6 and 7. However, there is always the danger when energy is being expressed unconsciously that it will act in ways that we don't want it to and will precipitate the very conditions we wish to avoid. Proxy wars are very dangerous.

---

[3] This belief is aptly expressed in the Preamble to the Constitution of UNESCO, which states: "War begins in the minds of human beings. Since this is so, the minds of human beings must also be capable of ending war."

As I have asserted repeatedly herein, war can be managed and contained and its energy dissipated. It cannot be "ended."

This is not to say that proxy wars between the Soviet Union and the United States should not take place—they may be a necessary evil—only that they are not conscious enough. Only by seeing them fully in terms of their function in superpower conflict will it be possible to structure them in a way where they optimally serve the function of averting direct war between the superpowers, thus making them relatively less necessary in the long term. The less consciousness the superpowers have about their proxy wars, the greater the danger that they will be inadvertently manipulated into direct warfare with each other. Two cases in point are Afghanistan and the Middle East conflicts, the Iran-Iraq war in particular.[4]

Some might argue, and rightly, that war games between the Soviet Union and the United States, even if they were feasible, would be highly dangerous. Once commenced, how would they be contained and kept from turning into the "real thing"?[5]

There *is* danger in reconstituting group ritual. But there may be a greater danger in not doing so. The answer to that crucial question may lie ultimately in structuring mixed teams of Soviet and American troops so that there would be no clearly discernible "side" to win or lose per se—the function of the exercise would be literally the dissipation of war-inducing energy. Given the persistence of the psychodynamic of pseudo-speciation throughout human history and the history of relations between the two countries, this suggestion may seem absurd.

However, what is considered to be absurd is relative to experienced

---

[4]The position taken by the Reagan administration in openly countenancing an international conference, including participation of the Soviet Union, on the Middle East, is a shift in this direction. All previous American administrations have officially opposed any formal Soviet participation in Middle East negotiations to preserve American hegemony in the area.

[5]Senator William S. Cohen (D-Maine), in correspondence addressing some of my proposals, observed: "His proposal for ritualized war games replicates a major objective of the Olympics. But I'm not satisfied that our psychic energy could be contained, or if so contained, could be stimulated in the first instance if there was foreknowledge that the sacrifice, and training was to be utilized for the equivalent of a chess game."

Senator Cohen's concern about containment is one that I share and one that must be addressed with great caution. His second point—that foreknowledge of the purpose of the game would eliminate psychic investment in the game—is contradicted by a mound of evidence (including raised blood pressure and adrenaline levels) on the tremendous psychic investment in (ritual) war games between groups at all levels of society. Additionally, the Pentagon would not be spending the hundreds of millions of dollars each year on war games if there were not evidence of their value in preparing troops psychologically as well as militarily.

reality and the state of the human psyche at any given point in history. We are living in an age of unprecedently rapid psychological, political, and social change. This book posits that the new psychodynamic of primary cooperation has become the dominant psychodynamic in the relationship between the Soviet Union and the United States. There is mounting evidence that primary cooperation may carry sufficient archetypal energy to neutralize or counter pseudospeciation under some circumstances.

In the not-too-distant future, the two superpowers will likely find themselves acting in concert to eliminate a threat of nuclear terrorism coming from a third country or group (for example, Iran, Libya, and Irish Republican Army [IRA], Abu Nidal, or the Red Brigade) in possession of a small nuclear (or chemical) device.[6] Chapter 7 proposes that the superpowers develop joint military or paramilitary strike forces in conjunction with their Nuclear Risk Reduction Centers[7] to operate against nuclear terrorism. If these joint strike forces are not created prior to the first incident of nuclear (or chemical or biological) terrorism, the odds are that they surely will be after that incident. The joint Soviet-American strike force will constitute the first mixed team of Soviet and American troops alluded to above. We will likely see such mixed teams before the turn of the century.

Perhaps out-and-out war games between the Soviet Union and the United States will never occur. Many would argue that they cannot occur, because the two countries are too polarized ideologically and politically. But conscious war games between the superpowers may take place eventually, *because* they are polarized. War games permit the dissipation of the instinct to aggression without requiring formal alliances or having to give up or change either country's ideological stance. It would constitute a kind of archetypal therapy.[8]

---

[6]The CIA estimates that by the year 2000 at least fifteen developing nations will have produced or be able to construct their own ballistic missiles. Some of these could be armed with chemical as well as nuclear warheads. Some of these countries are pooling their knowledge and technological and fiscal resources toward this end.

[7]If the Nuclear Risk Reduction Centers were to be eliminated, some other equivalent mechanism could function as well. Whenever I refer to Nuclear Risk Reduction Centers, I mean "or equivalent mechanism."

[8]Oftentimes when I work therapeutically with a couple in my clinical practice, the real work will begin only after the two have exploded at one another in my office. Frequently, one or the other or both will say, "We've been [cooperating in] holding off discussing this issue until we could see you today." The emotional "explosion" is like a cloudburst that dissipates the turbulent clouds and static electricity in the air so that the sun (that is, consciousness) can come through. Then meaningful communication between them can be facilitated.

Kull, Whitmont, and Neumann[c] have asserted that modern civilization has become too highly pluralized to recreate successfully collective psychic rituals like those found in primitive societies. It is their contention that rituals of the individual—inner intrapsychic symbolic rituals—are the only vehicles through which true transformation can take place. There is evidence to support their contention.

However, it seems that primary cooperation is constellating archetypal energies that are pointing to the reconstitution of a psychological need for collective ritual—at least in the limited areas discussed herein. CBMs (Confidence-Building Measures) are setting up a formal system to do this. The process of disarmament negotiations itself can be viewed as an ongoing ritual. It seems to me that a combination of direct and symbolic, individual and collective expression of the instinct to aggression, along with the implementation of primary cooperation, will serve as the primary vehicles for survival into the twenty-first century.

PEACE

> *The true object of war is peace.*
> —Sun Tzu

> *The problem in defense is how far you can go without destroying from within what you are trying to defend from without.*
> —Dwight D. Eisenhower, January 18, 1953[d]

Traditionally, peace has been viewed primarily as a state of being—that is, the absence of war—or as a policy in pursuit of that state of being. Since the Cold War, the word itself has become disparaged and often is seen as synonymous with appeasement, cowardice, inaction, weakness, and even treason.

Fundamentally, peace is not, *and cannot be,* the absence of war, because war is an archetypal energy that is universal and exists a priori. War was not invented by man, although man manifests and appropriates its energy, but rather derives from the aggressive instincts and power drive inherent in man's nature and the psychic derivatives (that is, archetypal dynamics) that influence his behavior. It is not within the realm of man's choice to abolish the archetype of war as an energy that induces warfare. What is within his choice is to channel, manage, and direct war-inducing energy (that is, energy, ensuing from the archetype of war, that is manifested as warfare.)

Peace as the absence of war is a static definition—and one that essentially misses the point. Peace as the active management of war-inducing energies—peace as an archetype—is a dynamic definition. Technically, it is one pole of the single archetype of War-Peace, war being the other pole. It is the Athena aspect of the Mars-Athena archetype.[9]

It is not accidental that in the mythological system that underpins the archetypal heritage of Western civilization, Mars (Ares) and Athena are brother and sister. They symbolize a paired psychodynamic in the Western psyche. The male component, Mars/Ares, represents the more hot-blooded heroic "macho" dynamic that views life as something to be approached with aggressive power as the primary, if not sole, force for dealing with conflict. It reflects the power drive par excellence.

The female component, Athena, represents a balance of wisdom with power. Power—force—is to be used in service to moral consciousness; it is to be used to bring an end to unmediated violence, not to carry it forward (that is, to bring about "conflict resolution"). Although she embodies the dynamic of conflict resolution, Athena just as well can, and does, represent conflict management through the wise use of force when necessary. Mythologically, this occurs when she appears on the battlefield in full armor, with her sword and shield. In this context she uses her superior martial powers to intervene in the battle on one side or the other in the name of higher moral principle—usually just in the nick of time. Her interventions oppose the principle of "might makes right" and aim at sub-

---

[9] It is not accidental that a primary archetypal symbol for peace in the Western psyche is a feminine figure. (It should be noted that Athena, as a feminine symbol, has a unique relationship to the masculine. Among her attributes is the fact that she is born a mature adult, in full battle gear, out of Zeus' head: she is a feminine principle born of the masculine.) The role of men in carrying the archetype of war is, and has been throughout history, undeniably dominant. The role of the feminine and women in manifesting the archetype of peace remains to be seen. I mean this in every sense of the word in which it is discussed herein. This work lacks any in-depth exploration of the archetypal suggestion that women and the feminine, in men as well as in women, will play a more crucial role in carrying the responsibility for and manifesting the archetype of peace. That is a most complex topic, needing to be a work in and of itself. For a beginning exploration the reader might wish to examine Edward C. Whitmont's *Return of the Goddess* and "Athena Today: Paradoxes of Power and Vulnerability," by Roger and Jennifer Woolger, in *Quadrant*, 20, [1] (1987).

Also see the discussion of Athena in Chapter 4.

ordinating an indiscriminate power principle to moral consciousness. In the myths she often confronts her hotheaded brother, Mars, and calms him down.[10] Interestingly, in the heat of brotherly-sisterly conflict, Mars usually comes up short.

Peace is a potential source of constructive power rather than—as it has come to be seen—the absence of power. It may not be possible always to prevent aggressive energies from being destructive, but humanity can play a significant role in determining how destructive energy might be channeled. Therefore, in most instances herein the term *peace* refers to a conscious ongoing process of managing and containing the archetype of war *both* in its manifest and latent states. This definition, of course, includes the discipline of conflict resolution.

PEACE TECHNOLOGY

Peace involves more than conflict resolution; some conflicts are not fully resolvable; for example, the conflicts in the Middle East. Conflict resolution—that is, psychodynamic negotiational process—as a technique is not sufficient to curtail and manage war on a sustained basis because it operates on the principle that the instinct to aggression always is subordinative to conscious ego control. In some cases, however, ritualized war games may be the only means for releasing pent-up energy ensuing from chronically unresolved tension.[11]

---

[10] Of note, H. W. Turney-High points out that in the case of some Indian tribes in the southeast United States, tribal leadership was shared between a war "chief" and a peace "chief," the latter being a civil and spiritual leader who was forbidden to shed blood. This sharing of power between two leaders is similar to the Mars-Athena model. Turney-High, *Primitive War* (Columbia: University of South Carolina Press, 1979), p. 65.

Similarly, in Navajo mythological cosmogony, the present world was made possible by a pair of heroes—Monster Slayer, who was psychodynamically the warrior, and Child-Born-of-Water, who was always present as an observer-reflector-spiritual presence who never took part in conflict.

[11] Such a situation might be one like that between Libya and the United States described in Chapter 7. Since rational negotiation or dialogue between Libya and the United States was impossible at the time, the naval "exercises" held by the United States may have been the *only* recourse, short of bombing and/or invading Libya, to release the frustrations of many months resulting from a feeling of national, political, and military impotence surrounding numberous kidnappings and terrorist attacks on United States citizens. As we know, those naval exercises (that

Although resolving international conflict remains the ultimate goal *when possible*, conflict management as a technology has not been seen as legitimate or desirable in its own right. For one thing, the very term acknowledges the unresolvability of a given conflict for the foreseeable future and shifts the focus and resources to another, less desirable, goal. It would acknowledge the real limitations of the human ego, particularly of politicians and bureaucrats, who are not noteworthy for their humility when it comes to the power drive. Moreover, conceptually, conflict resolution and conflict management go down two different streets. Conflict resolution contains an inherent negative bias toward human aggression that carries a negative (pathological) value in that context. Focusing on conflict resolution as presently formulated will yield limited insight and data in the area of conflict management, which is based on the principle that aggression is a permanent component of human psychology and is not always and fully able to be subordinated to the human ego. On the other hand, conflict management could broaden and enhance the discipline of conflict resolution.

Additionally, conflict resolution, with the limited exceptions noted, lacks the integration of archetypal theory essential for plumbing the deeper layers of psychodynamic process, particularly on the collective level between groups and nations.

Therefore it is essential that adequate resources be committed to develop a technology of peace to manage war on an ongoing basis, one that should have a status commensurate with war technology. An overwhelming portion of American economic and technological resources is devoted to improving war technology. Virtually no resources are formally committed to the development of a peace *technology*.[12] As of 1983, there were approximately two hundred thousand scientists and social scientists under federal contract who performed military-related work, compared with twenty thousand who were engaged in various kinds of nonmilitary work.[e] Probably not one percent of the latter worked on peace in the terms discussed here. Indeed, if anything the tide has been going the other way.[13]

---

is, ritual warfare) were not sufficient to stave off permanently the bombing of Libya.

[12] A notable limited exception is the National Peace Institute, established in October 1984. The institute will be discussed later in this chapter.

[13] The Center for Defense Information (CDI) reports that companies previously not normally associated with defense work have been redirecting their production in order to get a share of defense contracting dollars. "Singer, IBM, Goodyear Tire, Motorola, AT&T, and Westinghouse are just a few companies which have

A further complicating factor was the United States' decision to change the name of the "War Department" to the "Defense Department" in 1947. On the one hand, this suggests an advance in strategic thinking in the thermonuclear age, reflecting a realization that war had become much riskier for all sides—a concept that gave rise to modern-day deterrence theory. On the other hand, it subsumed into the context of war planning any real potential for developing a peace technology. Since then, war has been seen only as something the enemy (that is, the Soviet Union) does. The United States must "defend" against subversion and the threat of war from the Soviet Union.[14] This stance has tended to severely limit and constrict conceptualization and planning, as well as the allocation of resources and the development of infrastructures, for implementing an effective peace technology.

Psychologically speaking, this single act—changing the name of the War Department to the Department of Defense—split into "good" and "bad" the act of making war. No longer was war viewed as a legitimate and consciously willed act on the part of a nation. Bad countries (the Soviet Union) make war; good countries (the United States) don't—they just de-

---

crossed the line from civilian to military contracting. Some 80% of the Singer Company's revenues came from the firm's aerospace electronics business in 1985, compared to 15% ten years ago. Singer's nuclear-related contracts have included work on Trident and Pershing missiles, and simulators for the B-52 bomber." (*The Defense Monitor.* [Washington, D.C.: Center for Defense Information], 15, [3] [1986]: 3.)

CDI also reports that as of 1986, close to 70 percent of every federal dollar allocated for research and development (R&D) *in all areas of research* went to the military establishment. Overall military research spending since 1981 had increased by 62 percent above inflation, while funding for civilian research had decreased by 10 percent. Military R&D was predicted to rise to over $44 billion in FY 87 (*Defense Monitor*, ibid.).

[14] NSC-68, drafted by the National Security Council in 1950, stated this quite directly. It asserted that the "Soviet threat" was *the* basis upon which to build U.S. foreign and domestic policy. It stated, "The integrity of our system will not be jeopardized by any measures, covert or overt, violent or non-violent, which serve the purposes of frustrating the Kremlin design" (as reported in *The Defense Monitor*, 15, [3] [1986]: 2). Since the Soviet menace, *by definition*, was (and remains) *the* source of threat to national security and the survival of democratic principles (and for many, the source of evil itself), there can be no peace without the elimination of that threat. With the notable exception of "détente" during the Nixon administration, which was subsequently discredited by the Reagan administration as weakness, the virtual sole approach to the elimination of that Soviet threat has been through foreign and domestic policies of so-called "defense preparedness" and deterrence technology.

fend against them. By definition, then, any act of warfare by the United States would have to be a defense against something the Soviet Union did or perpetrated. This attitude has had the effect of making the United States blind to its own policies that provoke warfare. Vietnam is an example of this mind-set—the longest and most costly war of the United States, which from beginning to end was dubbed only in defensive and obtuse terms as the Vietnam "conflict." The Soviet Union plays out an identical dynamic, witness their "aid to a friendly neighbor": that is, Afghanistan.[15]

This split also has resulted in the development of a new lexicon that further distances governments from the motives behind their actions. Nicaraguan Sandinistas are "communists" and "Marxists" only, and the Contra guerrillas are dubbed "freedom fighters" only, by American government officials from the president to the secretaries of defense and state. If these groups were to develop views and promulgate policies that went beyond being "communists" and "freedom fighters," one would hardly learn about it, to read and listen to United States government statements about them.

The Reagan doctrine justified wars of liberation against Soviet-supported "Marxist governments" (for example, Nicaragua, Angola, Ethiopia). In the case of Chile, this split left no room for the discrimination that the "Marxist government" of Salvador Allende, which the United States subverted in 1972, was democratically elected and at the time of its demise observed a constitutional process that could have put it out of office by democratic electoral means. The point here is not the justification for or against such wars, overt or covert, but the commonplace words that are used to describe and "discuss" the issues involved. They reflect the paranoid defense discussed earlier, which is woven into the fabric of American foreign policy and, worse, into many levels of American perception of the international community.[16] Indeed, former President Reagan himself, during a press conference on February 19, 1982, became confused as to which side he was referring to, the words and labels had so little meaning!

Relatedly, since the War Department was converted to the Defense Department, the United States has fought two wars without ever having promulgated an official declaration of war. The word *war* has never been used to this day in official circles when referring to the Vietnam war,

---

[15] As recently as August 22, 1988, the Soviet party weekly *Arguments and Facts* was still talking about the provision of "external aid" and *Tass* was discussing "fraternal assistance" given to Czechoslovakia in 1968.

[16] See Chapter 8.

which still is referred to officially as the "Vietnam conflict." The Korean war was dubbed a "police action." Both wars were seen as essential to United States global policy and power needs in the Pacific. Yet the conditions giving rise to these two wars were radically different. The Korean War resulted from unprovoked invasion by North Korea of South Korea in clear violation of Soviet-American agreements on the partitioning of Korea at the 38th parallel.ᶠ The Vietnam war resulted from an American decision to move into a perceived power vacuum in the wake of French withdrawal from Indochina in the 1950s and the Eisenhower administration's decision to sabotage free elections in Vietnam when it became clear that American interests in that country would lose.ᵍ

Such obfuscation of the motives behind policy formulation on the parts of both the United States and the Soviet Union makes it difficult for even those "in the know" to be clear about the real motives behind foreign policy formulation, let alone for the Congress and the public-at-large. All of this becomes self-reinforcing and feeds shadow projection and psychological dissociation since, *by definition*, "freedom fighters" can only do good— notwithstanding ample and highly credible evidence to the contrary: for example, atrocities against civilians.

Another word used by both the Soviet Union and the United States that feeds shadow projection is *aggression*. The Viet Minh and the Viet Cong in Vietnam were "aggressors," while American bombers "interdicted" and "disrupted" supply lines in Cambodia. The Soviet Union supported a "friendly neighbor" against "counterrevolutionary aggression" in Afghanistan, et cetera.

In contemporary terms, virtually the entire approach to "peace" on the part of the Defense Department, and to a large extent on the part of the State Department as well, is some variant of deterrence theory.[17] Thus, in the thermonuclear age, with the exception of conflict resolution, previous efforts for the attainment of "peace" have been defined by a unilateral approach (that is, deterrence) that itself is part of the problem to be addressed.

I have used the phrase "peace *technology*" because the kind of peace that is essential for staving off nuclear holocaust is very different from the more passive and defensive concept of peace that has been pursued historically. The word *technology*—the application of scientific knowledge to practical purposes in a particular fieldʰ—like many other things, has become coopted and distorted by the defense establishment. What has to do

---

[17] For a significant exception to this statement, see Chapter 3, note 18.

with physics, mathematics, chemistry, engineering, et cetera, is "scientific" and legitimately technological. What has to do with psychology, ethics, and education is "soft" and therefore not legitimately scientific or technological. This approach amounts to applied research by dismissal.

It is one thing to pursue peace defensively through trying to settle disputes and conflicts during and after their genesis; it is another to realize that in dealing with the archetype of war per se, conflict must be anticipated. It is one thing to address the conscious and ostensible reasons for war; it is another to address the irrational and underlying psychological and archetypal factors that go beyond them and that generate and feed conflict.

The establishment of a peace technology that goes beyond the present technology of conflict resolution would carry implications for every sector of society. It would involve the development of archetypal profiles of the Soviet Union and the United States that would aid in better understanding the behavior of each; a science for predicting conflict and war; institutionalizing the development of Confidence Building Measures (CBMs) on an ongoing basis; an exploration of the full implications of "primary cooperation" as a new dynamic power between nations; a science of ritual warfare; systems for analyzing the underlying archetypal dynamics of specific conflict situations,[18] techniques to train others to make such analyses, and integration of those techniques into the science of conflcit resolution; techniques to reduce shadow projection and to further shadow integration; materials to train policymakers and negotiators in the utilization of the theory of psychological types at all levels in the foreign policy, intelligence, and military fields; techniques for identifying and managing, at all levels, paranoid process as it occurs between the superpowers; techniques for predicting, identifying, and reducing the danger of psychic inflation in those individuals who hold positions of major influence and power in government, including the military; research in the use of "feel-

---

[18] From the limited information available, it would appear that Peace and Common Security, of Berkeley, California, is engaged in the use of archetypal theory in developing approaches to conflict resolution.

Also, the Center for Middle East Peace and Development, of the City University of New York, to some degree utilized an archetypal approach to its work with some Middle East countries (Egypt, Israel, and Jordan) with some success. I have not been able to ascertain to what degree archetypal theory has been consciously employed in the project and the degree to which a simlar approach has been utilized unawares. This is an important distinction, since the real potency of a depth-psychological approach is in the full conscious use of the range of techniques available.

ing" as a technique to compensate for the tendency to overabstract the destructive potential of policy decisions; an economic science and industrial policy that would account for conditions of peace in economic formulas. And this is only a preliminary list.

At the same time, however, civilization as we know it is not ideally suited for peace. Therefore, it is necessary to research the social, economic, political, population, agricultural, et cetera, implications of prolonged peace and peace management. The development of a peace technology will need to focus a substantial part of that technology on the "problems" resulting from peace.

Ways will have to be found to make the establishment, and then the maintenance, of peace more profitable and labor-intensive. With the present commitment to a high allocation of resources toward war technology, there are few incentives for the development of a peace technology, and peace-waging itself simply is not profitable in the short term.[19] Those powerful institutions that have developed and sustained this country's war technology, with its particular orientation toward defense research and development and war hardware and high technology, should be given equally profitable incentives to use the same power and resources for the research and development of a peace technology.

As government presently subsidizes the military-industrial complex for

---

[19]The Center for Defense Information reports that as of 1986, the Department of Defense and the defense industries employed 6.5 million people in the United States, generating $146 billion in business between the Pentagon and private companies *each year*. This does not account for the accelerating outlays for SDI research and development. In addition, over thirty thousand companies are engaged in military production. Each day military agencies sign fifty-two thousand contracts—more than 15 million a year (*The Defense Monitor*, 15, [3] [1986]).

Relatedly, the increasingly multinational composition of large corporations is a complicating factor. For example, in 1987, the Toshiba Corporation of Japan (along with a Norwegian company) were found to have violated American as well as Japanese and Norwegian law in secretly passing on to the Soviet Union the technology and machinery for manufacturing quiet propellers for use in Soviet submarines, thus rendering virtually useless existing American antisubmarine-detection technology, with an estimated cost to the United States of more than $15 billion for a replacement technology. When the United States Congress formally moved to censure and prohibit the sale of Toshiba products in the United States for two years, to drive home its policy against passing on military technology to the Soviets, a number of American corporations and unions objected and brought counter political pressure because of the enmeshment of Toshiba Corporation with numerous American corporations and the implications for corporate profits and American jobs that might be lost or otherwise adversely affected. The issue of moral consciousness in corporate governance looms large in the decade of the nineties.

the development of war technology, so it could subsidize the same institutions, including existing think tanks, universities, and other public and private resources, to conduct research in the development of a peace technology. Tax incentives and set-asides within the overhead of defense contracts, if properly monitored, could provide uncomplicated and effective mechanisms for shifting resources from almost full support of war technology to at least partial support of an effective peace technology. A set-aside of one hundredth of one percent in the $44 billion allocated for defense R&D in FY 87 would have yielded $44 million for peace technology R&D.

As President Eisenhower forewarned in his farewell address, the then-developing military-industrial complex threatened to dominate the government's capacity to make "free" policy choices. Since that warning in 1961, the American military-industrial complex has become a dominating force in American foreign and defense policy-making.[20]

In addition, with the multi-billion-dollar contracts being negotiated with America's European allies for participation in the research and development of SDI ("Star Wars") technology, and the increasing envelopment of American research and industrial capacity into multinational corporate conglomerates, the military-industrial complex now carries the impetus of the economies and foreign policy support of the governments of much of Western Europe and Japan. Indeed, it has been argued that the Reagan administration's effort to sign on its European allies and Japan as contractors for SDI development represented nothing short of a buying-off of an initially skeptical, if not hostile, allied opposition to the SDI program. The inertial momentum of this institutionalized military-industrial complex threatens to carry the foreign policy apparatus with it rather than to be subject to it, not unlike the America Class aircraft carriers, which require a mile or more to negotiate a turn at sea and several miles to come to a stop.

The Defense Department is already a nearly equal and sometimes dominant participant in determining American foreign policy. Indeed, it played the major role in getting the Reagan administration to scrap the SALT II treaty in 1986 and in the fall of 1987, if not for congressional intervention, would have succeeded in bringing about the formal renunciation or effective nullification of the Anti-Ballistic Missile (ABM) Treaty

---

[20] Jerome B. Wiesner, science advisor to both presidents Eisenhower and Kennedy, in 1986, made the flat-out assertion, "It's no longer a question of controlling a military-industrial complex, but rather of keeping the United States from becoming a totally military culture" (*The Defense Monitor*, 15, [3] [1986]: 3).

between the United States and Soviet Union. Thus it would appear exceedingly difficult, if not impossible, to develop an independent peace technology as a complement to deterrence technology.

If the development of a peace technology as outlined herein is feasible at all, given the political realities, it will probably have to come about through the provision of incentives to shift existing resources of the military-industrial complex toward another goal without threatening its hold on a significant portion of the American economy, technology, and political power.[21]

However, at the same time, it is questionable whether government can or should be the primary vehicle for the development of a peace technology. It is axiomatic that the patient cannot treat himself. Neither superpower can separate itself from the problems it generates sufficiently to treat them. On the American side, the increase in the size, political influence, and power of the military-industrial complex since 1961 has been enormous. It would appear that, from the standpoint of the integrity of peace technology as a new technological field, a more realistic and hopeful approach will have to be taken *outside* existing institutions, government and private, particularly those operated by or in a position to be influenced by the United States government. The same argument and principles would apply in the case of the Soviet government as well. However, applying them might be even more difficult to accomplish in the case of the Soviet Union, since there virtually is no private sector and no public sector outside government organs.

Given the realities of power politics, the power of the military-industrial complex and economics on the United States side, and given the different, but equally formidable, blocks on the Soviet side to a politics-free vehicle for the development of a peace technology, probably a mix of the above approaches involving government, private, and newly created resources will reflect the limits of what is possible. A specific approach will be discussed later in this chapter. (See Appendix 1 for a case history of the development of the United States Institute of Peace, which serves as a case study of the pitfalls and real limitations inherent in a governmental approach to developing a viable peace technology.)

---

[21] Contributions from the twenty largest defense contractors through Political Action Committees (PACs) increased 225 percent since the early 1980s, totalling $3.6 million during the 1984 campaign. The amount of $440,000 was contributed to members of the Senate Armed Services Committee, which authorizes funds for military spending (*Defense Monitor*, 15, [3] [1986]: 3).

An additional approach would be to establish an Office of Peace Technology (OPT) within the executive office of the president. Peace technology would thus be brought to the defense, foreign policy, and intelligence fields and would be given legitimate standing and a significant position of advocacy within these arenas. The mandate of such an office would be to further the development and establishment of peace technology as a legitimate technological field in its own right and to implement and integrate the concepts of peace management and maintenance into the process and technology of warfare. This approach could change the ways in which war is perceived and conceptualized and the very nature of war technology itself: the means of containing and preventing warfare would be developed simultaneously with the legitimate military capabilities needed to defend the nation should that be necessary. This would be a radical shift.

It would reconnect the artificial split in the single War-Peace (Mars-Athena) archetype, which has left peace on the outside, a poor stepchild in the process, pounding on the door pleading to be let in. Peace would become a technological reality on its own terms. Conceptually, this is a critical point, since peace has been seen primarily as the absence of war or as a by-product of conflict resolution. It has not developed conceptually as a technological resource sufficiently powerful in its potential to constrain and manage the archetype of war on a sustained basis, rather than on a crisis basis.[22] Above all else, it would no longer be solely reliant on deterrence-like strategies that depend upon and augment nuclear arsenals and the threat of war, conventional as well as thermonuclear.[23]

IMPLEMENTING PRIMARY COOPERATION

Primary cooperation differs from détente in that the latter was essentially a voluntary policy agreed to by the superpowers out of their respective

---

[22] As mentioned in Chapter 7, CBMs represent the first direct development of one peace technology.

[23] To be fully effective, the OPT would have to use the coordination and oversight authority of the executive office of the president, in a manner similar to that of the Office of Management and Budget (OMB), in order to implement a policy of establishing a peace technology and interfacing and integrating it with war technology. Otherwise the Defense and/or State Department would overshadow and

perceived national interests; the former represents a dynamic that is forcing on the superpowers a relationship neither has directly chosen. Of course, the superpowers may choose to build upon and further aspects of the relationship into which they have been forced. But the basic dynamic that has resulted in primary cooperation was not chosen by either.

The idea behind détente was that an intermeshing of interests would be so profitable to both sides that neither would jeopardize them by disruptive actions. As a by-product, mutual trust would develop sufficiently to transform the entire relationship.[i] Of course, many of the presuppositions of the concept of détente, as we have seen, not only did not hold together, but much of it crumbled in the late 1970s and early 1980s. The concept did not account for the independent variables in the collective unconscious that operated to undermine many of the gains made through détente and for the fact that the instinct to aggression is not always subordinate to the will of the human ego.

In the case of primary cooperation, because the relationship in its fundamental terms is a forced one, aspects of it will remain in force no matter what transpires at a broader conscious policy level. Nish Jamgotch, Jr., in a comparative analysis of case studies on superpower cooperation in seven fields[24] reports that six of the seven areas were significantly affected by political exigencies on both sides, and that disruptive curtailments of cooperative arrangements occurred more on the American side than the Soviet. However, he observed that, to a greater or lesser degree, progress in these six areas continued throughout the darkest days of retrenchment from détente and that such cooperation yields dividends on both sides. The seventh area, problem-solving in crisis communications, was the least affected by political disruptions and indeed, there was some evidence that political disruptions increased impetus for forging progress in the crisis communications area.[j] (I prefer the term *Confidence-Building Measures* [CBMs], of which crisis communications is one part.)

Jamgotch, in his book, makes a case for the operation of the dynamic of "functionalism" in the cooperative agreements between the Soviet Union

---

dominate, if not absorb, the OPT into its (their) own framework(s), thus vitiating the real objectives of the OPT, if not subverting it altogether to supporting war technology. Such a situation occurred with the Arms Control and Disarmament Agency (ACDA) under the Reagan administration when it was used to abrogate or vitiate the Strategic Arms Limitation Treaty (SALT II) and the Anti-Ballistics Missile treaty (ABM).

[24] U.S.–Soviet problem-solving in the fields of crisis communications, trade, science, agriculture, environmental controls, space, and medicine.

and the United States. He defines functionalism as the teaching that "social inter-dependence is pervasive and all-embracing. International institutions based on problem solving in carefully limited and managed fields constitute the most promising basis for peace" (p. 2). In the context of the functionalism thesis, the relationship between the superpowers went to hell during the first three years of the Reagan administration with real concern at many levels, including within the United States government itself, that the United States was planning for a first strike against the Soviet Union (and/or would precipitate one from the Soviet Union).[25] Throughout this period, the cooperative agreements between the two countries functioned at a diminished level.

Primary cooperation, on the other hand, involves a forced relationship sealed and guaranteed by the permanent presence of nuclear weapons and guided-missile technology—sealed by the permanence of the threat of total death that they bring. Primary cooperation changes the primary relationship between the superpowers. No longer are they primary enemies of each other. Each shares the same primary enemy—nuclear war (and thus, all war). Therein each has become the secondary enemy of the other. In other words, the bond of the relationship itself, albeit forced, is the strongest and dominant dynamic that in turn will affect cooperative agreements and institutions (not the other way around, as held by the functional school). Inherent in the concept of primary cooperation is the notion that the forces that generate primary cooperation in the first place are sufficiently powerful to check many of the powerful forces of the collective unconscious that heretofore have always arisen to undermine positive developments in the superpower relationship.

With regard to CBMs, the first clear by-product of primary cooperation, they will command more resources—military, bureaucratic, and R&D personnel, technological and fiscal resources—as the problem of

---

[25] Early in the Reagan administration, a new strategy of planning for the "winnable" war with the Soviet Union developed and threatened to dominate U.S. strategic planning. This strategy was articulated in "Victory is Possible," by O. C. Gray and K. Payne in *Foreign Policy*, vol. 39 (1980). In it Gray says, "The United States should plan to defeat the Soviet Union and to do so at a cost that would not prohibit U.S. recovery. Washington should identify war aims that in the last resort would contemplate the destruction of Soviet political authority and the emergence of a postwar world order compatible with western values. . . .

A U.S. president . . . should not launch a strategic nuclear strike if expected U.S. casualties are likely to involve 100 million or more American citizens" (p. 21). Quoted in Steven Kull, "Nuclear Arms and the Desire for World Destruction," *Political Psychology*, 4 (3) (September 1983): 587.

managing the archetype of war grows in complexity, as no doubt it will. Inexorably and increasingly, they will intrude upon the fundamental thinking and planning that sustains contact between the superpowers, heightening an awareness of shared values, and will foster new attitudes and infrastructures on both sides.

The greater the increase in crisis-oriented communication, the greater the possibility of confrontation by both sides with their own shadow projections and paranoid defenses. But, most important, in the context of primary cooperation, they will be forced to do so *jointly* (not just cooperatively) on an increasing basis. This will heighten the possibility of withdrawal of shadow projections and the resolution of paranoid defenses.

In this connection, Jamgotch raises the interesting speculation that the personal closeness of the working relationship between Paul Nitze, the American negotiator, and Yuli Kvitsinsky, the Soviet negotiator at the INF negotiations in Geneva in 1982–1983, itself resulted in the famous "walk in the woods" agreement between the two.[k] In other words, the private discussions between the two men, removed from the tumult and paranoid process inherent in the formal negotiational process, permitted primary cooperation to enter in more readily and to transcend intransigent (paranoid) political positions (and the limits of their instructions) of their respective governments. Although the agreement reached during the "walk in the woods" subsequently was repudiated by both the American and Soviet governments in 1983, the essence of that agreement later became formalized by the Gobachev and Reagan administrations in September 1987 as the INF Treaty, the historic first treaty between any nations to eliminate an entire class of weapons (that is, intermediate-range nuclear missiles).

Most of what I have defined as the elements of a peace technology would have to be developed jointly with the Soviets to be effective. Thus primary cooperation will increase pressures for joint Soviet-American efforts across the board, but particularly in the area of CBMs.

THE ROLE OF DISARMAMENT

Disarmament will continue to play a prominent, but, it is hoped, not primary, role in the relations between the Soviet Union and the United States. I say "it is hoped not a primary" role because two things are clear about disarmament at the end of the 1980s:

1. Disarmament is a tricky and difficult business. Notwithstanding the

talk of the total elimination of nuclear weapons in the headiness that arose on both sides at Reykjavik and during the subsequent INF negotiations and Moscow summit of 1988, it is clear that total nuclear disarmament is not a realistic possibility, even if it were a desirable one.[26] There is zero precedent in human history for the voluntary elimination of a technology because it has been deemed undesirable. It is to be noted that the INF treaty agreed to in December 1987 between the two superpowers eliminates a class of weapons (intermediate-range nuclear missiles), not a technology. Despite the abolition of chemical warfare by the Geneva Convention, chemical weapons are back and were employed by Iraq in the Iran-Iraq war, and the two superpowers again find themselves, against their wishes, having stockpiled large arsenals of chemical and biological weapons.

Mr. Gorbachev has proposed (as have some in the United States) that 5 percent of the existing total arsenals possessed by the two countries would be sufficient for the protection of national security interests. Five percent retention of the existing arsenals would constitute a minimum of 2,500 warheads, a more than sufficient number to destroy life as we know it on the planet—and enough to assure the continued presence of primary cooperation as a governing dynamic in the superpower relationship.[27]

2. Ironically, since primary cooperation between the superpowers is "guaranteed" by the presence of their respective nuclear arsenals, total nuclear disarmament, even if it were possible, is no longer tenable. Since only given nuclear weapons—not nuclear technology itself—can be eliminated, "total disarmament" would open up a vacuum where small fanatical groups (for example, Abu Nidal and the Irish Republican Army) and nations (for example, Libya, Iran, South Africa) could dominate world politics with a small number of nuclear weapons, which they might steal or manufacture. Furthermore, given the relative ease with which small nuclear weapons can be made, and the relative availability, illegally if not legally, of the necessary materials and technology, the most that the super-

---

[26] At a joint press conference on December 8, 1987, following the formal signing of the INF Treaty, General Secretary Gorbachev, in referring to the treaty, stated, "This will, of course, be the first step down the road leading to a nuclear-free world." President Reagan echoed those sentiments (*Washington Post*, December 9, 1988, p. A24).

[27] I am indebted to Jeanne Vaughn Mattison Gayler, formerly director of the American Committee on East-West Accord, for pointing me early in 1985 to the concept of "minimum sufficiency," which she helped conceptualize and which is rapidly becoming a cornerstone concept in disarmament negotiations between the superpowers.

powers could guarantee would be their own mutual nuclear impotence, since they cannot guarantee the elimination of nuclear weapons everywhere in the world.

Continued efforts at nuclear disarmament by the two superpowers is essential because the shrinking of their nuclear arsenals, particularly the excessive number of missiles carrying multiple nuclear warheads, will significantly reduce the dangers of unintended nuclear war through error, miscalculation or guile.[28] The reduction of superpower stockpiles of nuclear weaponry also will diminish the spreading of nuclear technology either through design or theft and will make nuclear nonproliferation more possible.

Eventually the most difficult problem will be the continued need to determine the point at which the type and size of superpower nuclear arsenals are at the same time maximally reduced to eliminate inadvertent nuclear war as discussed above, but sufficiently large to discourage a resurgence of conventional (that is, nonnuclear) warfare and to guarantee primary cooperation. It is unlikely that this "point" will be a fixed one. Rather, it will fluctuate as a function of changing world political realities and technological developments as well as the evolution of individual and collective moral consciousness and the development of a comprehensive peace technology. By the turn of the century, this latter concern may well dominate the superpower relationship.

We have, in the 1980s, entered into an age of paradoxical realism. Seemingly clear choices of the past (for example, nuclear weapons are bad and disarmament is good) are rapidly giving way to paradox. Increasingly we are called upon to choose between forms of conflict, rather than conflict resolution per se. Indeed, for the future it appears that survival is dependent upon the preservation, as well as the resolution and management, of specific forms of conflict. This calls for a new kind of consciousness—a conflict-bearing consciousness—that can live with the psychological tension of perpetual conflict and paradox; a consciousness that does not have to "resolve" all forms of conflict. Such a consciousness will not come easily to the western patriarchal psyche.[29, 1]

---

[28] With the elimination of intermediate-range nuclear missiles under the INF Treaty, the minimum retaliatory time for a nuclear counterstrike by either side will have been restored to 35 minutes from 12–17 minutes.

[29] I believe this paragraph to be true notwithstanding the lessening of conflict between the superpowers and the dramatic lessening of regional conflicts in the last few years.

In the five to ten years preceding the advent of the Gorbachev administration, there had been a slowly evolving shift from Stalinist orthodoxy with its world view that saw all considerations between nations in the context of irreconcilable conflict between capitalism and socialism. The new view that emerged was called "internationalist thinking" and later came to be known simply as "*globalistika*."[m]

Globalistika holds that the great survival issues facing the nations of the world today impinge upon all nations—that is, the arms race, environmental problems, a global economy, world hunger, overpopulation, et cetera. Irrespective of their specific roles in generating those problems, all nations are threatened by their impact and thus find themselves in an interdependent relationship with all other nations concerning these issues.

Under Gorbachev, *globalistika* has become a cornerstone of the Soviet world view and has taken on an accelerated urgency. In Gorbachev's own words:

> The most important thing now is this: either we survive cooperating and preserving the earth, the ocean, the skies, the whole environment, or we lead civilization to disastrous consequences. We must get rid of the outdated notion that the world is someone's domain. The world of today means co-existence of nations and states. It is a multitude of countries, each with a history of its own and each at its own stage of development. We must work and create relations of a new type in international and interstate affairs. Neither the Soviet Union nor the United States will be able to be in command of the world. The world has changed.[n]

At the same time it is well known that the Soviet Union has one of the worst environmental records on all fronts of any industrialized nation in the world. Chernobyl is but one example of the historic backwardness of Soviet society. Because of this fact, there are many in America, including a number of policymakers, who are quick to dismiss *globalistika* as a propaganda policy ploy to shift focus away from the shabby condition of the Soviet economy and its own dismal environmental record.

However, the record under Gorbachev is beginning to paint a different picture. The Soviet Union took the initiative in supporting the development of a joint U.S.–Soviet project to demonstrate conservation methods in Madagascar, which has lost half of its tropical rain forests because of agricultural pressures and the use of wood for fuel. As of 1987, the project received initial approval by the U.S. and Soviet governments. The destruction of the world's tropical forests will alter global climate, create deserts, and lead to the extinction of millions of species of plants and animals, as well as to the starvation of millions of people. The Environmental Policy Institute estimates that virtually all of the world's tropical forests will be destroyed in the next thirty years unless the trend is reversed and that up to one billion people will starve to death in the tropics. Although the Soviets took the lead in supporting a joint U.S.–Soviet project in Madagascar, neither the United States nor the Soviet Union has tropical forests. The project reflects the increasing concern on the part of both countries that localized problems carry serious global implications such as the greenhouse effect.[30]

In July 1987, the Soviet Union sent a delegation of three top Soviet scientists to testify before the House Subcommittee on International Scientific Cooperation on the subject of international efforts to deal with changes in the global life-support system of air, water, and forests and in other environmental areas as a result of human activity. It is noteworthy that Western European nations and Japan declined their invitations from the subcommittee to testify.

Indeed, a partial listing of joint U.S.–Soviet agreements encompass a rapidly growing list of national and global imperatives: long-term weather forecasting; a joint effort to halt depletion of atmospheric ozone; a study by Soviet legal scholars of U.S. environmental law: research on environmental warming and the greenhouse effect as a result of atmospheric pollutants (of which the two countries are the major producers); and the effects of acid rain and heavy metals on young fish.

Moreover, at a meeting on October 24 and 25, 1986 in Washington, D.C., between the American National Academy of Sciences and the

---

[30]The *Washington Post*, April 24, 1987, p. A21, and *Surviving Together*, March 1987, no. 11.

The greenhouse effect results from an overabundance of carbon dioxide in the atmosphere as a result of human activity—for example, deforestation and industrial pollution of the atmosphere. The carbon dioxide buildup prevents sufficient reflection of solar radiation, resulting in a gradual, but inexorable, heating of the earth's temperature with disastrous consequences such as the melting of the polar ice caps.

It should be noted regarding the greenhouse effect that the earth has experienced a natural warming trend of about one degree celsius per one thousand years of geologic history. Some scientists predict a three- to five-degree (celsius) increase in the earth's temperature over the next *thirty to fifty years!* The implications of such an atmospheric upheaval are not yet fully fathomable.

Academy of Sciences of the U.S.S.R., the two academies agreed to sponsor bilateral workshops on the following topics: precursors of earthquakes, development of vaccines, use of lasers in photochemistry, and condensed matter theory. In addition, they identified the following areas for the development of cooperative projects: energy conservation, effects of exposure to nuclear radiation, and behavioral and social science research and nuclear war.[o]

Most of the areas of joint cooperation between the two superpowers reflect the dynamic of "functionalism" described by Jamgotch.[31] However, since 1984 one can see the dynamics of primary cooperation at work as it is beginning to force radical shifts in foreign policy on the part of both superpowers.

The Soviet Union and the United States in 1987 moved much closer to a joint U.S.–Soviet effort to impose an end to the Iran-Iraq war. After initial American indecision regarding the reflagging of Kuwaiti oil tankers, Kuwait approached the Soviet Union in November 1987, either to charter tankers to Kuwait or to reflag some Kuwaiti tankers. Subsequently the United States agreed to reflag Kuwaiti tankers and decided to put a sizable naval presence in the Persian Gulf. The Soviets reflagged three Kuwaiti ships to Soviet registry and these subsequently were escorted by a contingent of three Soviet minesweepers.[p]

There have been signs that the Soviets cooperated with American ships in the Persian Gulf through the sharing of communications intelligence and through other means. The presence of the two superpowers in the Persian Gulf has served to limit the escalation of the sea war and attacks on the world's oil supplies by both antagonists in the war.

---

[31] Although for the most part American policymakers of both parties to date have not acknowledged the importance of this rapidly occurring trend, it is already being talked about in some private, but important and potentially influential circles. At the May 17, 1983, meeting of the American Committee on East-West Accord, Professor George F. Kennan observed: "The area of common interest between the Soviet Union and ourselves is not limited to the needs of both these peoples to see world peace preserved. Both are great industrial powers. As such, they have a growing number of common problems. Prominent among these are the environmental ones. Both of these countries occupy major portions of the environmentally endangered northern hemisphere. The Soviet leaders are no less aware than we are of the extent to which this hemisphere, even if it should escape nuclear disaster, would still be threatened by environmental pollution and deterioration. They know that these problems will not be mastered just by measures taken within any single country—that their solution will require international collaboration" (Nish Jamgotch, Jr., *Sectors of Mutual Benefit in U.S.–Soviet Relations* [Durham, N.C.: Duke University Press, 1985], pp. 169–170).

Indeed, at one point joint Soviet-American cooperation to end the Iran-Iraq war, including military cooperation in the Persian Gulf, seemed close at hand. A House committee report on United States policy in the Persian Gulf observed:

> White House Chief of Staff Howard Baker at one point spoke favorably of cooperation between the United States and the Soviet Union in policing Persian Gulf shipping. Baker subsequently recanted that position, but President Reagan, in his June 11 news conference following the Vienna summit, seemed to leave the door open to joint US-USSR efforts. He noted that the Soviet Union "has some vessels" in the Persian Gulf and acknowledged that "they have a stake, too, in peaceful shipping and the openness of the international waters."[q]

The report goes on to discuss the "ideal opportunity for a joint US/USSR force" in the Persian Gulf and the "rare opportunity for cooperation rather than confrontation with the Soviet Union" that the Iran-Iraq war provided.[r] However, the White House subsequently succumbed to pressure from the Defense Department, and the impetus for a "joint US/USSR force" gave way to other, more traditional, approaches for cooperation between the superpowers. (It is not too far-reaching to imagine that the current administration will be less hostage to its own Defense Department and that joint military cooperation—not just the avoidance of "incidents"—between the superpowers will become a reality even by the end of the decade of the 1980s.)

The Middle East is not the only place where each side is backing off from previously entrenched positions and moving more toward one of cooperation. Each has significantly toned down its rhetoric concerning the other's adventures in such trouble spots as Afghanistan and Nicaragua. Indeed, the United States, notwithstanding its continued supply of weapons to the Afghan rebels, played an instrumental role in helping the Soviets find a politically workable and sufficiently face-saving formula for their subsequent withdrawal from Afghanistan.

Given the enormous disparity between the technological and economic development of the two superpowers, clearly it will be some time before the Soviet Union will be able to contribute as much as the United States to the material development of *globalistika* as a major economic and technological force on the world scene. However, at the political psychological levels, particularly if Gorbachev's stated commitment is realized to shift economic and industrial resources from war technology and the maintenance of large land forces in Europe to the development of Soviet domestic economy, considerable pressure will be put on American governments to make similar shifts.

Most important, primary cooperation will see to it that survival will be defined more and more in nonmilitary terms. The two superpowers increasingly will find themselves having to impose survival policies on others—through joint foreign policy initiatives, and strong policies, backed by economic resources and pressure, and, only as a last resort, through coordinated or even joint military intervention, to protect global economic and ecological life-support systems.[32]

By the turn of the century the two superpowers may be faced with a situation of accepting the destruction of the global ecology with irreversible disastrous consequences on *their* peoples and economies, or, because the political processes necessary to save the tropical rain forests—all of which are on the soil of other nations—are too slow to be effective, taking joint military action to bring about a forced change in the policies and actions of the offending nations. (The military action would have to be joint to make it politically palatable to the rest of the world and to keep the focus on the ecological objective, rather than falling back into the archaic political pattern of hegemonic control, which could lead to war between the superpowers.)[33]

For example, in the fall of 1988, the São Paulo–based Institute for Space Research reported that fires, intended to clear land for planting and pastures for white settlers in the Amazon, in an eighty-day period in 1987 alone, destroyed eighty thousand square *miles* of forest—an area composing 4 percent of the entire Amazon region and larger than Denmark, Belgium, Austria, and Switzerland combined. Scientists reported that the nearly five thousand daily fires started between July and October dumped

---

[32] Such a situation may be looming as a result of the proliferation of ballistics missiles and weapons of chemical and biological warfare in the hands of the nations of the Middle East.

[33] Although it is anticipated that both superpowers will endeavor to seek to increase and restructure the role of the United Nations to encompass the role of policeman/enforcer of global survival interests, such a ploy does not seem likely to work. The cumbersome bureaucracy of the United Nations, along with its dominance by Third World nations (many of which will be the object of the policing/enforcement efforts), will make it virtually impossible to get the kind of quick and decisive action that will be necessary to prevent irreversible actions that could decide the ultimate fate of the globe and all of its inhabitants (for example, the destruction of atmospheric ozone or the elimination of the tropical rain forests).

millions of tons of particulate matter and carbon dioxide into the atmosphere and will contribute significantly to polluting the air in the Western Hemisphere.

The report went on to say: "This phenomenon . . . will certainly be linked in the near future to atmospheric alterations of our planet, and quite probably to the problem of the [depletion of] the Antarctic ozone, where the winds transport the emissions from the burnings." An American scientist attached to the institute went on to say that the seasonal fires could contribute to the "greenhouse effect." It is noteworthy that the institute puts most of the blame for the situation on the Brazilian government's own Institute for Forestry Development.[5]

If the Brazilian government or other governments do not drastically curtail such ecologically destructive practices, which directly affect the livelihood—even the literal survival—of peoples in other nations and continents, including those of the two superpowers, what recourse will the affected nations have? What responsibility do the latter have to their own people? What are the political, socioeconomic, health, moral, and other considerations involved here?

Moreover, by the turn of the century, we are likely to see a scenario wherein the United States will find itself in the unique position of being forced to help the Soviet Union maintain stability in its eastern bloc and even in some of its own constituent republics, which are growing increasingly unstable due to socioeconomic pressures. This instability, long dormant in these regions, will likely accelerate as a function of *glasnost* and *perestroika*. In such a scenario, the United States may find that it must assist a moderate Soviet regime to maintain stability and order in those areas to protect its own larger global interests (for example, critical ecological concerns, the global economy, the advance of radical Muslim fundamentalism—especially in the Soviet Union). Politically, the United States increasingly will have the need for another superpower partner to maintain essential world order in the interest of its own survival. The same will be true for the Soviet Union. The "partnership" will serve to keep both superpowers "honest" with regard to the pursuit of real global (and thus national) survival issues, rather than regress to the level of power politics in the archaic sense of the word.

Ultimately the threat to survival by such issues as the greenhouse effect, the depletion of the ozone layer, overpopulation, depletion of fossil fuels and natural resources, medical catastrophes such as the AIDS epidemic, and global economic crises, among others, is as great, albeit not as dramatic and sudden, as that posed by nuclear weapons. Paradoxically, it is the threat from the latter that is bringing about the primary cooperation needed to address the former before it is too late to be effective.

Indeed, the world has already crossed the threshold where international problems, conflict, and survival are being replaced rapidly by global problems, conflict, and survival. For the very first time in history, the fate of the "great" civilized nations of the world *and each and every one of their citizens* lies in the hands of the lowliest—the least powerful and the most impoverished. And their survival will rest on the ability of those "great" civilized nations, the two superpowers in particular, to prevent— in some cases, through the joint use of force—and bring about necessary cooperation to forestall global catastrophe.

We are transitioning irreversibly into a dimension where virtually all survival issues facing the peoples of the world will be global and where, for the foreseeable future, their solution and management will have to be guaranteed by the two superpowers. It is unlikely that existing or anticipated global mechanisms like the United Nations will be sufficiently effective until well into the twenty-first century in protecting the survival of the species and the planet. New kinds of global mechanisms will have to be forged, and we will have to learn to think in a wholly different manner to address the survival crises that will be facing the world in the next decade and into the next century.

Ironically, the Soviet system, because of its lack of democratic process and the absence of capitalism, holds the potential for more rapid and aggressive efforts than the capitalist system per se. The Soviet government would not have to contend with powerful competing economic and private self-interest groups deeply entrenched in capitalist systems. (The Fortune 500 and the trade unions are but two examples of the latter.) However, this would be possible only to the extent that Mr. Gorbachev and his successors can overcome the backwardness and inertia of Soviet bureaucracy.

Finally, primary cooperation is bringing about between the two hostile systems an interface unprecedented in world politics. Such activities as the "CongressBridges" project—six public dialogues by satellite during TV prime time, between members of the U.S. Congress and the Supreme Soviet, and "SpaceBridges," with Soviet journalists in Moscow joining in dialogue with members of the American Society of Newspaper Editors in San Francisco, all of which are broadcast live and uncensored on Soviet and American TV and radio—hold promise for bridging the perceptual distortion and the communication gulf created by years of shadow projection between the two countries.

At the same time, it would be unrealistic to see primary cooperation as the panacea that will solve all of the world's problems, let alone those of the two superpowers. At best, it will create new perceptions and new possibilities. To be sure, they are indeed profound new perceptions and profound new possibilities. However, in the last analysis the question remains one of moral consciousness, moral choice, and moral courage. It is still easier to opt for political expediency and the intoxication of power— the ego rewards are much greater and quicker to hand.

Concerning our two governments, we are beginning to recognize that the issue is not as much our respective systems per se, but rather moral consciousness and moral leadership. What is needed is a redefinition of power along Athena lines. Primary cooperation is providing the impetus and setting the stage for such a redefinition. However, at the moment we have no infrastructure to evolve or define this twenty-first-century conception of power. I would define it as "peace as power."

A SOVIET-AMERICAN INSTITUTE FOR WAR-PEACE RESEARCH AND TECHNOLOGY DEVELOPMENT

Primary cooperation has brought the two superpowers and the world to the threshold of a new age where "fist" power as we have known it since the dawn of civilization is no longer tenable, and where *peace as power* will be the only legitimate and survivable form of power possible. The choices before us are to work consciously with the impetus that primary cooperation brings or to continue to be dragged along by it with a higher risk of self-annihilation.

Working with the impetus of primary cooperation means learning to perceive and think in a manner that is not only radically different, but one that will be, in some cases, 180 degrees opposite to what has been considered rational and consistent with national security. An example of the latter is the reflexive manner in which the two superpowers have pulled back from previous strong positions regarding on-site inspection in conjunction with disarmament treaties. In particular, the United States, after years of often valid self-righteous finger-pointing at the Soviets for resisting any on-site inspection, suddenly found itself at odds with its own position when the Soviet Union was forced to agree to rigorous on-site inspection provisions in order to pursue its own self-interested goal of disarmament. After having pulled back from their initial positions, the two superpowers were again forced to adopt modified on-site inspection provisions in conjunction with the INF Treaty signed between the two countries on December 7, 1987.[34]

Primary cooperation is bringing with it a whole set of new mandates, possibilities, resources, and issues as yet unknown. One mandate, it seems, is the requirement that the two superpowers work together in a joint effort to explore and define the implications of *peace as power* and the development of the technology necessary to implement it. At present virtually all research on superpower conflict is focused on the split relationship between the two superpowers and how to manage or bridge the split. Virtually none of it consciously recognizes the impetus of primary cooperation as a dynamic that is intrinsically aimed at healing that split. Virtually none of it focuses on the archetypal underpinnings of superpower conflict and inherent in primary cooperation, and none is devoted to the development of a peace technology as such. Virtually all of it is conducted in parallel by each superpower and, to the extent there is an interface, it is at best cooperative and not joint.[ ] Jamgotch proposes an "intellectual Marshall Plan," based on the National Defense Education Act model of the 1950s, as a way of stimulating research in Soviet studies in the United States and in the six subject areas outlined in his book. He suggests large grants that "would serve to focus, direct and simulate scattered research efforts usually undertaken in a more spontaneous and haphazard way." He proposes that the Soviet government undertake a similar plan of its own.

These are laudable and important proposals, which should be explored. However, they accept the split in the Soviet-American relationship and would perpetuate it through essentially parallel research efforts, notwithstanding the fact that Jamgotch supports and presses for greater cooperative and collaborative ventures. In addition, the intellectual Marshall Plan idea would largely expand and broaden the scope of research and development as presently conceived and would not focus on the implementation of primary cooperation, *peace as power*, and the development of a peace technology.

---

[34] The *Washington Post*, on November 26, 1987, quoted Secretary of State George P. Shultz as having remarked that the inspections go "far beyond anything that's ever been attempted before," and Defense Secretary Frank C. Carlucci as calling them "mind-boggling."

Harold Brown, defense secretary in the Carter administration, was quoted as stating, "If somebody had asked me about this 10 years ago, I would have said it's wildly improbable."

One Soviet negotiator remarked that he "would have been shot" for treason if he had provided such information on Soviet missiles just one month earlier (p. A52).

I propose that the Soviet Union and the United States establish an independent Soviet-American institute for war-peace research and technology development. The hyphen in *war-peace* is important, since the artificial split between the archetype of war-peace must be redressed if we are to facilitate the transition to *peace as power*.

Such an institute would have the following functions:

1. Review, evaluate, and pull together the separate, scattered, and disjointed research on conflict and conflict resolution into a single information data bank, establishing a single comprehensive source of information.[35]

(The review and evaluation process alone would provide a perspective on problem definition and research findings that would bridge shadow problems by viewing the same material from the perspective of the other country or culture as well as one's own, providing a context for each superpower to see itself empathically through the eyes of its adversary.)

2. Develop a joint Soviet-American agenda for researching the implementation of primary cooperation. (One of the primary objectives in this context would be to provide sufficient incentives—monetary and moral—to shift existing resources from their exclusive focus on war technology to the development of peace technology.)[36]

3. Develop the specific components of a peace technology. (This would provide the technological infrastructure for facilitating the conscious implementation of primary cooperation.)

4. Serve as a training center for diplomats, and military and intelligence personnel, as well as civilian government personnel (including the Congress and the Supreme Soviet) and other professionals presently en-

---

[35] Each nation would identify the subject area of any research undertaken but withheld on national security grounds, when possible, and would withhold identification of projects where such identification would be deemed detrimental to national security interests.

To make such a provision viable, each nation would have to establish a panel of scientists and other scholars (or some other equivalent mechanism), all of whom would hold the appropriate security clearances, picked by the scientists and scholars of the other country, to review those projects withheld on national security grounds. For example, the American Academy of Sciences would designate a panel of Soviet scholars and scientists and the Soviet Academy of Sciences would designate a panel of American scientists and scholars who would review all such research projects of their respective countries and file a report with the respective government requesting a review and reconsideration of any project it deems inappropriately withheld from the information bank on the grounds of national security.

[36] This would entail a combination of in-house research and contracts as well as grants to other individuals and resources.

gaged in conflict resolution, as well as the new cadre of technicians that a fully functional peace technology will spawn.

5. Provide technical assistance to Soviet and American government efforts involved with the implementation of primary cooperation.[37]

6. Generate jointly developed educational materials, for use by both governments in educating their populace in the objectives and results of *peace as power* at all levels of society.[38]

It is stressed that the proposed institute would be apolitical. The institute is conceived as a mechanism for institutionalizing and objectifying primary cooperation as the major dynamic working to effect *peace as power*. Were it to become involved in the political agenda of either superpower, the effect would be to remove the hyphen in "war-peace," and to heighten the existing split between the two superpowers. The entire spirit and purpose of the institute would be vitiated and it would lose its capacity to achieve most, if not all, of the goals outlined above.

The idea of a *joint* Soviet-American institute for war-peace research and technology development is difficult to conceive of at this junction in the superpower relationship. Appendix 2 presents a hypothetical structure for such an institute—one that takes into consideration many of the pitfalls and problems that no doubt will arise in such an approach. The structure in Appendix 2 is limited in scope, but, it is hoped, sufficient to give the idea plausibility as a viable entity.

It is not likely that a Soviet-American institute for war-peace research and technology development will be realized early in the decade of the 1990s. For one thing, the level of political and psychological maturity necessary to undertake such an enterprise seems to be lacking on both sides. However, by the mid-1990s, we may well see the implementation of this concept. Primary cooperation is moving the world along at an amazingly rapid rate—the superpowers in particular. One can hardly catch one's breath, let alone assimilate the changes of the last six months, before new

---

[37] This might include, among other activities, reviewing proposed disarmament agreements and recommending specific provisions that would prevent further splitting as a result of a given treaty, providing a specialist trained in psychological typology to facilitate communication between the superpowers during crucial negotiations, and providing alternatives for existing regional conflicts that threaten to expand into uncontainable conflict. It could provide technical assistance to other governments as well.

[38] It is implicit that educational materials would be jointly developed and jointly presented to the people of both superpower nations as well as third-party countries and groups. Jointly developed materials would markedly reduce splitting and shadow projection.

and even more radical changes emerge on the scene. One need only compare the Soviet Union in the pre- and post-Gorbachev eras and observe the archenemy (Ronald Reagan) of the "evil empire" meeting with its leader to sign a disarmament agreement, to see how far things have come in a very short period of time. It is important to remember that it is not only politics that is changing, but perhaps more important are the changes in the nature of the human psyche with respect to the development of moral consciousness and the psyche's capacity to live with paradox. What was deemed impossible three years ago is reality today. If we do not succumb to our nihilistic tendencies, I believe that we will see the realization of a mechanism such as a joint Soviet-American institute before the turn of the century.

IN AUGUST of 1987, the world crossed an important threshold. It had been forty-two years since the end of World War II, exactly twice as long as the interval between World War I and World War II. Ironically, the sometimes shaky and bloody peace that has ensued since then has been "guaranteed" by our nuclear arms and missile technology. The future of the world lies in a growing moral consciousness and an emerging technology of peace. Primary cooperation has already begun to demonstrate the power to change the single greatest threat to the survival of life—the human psyche. Therein lies the hope.

Appendix ① Case History of the United States Institute of Peace

The concept of the United States Institute of Peace (USIP) has for years been the hope of many inside and outside of government for the creation of an effective vehicle for researching and implementing peace strategies that would not be overly subject to influence by government or the military-industrial complex. A close look at the history of the development of the USIP, which came into being on October 19, 1984, is instructive as to why such a mechanism must be insulated from government influence.

The purpose of the institute is to "provide the means for scholars and leaders in peace from the U.S. and abroad to pursue scholarly inquiry on international peace and conflict resolution and to share their insights." Specific areas of focus for the institute are researching the causes of international conflict and elements of peace among nations; promoting education on the broad area of international peace and conflict resolution; enhancing the skills of policymakers; developing printed materials that inform interested parties; examination of conflict between free trade unions and Communist organizations in the context of protecting human rights.[1]

The idea for a peace academy or peace institute had been alive in the United States since 1935, when Senator Matthew Neely, of West Virginia, introduced a bill to establish a Department of Peace. The National Peace Academy Campaign, a private nonprofit group, was formed in 1976, and lobbied for several years for the establishment of a "peace academy" on the model of the military academies. A 1981 Senate study, the "Matsunaga report," favorably recommended the creation of a peace academy. In the compromise reached with the White House and other political interests, the name was changed from "the U.S. Peace Academy" to "the United

---

[1] *Peace Institute Reporter* (September 1986), p. 5. (Published by National Peace Institute Foundation, Washington, D.C.)

States Institute of Peace" (USIP). The compromise reached prevented the institute from directly training individuals for the "profession" of peace and from receiving funds from private resources.

The Peace Academy Campaign took great pains to keep the concept of a peace academy (institute) from becoming politicized, recognizing that for such a body to have credibility as an objective research, educational, and evaluative body, it could not be beholden to any individual or interest group. Various bills introduced into the Congress over the years would pass one house or the other, but never cleared both houses of Congress until early in the Reagan administration. The Reagan administration was opposed to the creation of the USIP, officially for reasons of fiscal restraint. (The USIP's initial budget was a modest $4.2 million.)

When forced because of political pressure to sign the bill creating the institute, the Reagan administration forged several crucial compromises, the major one being the composition of the institute's fifteen-member board of directors, all of whom were to be appointed by the president with confirmation by the United States Senate. The Peace Academy Campaign fought a hard, bitter, and losing battle for the political integrity of the institute. At one point the campaign seriously considered opposing the establishment of the institute at the cost of such an extreme compromise. In the end, a seriously compromised, if not crippled, USIP was established.

Once the political handwriting was on the wall concerning the establishment of a politically "clean" institute, the Peace Academy Campaign transformed itself into the National Peace Institute Foundation. The latter lobbied for a while to get Congress to change the structure of the institute's board as proposed by the Reagan administration, and when it lost that battle, it set itself as a monitor of the activities of the USIP.

Aside from the fact that the president appoints all of the members of the board, there are four ex-officio members: the secretaries of State and Defense, the director of the Arms Control and Disarmament Agency, and the president of the National Defense University. Eleven members are to be private citizens with academic or practical experience in peace and conflict resolution efforts of the United States. The first chairperson of the board was to be selected by the president for a three-year term. Subsequent chairpersons were to be elected by the board from among its private-citizen members. The board appoints the institute's president, who will employ appropriate staff members to carry out the purposes of the institute. The initial ex-officio members of the board were Kenneth L. Adelman, director of the Arms Control and Disarmament Agency; Richard

Schifter (designate of the Secretary of State), Assistant Secretary of State for Human Rights and Humanitarian Affairs; Lieutenant General Bradley C. Hosmer, president of the National Defense University; Richard N. Perle (designate for the Secretary of Defense), Assistant Secretary of Defense for International Security Policy.

The following chronology of events[2] serves as a laboratory example of how a mechanism such as a "peace institute" cannot maintain independence of purpose and program and credibility with respect to its own mission and in the eyes of the world when it is politically compromised:

1984	*October 19:* The president signs H.R. 5167 into law as Public Law 98-525. The United States Institute of Peace Act is Title XVII of this law.
1985	*April 12:* The Department of State proposes seventeen amendments to the institute's charter. If accepted by Congress, these amendments would convert the institute from an independent national educational institution into a very small grant-giving agency under the control of the State Department.
1985	*April 18:* Representatives Dan Glickman (D.-Kan.) and Newt Gingrich (R-Ga.) send a letter to President Reagan, noting the deadline of April 20 specified by law for the appointment of the institute's board of directors.

April 20: The statutory deadline of April 20 for submission of presidential nominees for the institute's board of directors passes without the president's taking action.

April 24: Twenty-four senators send a letter to President Reagan, urging compliance with the law concerning nominations for the institute's board of directors.

May 8: Congress passes a sense-of-congress resolution reminding the president that nominations to the board of the U.S. Institute of Peace should be submitted to the Senate without delay "to permit implementation of the Congressional mandate."

May 21: Eighty-five representatives send a letter to President Reagan urging him to comply with the law by nominating the institute's board of directors.

June 3: The Senate Appropriations Committee votes an amend-

---

[2]This chronology has been taken, much of it verbatim, from, "The United States Institute of Peace: An Update: July, 1987." National Peace Institute Foundation, Washington, D.C.

ment to the Spring Supplemental H.R. 2577 disapproving the President's deferral of funds for the institute.

June 21: The Senate disapproves the president's deferral of funds for the institute.

July 16: Senator Mark Hatfield (R-Ore.) urges the president from the Senate floor to nominate the institute's board of directors and gives warning that Senate confirmation procedures should not be bypassed by making appointments to the board during the August Senate recess.

July 22: Senator Robert Stafford (R-Vt.), chairman of the Subcommittee on Education, Arts and Humanities, writes a letter to President Reagan requesting his nominees immediately—before Senate recess in August. He declares unacceptable that nominations be submitted as recess appointments.

July 31, August 1: The House and Senate disapprove the presidential deferral of institute funds in an amendment to the Spring Supplemental (H.R. 2577).

September through December: The president submits all but one nomination to the Senate for confirmation.

In addition to the above, the initial board included no business leaders, no labor leaders, no women, no minorities, and no professionals in the field of conflict resolution. A General Accounting Office (GAO) report of January 13, 1986, found that one of the criteria used by the White House to select board nominees was "commitment to the President's policy agenda."[3]

---

[3] *Peace Institute Reporter* (February 1986), p. 3.

Appendix ② A Hypothetical Structure for a Soviet-American Institute for War-Peace Research and Technology Development

A Soviet-American Institute for War-Peace Research and Technology Development is envisioned as having an independent board of directors. By "independent" is meant "with free authority to establish whatever policies, procedures, and fiscal guidelines it deems in the best interest of the institute without *any* constraints whatsoever imposed by either government." It would have an equal number of board members, perhaps ten each, appointed by each government *and* ratified by an independent body with no political or fiscal ties to either government—perhaps the International Physicians for Prevention of Nuclear War or an equivalent group acceptable to both governments. Thus it would take the ratification of each designated board member by the agreed-upon international organization for the appointment to the board of the institute to be valid.

The idea behind the ratification by an independent international body of the board members of the institute is to provide some kind of check to the inevitable tendency of each government to make appointments to the board on the basis of self-serving political expediency rather than the ultimate purposes and aims of the institute itself. The mechanism is admittedly faulty—but then, any mechanism would be.

Eight-year staggered terms for the board members is proposed. All members of the initial board would serve at least four years. At the end of the fourth year, one Soviet and American member each would rotate off the board (or be reappointed for another eight-year term) and be replaced by a new board member with an eight-year appointment. Thus eight members (four American and four Soviet) would serve a minimum of four years, but less than eight years, and a possible six would serve more than eight years. After the fourteenth year, all board members would have been appointed for eight-year terms.

The purpose of eight-year terms would be to provide for sufficient time for board members to develop wisdom and insight into the functions and operation of the institute and to take advantage of the expertise and wisdom that will accumulate over the years. Since moral consciousness is a powerful and growing influence in primary cooperation, time will be needed to permit it to knit a unifying spirit and operational dynamic between the Americans and Soviets serving on the institute board.

The board would operate under the co-chair of an American and a Soviet elected by the board. They would serve at the discretion of the board. However, should the board determine to unseat one of the co-chairs, the other co-chair would automatically be unseated and the board would have to elect new co-chairs (one Soviet and one American). The "other" co-chair could be reappointed by the board after a two-year period out of office. The purpose here would to be assure an investment by each co-chair in the "success" of the other and to avoid the natural tendency to split that has been inherent in the Soviet-American relationship.

All "decisions" by the board would be made by consensus, with the single exception of official authorization for the expenditure of funds, in which case both co-chairs (and their designates) would have joint sign-off. The aim would be to prevent power politics from entering into the deliberations of the board. There would be no formal votes per se, with the single exception being in the case of the removal of a board member. In the latter situation, a vote by two-thirds of the entire board (both American and Soviet members) and ratification by a majority of the ratifying international body would be necessary to remove a given board member. The appointing country would appoint a replacement member for the balance of the removed member's term. The replacement process would require ratification by the ratifying international body, as specified above.

It is recognized that consensus can be an initially slow and cumbersome mechanism for conducting business. However, the work of the institute should be slow in gaining momentum and the primary determinant of "success" will be the degree to which both Soviet and American board members can develop the essence and the "spirit of the hyphen."[1] Consensus can be a powerful dynamic for forcing shadow confrontation (with one's own shadow) and an investment in the point of view of the other side. Given sufficient time to become an accepted and integrated procedural dynamic, it should result in much more being accomplished over time than the politicizing and splitting process of vote-taking, particularly in the context of a board made up of individuals representing two opposite value systems and ideologies.

For such an institute to be viable, it would have to have substantial funding. It is proposed that the institute be funded by a ten-year, lump-sum (not annual) nonrevokable *appropriation* received from all sources,[2] including either or both superpower or third-party governments. However, the charter of the institute would contain a provision stipulating that no funds may be received if there is *any* stipulation of any kind regarding the use of the funds. The charter would also prohibit the commingling of the institute's funds with those from any other source not directly appropriated to the institute. This would mean specifically that no "outside" funds could be used to supplement institute funds. This provision would be aimed at keeping the institute's work from becoming politically subverted by outside interests.

Although the institute would be empowered to receive funds from any noncommercial source, providing the above stipulations were met, it is envisioned that the primary source of funding would be the governments of the Soviet Union and the United States of America.

For the initial start-up phase, a total appropriation of $20 million for each of the first two years of operation is suggested, with subsequent appropriations to double in each of the subsequent four years. This would result in an operating budget of $320 million by the sixth year of operation—not in the least excessive for the scope and depth of the research and development effort outlined above.[3] By the end of the sixth year the institute should have achieved definition of itself and its work, developed a four-year plan, and have convinced both superpowers of its importance.

---

[1] As in the archetype of war-peace.

[2] "All sources" means government and nonprofit resources. No funds would be received from any commercial entity. The ten year appropriation would kick in at the end of the sixth year of operation to allow for an initial start-up phase.

[3] I do not propose a ceiling of $320 million. Appropriations beyond the sixth year are not addressed here because it is difficult to envision the fiscal needs of the Institute beyond that period of time.

At that time, long-term funding based on the principles outlined above would be in order.

Even if the work of the institute ultimately were considered to be a 100 percent failure, the expenditure of funds over the entire ten-year period would be negligible compared to the amount of funds expended by each superpower on past and present failed weapons systems. In other words, the experiment should be undertaken as a *full-risk venture*, without impinging on the freedom of the effort through controls or constraints of any sort. Such an experiment would constitute the first effort of its kind.

Notes

Chapter 2. Jung's Theory of the Collective Unconscious and Archetypes

a. Edward C. Whitmont, *Symbolic Quest* (Princeton: Princeton University Press, 1969), p. 81.

b. Mircea Eliade, *Myths, Dreams and Mysteries* (New York: Harper and Row, 1960), pp. 25–26.

c. C. G. Jung, *The Collected Works*, vol. 8, p. 134.

Chapter 3. The Archetype of the Shadow

a. The *Washington Post*, February 8, 1984, pp. A1, A22.

b. From the talk entitled "Approaches to the Resumed START Negotiations," given at the Kennan Institute for Advanced Russian Studies of the Wilson Center, in Washington, D.C., on March 20, 1985.

c. A paper entitled "The Assumption of Hostility in U.S.–Soviet Relations," June 4, 1980, pp. 13, 11.

d. Strobe Talbott, *Deadly Gambits: The Reagan Administration and the Stalemate in Nuclear Arms Control* (New York: Knopf, 1984), p. xii.

e. Source: a U.S. government official in the intelligence field who requested anonymity.

f. Carl G. Jung, The Collected Works, vol. 7, pp. 53–54.

g. Jerome S. Bernstein, "Power and Politics in the Thermonuclear Age: A Depth-Psychological Approach." *Quadrant*, 18 (3) (Fall 1985): 17.

h. Edward C. Whitmont, *Symbolic Quest*, pp. 160–169. Jung, Carl G. "Approaching the Unconscious," in *Man and His Symbols*. London: Aldus Books, 1964, pp. 18–103.

i. Mikhail Gorbachev, addressing a labor union convention, Moscow, February 25, 1987. As reported in *Surviving Together*, March 1987, No. 11, p. 13.

j. The comment was made on U.S. television immediately before the May-June 1988 summit, as reported in *Parade Magazine*, July 10, 1988, p. 2.

k. Carl G. Jung, *The Collected Works: Psychological Types*, vol. 6.

l. Highly placed confidential source.

m. Strobe Talbott, *Deadly Gambits*, n. 96.

Chapter 4. The Hero Dynamic

a. See Joseph Campbell, *The Power of Myth* (New York: Doubleday, 1988). This book is the result of a six-part series of interviews with Joseph Campbell, world-renowned mythologist, shortly before his death. The series was aired on public television in 1988.

b. *Washington Post,* June 3, 1988, pp. A1, A26.

c. In a speech before the World Affairs Council of Northern California on June 29, 1988. *Washington Post,* June 30, 1988, p. A14.

Chapter 5. Power

a. From the Bhagavad Gita, as quoted in *Bartlett's Familiar Quotations,* 15th ed., ed. Emily Morison Beck. (Boston: Little, Brown, 1980), p. 861n.

b. Eric Partridge, *A Short Etymological Dictionary of Modern English Origins.* (New York: Macmillan, 1977), p. 517. Onions, C.T., ed. *The Oxford Dictionary of English Etymology* (London, New York: Oxford University Press, 1978), pp. 702, 699.

c. Carl G. Jung, *The Collected Works,* vol. 8, p. 4.

d. Ibid., vol. 5, p. 199.

Chapter 6. War

a. Maurice R. Davie, *The Evolution of War* (New Haven: Yale University Press, 1929), p. 9.

b. Ruth L. Sivard, "Deaths in Twentieth Century Wars," in *World Military and Social Expenditures 1985* (Washington, D.C.: World Priorities, 1985), p. 9.

c. *The Defense Monitor,* published by the Center for Defense Information, Washington, D.C., 12, no. 1 (1983): 1.

d. See Anthony Stevens, M.D., "The Archetypes of War," in *The Anatomy of Conflict,* ed. Ian Fenton (London: Coventure, 1985).

e. Davie, pp. 219–233.

f. Bigelow, *The Dawn Warriors,* p. 57; Schmookler, *The Parable of the Tribes.*

g. Bigelow, p. 95.

h. Jerome S. Bernstein, "The Decline of Rites of Passage: The Impact on Masculine Individuation," unpublished thesis, C. G. Jung Institute of New York, June 1980. Also see *Betwixt and Between: Patterns of Masculine and Feminine Initiation,* ed. Mahdi, Foster, and Little (La Salle, Ill.: Open Court, 1987), pp. 135–158.

i. The Center for Defense Information, Washington, D.C., July 1987.

j. Bigelow, pp. 197–198.

k. Schmookler, p. 76.

l. Ezra B. W. Zubrow, *Prehistoric Carrying Capacity: A Model,* in Cummings

Archaeology Series, ed. Lamberg-Karlovsky and Jeremy Sabloss (Menlo Park, Calif.: Cummings, 1975), Appendix I, p. 123.

m. Statement on Violence, Seville, Spain, May 16, 1986, as provided by Psychologists for Social Responsibility, Washington, D.C.

n. *APA Monitor* 18, no. 10 (Washington, D.C., October 1987): 8.

o. Steven Kull, "Nuclear Arms and the Desire for World Destruction," *Political Psychology* 4, no. 3 (September 1983): 565.

p. Whitmont, *Return of the Goddess*, p. 32.

q. As reported by Winifred Gallagher, "Sex and Hormones," *Atlantic Monthly* 261, no. 3 (March 1988): 79.

r. H. W. Turney-High, *Primitive War: Its Practice and Concepts*. (Columbia: University of South Carolina Press, 1979), pp. 147, 167.

s. Davie, p. 148.

t. Ibid., pp. 148–149.

u. James Robert Moriarty, "Ritual Combat: A Comparison of the Aztec 'War of Flowers' and the Medieval 'Melée.'" Paper presented at a meeting of the Southwestern Monuments Association, Fall 1968, p. 10.

v. Whitmont, p. 236.

w. Turney-High, p. 143.

x. Davie, p. 149.

y. Whitmont, p. 26.

z. General Kraft reported this episode at a conference entitled "Communicating with the Russians," March 24, 1984, at the Newport Institute, Newport, R.I.

aa. Vamik D. Volkan, "The Narcissism of Minor Differences in the Psychological Gap between Opposing Nations," *Psychoanalytic Inquiry* 6, no. 2 (1986): 189–190.

Chapter 7. Primary Cooperation

a. See Carl G. Jung's essay "The Transcendent Function," in the *Collected Works*, vol. 8, pp. 67–91.

b. "Document of the Stockholm Conference: Final Report," unpublished copy, dated September 19, 1986, of the official conference report on Confidence- and Security-Building Measures and Disarmament in Europe. U.S. Department of State, December 1986, pp. 7–8, 12.

c. Ibid., p. 15.

d. *CDE Implementation Report*, U.S. Arms Control and Disarmament Agency, U.S. Department of State, September 14, 1988. The data in this report were updated by Cameron McCall, Foreign Affairs Specialist in the ACDA office, by telephone interview on December 14, 1988.

e. See Bernstein, "Power and Politics in the Thermonuclear Age," *Quadrant* (Fall 1985).

f. Source: The *Washington Post*, February 13, 1986, p. A28.

g. See Jenkins, Brian Michael, "Nuclear Terrorism and Its Consequences" *Society*, 17, (5) (July/August 1980), for an excellent analysis of this issue from the U.S. standpoint.

h. See Ury, William L., *Beyond the Hotline* (Boston: Houghton Mifflin, 1985), pp. 69–71.

i. Hildreth, Steven A. "Nuclear Risk Reduction Centers," Congressional Research Service, United States Congress, Updated May 19, 1987, p. 4.

j. Ibid., p. 6.

k. See Ury, *Beyond the Hotline*, especially the chapter entitled "A Joint Crisis Control Center," pp. 57–73.

l. Kupperman, Robert H. "Leaders and Crisis: The CSIS Crisis Simulations." Significant Issues Series, vol. 9, no. 5 (Washington, D.C.: Center for Strategic and International Studies), pp. 58–74.

m. Ibid., p. 63.

n. Ibid., pp. 37–38.

o. Ibid., p. 48.

Chapter 8. Paranoia between Groups and Nations

a. Gould, Stephen Jay, in *The Yale Review*, 73, (4) (July 1984): 490.

b. Charles A. Pinderhughs, "Differential Bonding from Infancy to International Conflict" *Psychoanalytic Inquiry* 6, no. 2 (1986): 157.

c. Ibid., pp. 158, 162–165.

d. Ibid., p. 159.

e. *Webster's Ninth New Collegiate Dictionary.* (Springfield, Mass.: Merriam-Webster, 1983), p. 1364.

f. Ibid., p. 854.

g. Meissner, W. W. *The Paranoid Process* (New York: Jason Aronson, 1980), pp. 120–121.

h. Notes taken from a lecture on Soviet foreign policy given at the National War College, Washington, D.C., 1985.

i. Meissner, *The Paranoid Process*, p. 801.

j. Ibid., p. 134.

k. Ibid., p. 75.

l. Ibid. pp. 76–77.

m. 1979 Soviet census.

n. Meissner, *The Paranoid Process*, pp. 805–806.

o. Ibid., p. 798.

p. Ibid., p. 107.

q. *Washington Post*, December 10, 1987, p. A30.

r. In a talk called "Russian Society and U.S.–Soviet Relations" at the Kennan Institute for Advanced Russian Studies, Washington, D.C., on November 13,

1986, as provided in the *Meeting Report* (Washington, D.C.: Wilson Center, Smithsonian Institution, 1986). (See also my note 38.)

s. *Washington Post*, September 22, 1987.

t. In Meissner, *The Paranoid Process*, pp. 114–115.

u. In Jamgotch, Nish, Jr. pp. 174–175.

v. *Washington Post*, March 3, 1987.

w. Ibid., January 11, 1987, p. A5.

x. A reliable source not wishing to be identified.

y. Meissner, *The Paranoid Process*, p. 170.

Chapter 9. Conclusion

a. Both excerpts as reported in *Surviving Together*, (published by the Institute for Soviet-American Relations), 10 (November 1986): 2.

b. *Washington Post*, January 11, 1987, p. A5.

c. "On the Psychological Measuring of Ritual."

d. In *Defense Monitor*, 16, (4) (1987): 6.

e. From a speech by Senator Jennings Randolph (D.-W.Va.) given before the Senate and reported in National Peace Academy Campaign, *Campaign Update*, 6, (1) (Winter 1983).

f. General Order No. 1 of the Japanese surrender, 8/11/45.

g. George C. Herring, *America's Longest War: The United States and Vietnam, 1950–1975*, 2nd ed (New York: Knopf, 1979), p. 55.

h. *Webster's Third New International Dictionary, Unabridged* (Chicago: R. R. Donnelley and Sons Co., 1966), p. 2348.

i. Fred Warner Neal, "Foreword," in Jamgotch Jr., p. xvi.

j. Jamgotch, Jr., p. 152ff.

k. Jamgotch Jr., p. 234, n. 12.

l. See Charles Taylor, "Apocalyptic Power and Human Care," *Yale Review*, 1984.

m. Joel S. Hellman, American Committee on US-Soviet Relations. In *Surviving Together*. Institute for Soviet-American Relations, Washington, D.C.: November 1986, no. 10, p. 7.

n. From a speech delivered in Moscow on July 14, 1986. Ibid., p. 2.

o. Hellman, *Surviving Together*.

p. "National Security Policy Implications of United States Operations in the Persian Gulf," Report of the Defense Policy Panel and the Investigations Subcommittee of the Committee on Armed Services, U.S. House of Representatives. U.S. Government Printing Office, Washington, D.C., July 1987, pp. 9–10.

q. Ibid., pp. 38–39.

r. Ibid., pp. 41–42.

s. As reported in the *Washington Post*, September 8, 1988, pp. A31, 39.

t. Jamgotch Jr., p. 167.

Bibliography

Public Documents

Conference on Security and Co-operation in Europe. *Final Act of the Conference* (Helsinki Summit), Helsinki, August 1, 1975.

The Constitution of the U.S.S.R. Adopted at the Seventh (Special) Session of the Supreme Soviet of the U.S.S.R., Ninth Convocation, on October 7, 1977.

Document of the Stockholm Conference. January 17, 1984–September 19, 1986.

Federal Emergency Management Agency. *How Can Terrorism Be Stopped?: The Domestic Front.* Remarks by the Honorable Louis O. Giuffrida, Director. June 25, 1985.

U.S. Commission on Proposals for the National Academy of Peace and Conflict Resolution. *Report: To Establish The United States Academy of Peace,* 1981.

U.S. Congress Joint Economic Committee. *Statement by Robert Gates, Deputy Director for Intelligence, CIA, on The Allocation of Resources in the Soviet Union and China, 1984, before the Subcommittee of International Trade, Finance, and Security Economics.* November 21, 1984.

U.S. Department of State Bureau of Public Affairs. *Combating International Terrorism* (Current Policy No. 667). March 5, 1985.

U.S. Department of State Bureau of Public Affairs. *The Impact of International Terrorism* (Current Policy No. 340). October 29, 1981.

U.S. Department of State Bureau of Public Affairs. *Implementation of Helsinki Final Act* (Twelfth Semiannual Report, Special Report No. 100). December 1981–May 31, 1982.

U.S. Department of State Bureau of Public Affairs. *Implementation of Helsinki Final Act* (Nineteenth Semiannual Report). April 1, 1985–October 1, 1985.

U.S. Department of State Bureau of Public Affairs. *International Terrorism: A Long Twilight Struggle* (Current Policy No. 608). August 15, 1984.

U.S. Department of State Bureau of Public Affairs. *International Terrorism: Current Trends and the U.S. Response* (Current Policy No. 706, by Robert Oakley).

U.S. Department of State Bureau of Public Affairs. *Terrorism and the Modern World* (Current Policy No. 629). October 25, 1984.

U.S. Department of State Bureau of Public Affairs. *Terrorism: The Challenge to the Democracies* (Current Policy No. 589). June 24, 1984.

U.S. Department of State Bureau of Public Affairs. *Terrorism: The Problem and the Challenges* (Current Policy No. 586). June 13, 1984.

U.S. House of Representatives Committee on Armed Services. *Report of the De-*

fense Policy Panel and the Investigations Subcommittee on National Security Policy Implications of United States Operations in the Persian Gulf. July 1987.

U.S. House of Representatives Foreign Affairs Committee. *Testimony before International Security Subcommittee of House Foreign Affairs Committee on November 9, 1983.* November 9, 1983.

U.S. Pentagon. *Awards Issued to Participants in the Grenada Rescue Mission* (as of August 26, 1985).

U.S. Pentagon. *Press Conference by Secretary of Defense Caspar W. Weinberger.* October 28, 1982.

U.S. Pentagon. *Remarks Prepared for Delivery by the Honorable Caspar W. Weinberger, Secretary of Defense, to The National Press Club.* November 28, 1984.

U.S. Pentagon. *Statement by Admiral Wesley L. McDonald, Commander in Chief, U.S. Atlantic Command, before the House Armed Services Committee.* January 24, 1984.

U.S. Pentagon. *Statement by Colonel James M. Sims, USMC, Organization of the Joint Chiefs of Staff, before the Senate Armed Services Committee on Strategy and Wargaming.* January 14, 1987.

U.S. Senate. *Senate Resolution 329—Relating to Nuclear Risk Reduction Centers.* 98th Congress, Second Session, February 1, 1984.

U.S. Senate. *Treaty on the Limitations of Strategic Offensive Arms and Protocol Thereto (SALT II Treaty). Message from the President of the United States.* 95th Congress, 1st Session, June 25, 1979.

U.S. Senate, Committee on Foreign Relations. Staff Report: *The United States and the Soviet Union: Prospects for the Relationship.* 98th Congress, 1st Session, June 1983.

U.S. Senate, Committee on Labor and Human Resources. *S. 1889 To Establish the United States Academy of Peace,* November 24, 1981.

U.S. White House Office of the Press Secretary

Inaugural address of President Ronald Reagan. January 20, 1981.

Press Conference No. 1 of the President of the United States. January 29, 1981.

Remarks of the President at the Eureka Commencement Ceremony. Eureka College, Peoria, Illinois. May 9, 1981.

Announcement by the President on Strategic Weapons Systems. October 2, 1981.

Address of the President to the National Press Club on the Deployment of Nuclear Weapons. November 18, 1981.

Address of the President to the Nation. December 23, 1981.

Text of an Address by the President on the State of the Union before a Joint Session of Congress. January 26, 1982.

Address of the President to Members of Both Houses of Parliament. The Palace of Westminister. June 8, 1982.

Address of the President to the United Nations. June 17, 1982.

Remarks of the President at Signing Ceremony for Captive Nations Week Proclamation. July 19, 1982.

Statement by the President. November 22, 1982.

Remarks of the President and a Question and Answer Session with Reporters. October 25, 1983.

Remarks Announcing the Appointment of Donald Rumsfeld. November 3, 1983.

Remarks of the President at the White House Ceremony for the Medical Students from Grenada and U.S. Military Personnel. November 7, 1983.

Question and Answer Session of the President with Student Participants in the Close-up Foundation Program. December 2, 1983.

Address by the President to the Nation. February 26, 1986.

United States White House. *Presidential Documents.*

President Dwight Eisenhower's News Conference of May 11, 1960.

Statement by President Lyndon B. Johnson Calling on the Warsaw Pact Allies to Withdraw from Czechoslovakia. August 21, 1968.

Inaugural Address of President Jimmy Carter. January 20, 1977.

Letter of President Ronald Reagan to the Speaker of the House and the President Pro Tempore of the Senate. October 25, 1983.

Letter of President Ronald Reagan to the Speaker of the House and the President Pro Tempore of the Senate. December 8, 1983.

U.S.S.R. Embassy of the U.S.S.R. Public Information Office.

Brezhnev Addresses Army, Navy Officers in Kremlin. October 27, 1982.

Carrying on the Cause of the Great October Revolution: Speech by Victor Vasilyevich Grishin. November 5, 1982.

K.U. Chernenko Award Ceremony Speech. October 29, 1982.

Books

Adams, Ruth, and Susan Cullen, eds. *The Final Epidemic.* Chicago: Educational Foundation for Nuclear Science, 1981.

Adler, Gerhard, ed. *C. G. Jung Letters.* Princeton: Princeton University Press, 1973.

Aitmatov, Chingiz. *The Day Lasts More Than a Hundred Years.* Moscow: Novyi Mir, 1980. (English translation: Bloomington: Indiana University Press, 1983.)

Alexander, Yonah, and John M. Gleason. *Behavioral and Quantitative Perspectives on Terrorism.* New York: Pergamon Press, 1981. "Super Terrorism" by Yonah Alexander.

Amter, Joseph A. *The Vietnam Verdict.* New York: Continuum, 1982.

Arbatov, Georgi, and Willem Oltmans. *The Soviet Viewpoint.* New York: Dodd, Mead, 1983.

The Bhagavad Gita. Baltimore: Penguin Books, 1962.

Bigelow, Robert. *The Dawn Warriors*. London: Hutchinson, 1969.

Brandon, S. G. F. *Man and God in Art and Ritual*. New York: Scribner's, 1975.

Leonid I. Brezhnev: His Life and Work ("Written under the auspices of the Academy of Sciences of the USSR"). New York: Sphinx Press, 1982.

Cahn, Edgar S., and Barry A. Passett, eds. *Citizen Participation: Effecting Community Change*. New York: Praeger, 1971. "Manpower-T.W.O. and the Blackstone Rangers" by Jerome Bernstein.

Caldicott, Helen. *Missile Envy*. New York: Bantam Books, 1984.

Campbell, Joseph. *The Hero with a Thousand Faces*. Princeton: Princeton University Press, 1949.

————. *The Masks of God: Primitive Mythology*. New York: Viking Press, 1970.

Campbell, Robert J., and Leland E. Hensie, eds. *Psychiatric Dictionary*. 4th ed. New York: Oxford University Press, 1970.

Capra, Fritjof. *The Tao of Physics*. Berkeley: Shambhala Publications, 1975.

Carter, Jimmy. *Keeping Faith: Memoirs of a President*. New York: Bantam Books, 1982.

Clay, Jenny Strauss. *The Wrath of Athena: Gods and Men in the Odyssey*. Princeton: Princeton University Press, 1983.

Clausewitz, Carl von. *On War*. Princeton: Princeton University Press, 1976.

Cox, Arthur Macy. *Russian Roulette: The Superpower Game*. New York: Times Books, 1982.

Cushing, Frank Hamilton. *Zuni Fetishes*. Las Vegas: K.C. Publications, 1974.

Davie, Maurice R. *The Evolution of War*. New Haven: Yale University Press, 1929.

deMause, Lloyd. *Reagan's America*. New York: Creative Roots, 1984.

Downing, Christine. *The Goddesses: Mythological Images of the Feminine*. New York: Crossroad, 1981.

Dumezel, Georges. *The Destiny of the Warrior*. Chicago: University of Chicago Press, 1969.

Eliade, Mircea. *Gods, Goddesses, and Myths of Creation*. New York: Harper and Row, 1967.

————. *Myth and Reality*. New York: Harper and Row, 1963.

————. *Myths, Dreams, and Mysteries*. New York: Harper and Row, 1957.

Falwell, Jerry. *Nuclear War and the Second Coming of Christ*. Lynchburg, Va.: Old Time Gospel Hour, 1983.

Feest, Christian. *The Art of War*. London: John Calmann & Cooper, 1980.

Field, D. M. *Greek and Roman Mythology*. New York: Chartwell Books, 1977.

Freedman, Lawrence. *The Evolution of Nuclear Strategy*. New York: St. Martin's Press, 1981.

Frey, Robert Seitz, and Nancy Thompson-Frey. *The Imperative of Response: The Holocaust in Human Context*. New York: University Press of America, 1985.

Van Gennep, Arnold. *The Rites of Passage*. London: Routledge and Kegan Paul, 1960.

Ginzberg, Louis. *Legends of the Bible*. Philadelphia: Jewish Publication Society of America, 1975.

Gorbachev, Mikhail. *Perestroika*. New York: Harper and Row, 1987.

———. *Towards a Better World*. New York: Richardson and Steirman, 1987.

Graves, Robert. *The Greek Myths: 1*. Middlesex: Penguin Books, 1955.

———. *The Greek Myths: 2*. Middlesex: Penguin Books, 1955.

Gray, Louis Herbett, ed. *The Mythology of All Races*. Vol. I *Greek and Roman*. New York: Cooper Square Publishers, 1969.

Guirand, Felix, ed. *New Larousse Encyuclopedia of Mythology*. London: Hamlyn Publishing Group, 1968.

Halle, Louis J. *The Cold War As History*. New York: Harper and Row, 1967.

Harding, M. Esther. *Psychic Energy: Its Source and Goal*. Washington, D.C.: Pantheon Books, 1947.

Hillman, James, et al., eds. *Facing the Gods*. Irving, Tex.: Spring Publications, 1980.

Hirst, David, and Irene Beeson. *Sadat*. London: Faber and Faber, 1981.

The Holy Bible. New York: Thomas Nelson and Sons.

Jamgotch, Nish, Jr., ed. *Sectors of Mutual Benefit in U.S.-Soviet Relations*. Durham: Duke University Press, 1985.

The Jerusalem Bible. New York: Doubleday, 1966.

Jung, C. G. *The Collected Works of C. G. Jung*. Bollingen Series XX. Vols. 3–18. Princeton: Princeton University Press,

———. *Man and His Symbols*. Garden City, N.Y.: Doubleday, 1964.

Kaplan, Fred. *The Wizards of Armageddon*. New York: Simon and Schuster, 1983.

Keen, Sam. *Faces of the Enemy: Reflections of the Hostile Imagination*. San Francisco: Harper and Row, 1986.

Kennedy, Robert F. *Thirteen Days: A Memoir of the Cuban Missile Crises*. New York: W. W. Norton, 1969.

Kerenyi, C. *The Gods of the Greeks*. London: Thames and Hudson, 1951.

———. *The Heroes of the Greeks*. London: Thames and Hudson, 1959.

———. *Athene: Virgin and Mother in Greek Religion, A Study of Pallas Athene*. Zurich: Spring Publications, 1978.

Kissinger, Henry. *White House Years*. Boston: Little, Brown, 1979.

Larousse Encyclopedia of Mythology. London: Batchworth Press, 1959.

Lauterbach, W. *Soviet Psychotherapy*. Oxford: Pergamon Press, 1984.

Loomis, Julia Wolfe. *Mythology*. New York: Monarch Press, 1965.

Macy, Joanna Rogers. *Despair and Personal Power in the Nuclear Age*. Philadelphia: New Society Publishers, 1983.

Mahdi, Louise Carus, Steven Foster; and Meredith Little, eds. *Betwixt and Between: Patterns of Masculine and Feminine Initiation*. La Salle, Ill.: Open Court, 1987.

Mansfield, Sue. *The Gestalts of War: An Inquiry into Its Origins and Meanings As a Social Institution*. New York: Dial Press, 1982.

Marx, Karl. *Capital.* New York: Random House, 1906.

Medvedev, Roy. *Khrushchev.* Garden City, N.Y.: Anchor Press/Doubleday, 1983.

Meissner, W. W. *The Paranoid Process.* New York: Jason Aaronson, 1978. "The Paranoid Process in Adaptation."

Montagu, Ashley. *The Nature of Human Aggression.* New York: Oxford University Press, 1976.

The Navaho War Dance: A Brief Narrative of Its Meaning and Practice. St. Michaels, Ariz.: St. Michaels Press, 1946.

Odajnyk, Volodymyr W. *Jung and Politics: The Political and Social Ideas of C. G. Jung.* New York: Harper and Row, 1976.

O'Keefe, Bernard J. *Nuclear Hostages.* Boston: Houghton Mifflin, 1983.

Onions, C. T., ed. *The Oxford Dictionary of English Etymology.* Oxford: Clarendon Press, 1966.

Partridge, Eric. *A Short Etymological Dictionary of Modern English Origins.* New York: Macmillan, 1958.

Perera, Sylvia B. *Descent to the Goddess.* Toronto: Inner City Books, 1981.

Perowne, Stewart. *Roman Mythology.* London: Hamlyn Publishing Group, 1969.

Pospisil, Leopold. *The Kapauku Papuans of West New Guinea.* New York: Holt, Rinehart and Winston, 1963.

Powers, Thomas. *The Man Who Kept Secrets.* New York: Pocket Books, 1979.

———. *Thinking about the Next War.* New York: New American Library, 1976.

Rangell, Leo, M.D. *The Mind of Watergate.* New York: W. W. Norton, 1980.

Rapoport, Anatol. *The Big Two.* New York: Pegasus, 1971.

Read, Kenneth E. *The High Valley.* New York: Scribner's, 1966.

Report from Iron Mountain on the Possibility and Desirability of Peace. New York: Dell, 1967.

el-Sadat, Anwar. *In Search of Identity: An Autobiography.* New York: Harper and Row, 1977.

Sagan, Eli. *Cannibalism.* New York: Psychohistory Press, 1974.

———. *The Lust to Annihilate: A Psychoanalytic Study of Violence in Ancient Greek Culture.* New York: Psychohistory Press, 1979.

Scheer, Robert. *With Enough Shovels: Reagan, Bush, and Nuclear War.* New York: Random House, 1982.

Schell, Jonathan. *The Abolition.* New York: Alfred A. Knopf, 1984.

———. *The Fate of the Earth.* New York: Alfred A. Knopf, 1982.

Schmookler, Andrew Bard. *The Parable of the Tribes.* Berkeley: University of California Press, 1984.

Schwab, Gustav. *Gods and Heroes.* New York: Pantheon Books, 1946.

Sheldrake, Rupert. *A New Science of Life.* Los Angeles: J. P. Tarcher, 1981.

Shevchenko, Arkady N. *Breaking with Moscow.* New York: Alfred A. Knopf, 1985.

Shipler, David K. *Russia: Broken Idols, Solemn Dreams.* New York: Times Books, 1983.

Simpson, D. P. *Cassell's Latin Dictionary*. London: Cassell, 1959.

Singer, June. *Boundaries of the Soul*. Garden City, N.Y.: Anchor Press/Double-day, 1971.

Smith, Charles Duryea, ed. *The Hundred Percent Challenge*. Washington, D.C.: Seven Locks Press, 1985.

The Soviet Union: Facts, Problems, and Appraisals. Moscow: Novosti Press Agency Publishing House, 1986.

Stevens, Anthony. *Archetypes*. New York: Quill, 1983.

———. "The Archetypes of War," in *The Anatomy of Conflict*, ed. Ian Fenton. London: Coventure, 1985.

Sun Tzu. *The Art of War*. New York: Delacorte Press, 1983.

Talbott, Strobe. *Deadly Gambits*. New York: Alfred A. Knopf, 1984.

———, trans. *Khrushchev Remembers*. New York: Bantam Books, 1970.

Tiger, L. 1970. *Men in Groups*. New York: Vintage Books.

Timerman, Jacobo. *The Longest War: Israel in Lebanon*. New York: Alfred A. Knopf, 1982.

Tolstoy, Leo. *War and Peace*. Vol. 2. New York: Heritage Press, 1938. First and Second Epilogues.

Truman, Harry S. *Memoirs: Year of Decisions*. Garden City, N.Y.: Doubleday, 1956.

———. *Memoirs: Years of Trial and Hope*. Garden City, N.Y.: Doubleday, 1956.

Ury, William L. *Beyond the Hotline*. Boston: Houghton Mifflin, 1985.

USSR Academy of Sciences. *Political Consciousness in the U.S.A.: Traditions and Evolution*. Moscow: Progress Publishers, 1980.

Valenta, Jim, and William Potter, eds. *Soviet Decisionmaking for National Security*. London: George Allen and Unwin, 1984.

Vanggaard, Thorkil. *Phallos: A Symbol and Its History in the Male World*. New York: International Universities Press, 1969.

Vitukhin, Igor, ed. *Soviet Generals Recall World War II*. New York: Sphinx Press, 1981.

Walsh, Roger, M.D. *Staying Alive*. Boulder: Shambhala/New Science Library, 1984.

Warner, Rex, trans. *War Commentaries of Caesar*. New York: New American Library, 1960.

Waters, Frank. *Book of the Hopi*. New York: Ballantine Books, 1963.

White, Ralph K. *Fearful Warriors*. New York: Free Press, 1984.

Whitmont, Edward C. *Return of the Goddess*. New York: Crossroad Publishing, 1982.

———. *The Symbolic Quest*. Princeton: Princeton University Press, 1969.

Wieseltier, Leon. *Nuclear War, Nuclear Peace*. New York: Holt, Rinehart and Winston, 1983.

Willens, Harold. *The Trimtab Factor*. New York: William Morrow, 1984.

Articles and Periodicals

Adelman, Kenneth L. "Arms Control with and without Agreements." *Foreign Affairs* 63, no. 2 (1984): pp. 240–263.

Adler, Gerhard. "Psychology and the Atom Bomb." *Psychological Perspectives* 16, no. 1 (1985): 13–28.

Armstrong, Barbara. "Group Therapy for the Middle East." *Washington Post Magazine*, June 24, 1984, pp. 6–7.

Bell, Coral. "From Carter to Reagan." *Foreign Affairs* 63, no. 3 (1985): 490–510.

Bernstein, Jerome S. "Jung, Jungians and the Nuclear Peril." *Psychological Perspectives* 16, no. 1 (1985): 29–39.

———. "Power and Politics in the Thermonuclear Age: A Depth-Psychological Approach." *Quadrant* 18, no. 2 (Fall 1985).

Bialer, Seweryn. "The Psychology of U.S.–Soviet Relations." *Political Psychology* 6, no. 2 (June 1985): 263–273.

Blechman, Barry M., and Michael Krepon. "Nuclear Risk and Reduction Centers." *Significant Issues Series*, Center for Strategic and International Studies, vol. 8, no. 1 (1986).

Bolen, Jean Shinoda. "Healing the Psyche, Healing the Earth." *Psychological Perspectives* 18, no. 1 (Spring 1987): 26–37.

Borenzweig, Herman. "*Perestroika* by Mikhail Gorbachev." *Psychological Perspectives* 19, no. 2 (Spring-Summer 1988): 164–169.

Bronfenbrenner, Urie. "The Mirror Image in Soviet-American Relations: A Social Psychologist's Report." *Journal of Social Issues* 17, no. 3 (1961): 45–56.

Bundy, McGeorge, George F. Kennan, Robert S. McNamara, and Gerard Smith. "The President's Choice: Star Wars or Arms Control." *Foreign Affairs* 63, no. 2 (1984): 264–278.

Cannon, Lou. "President Points to Release of Three Hostages." *Washington Post*, November 20, 1986, p. A1.

———. "Reagan: Poindexter and 'Honorable Man.'" *Washington Post*, April 29, 1987, p. A1.

———. "Reagan Silent on Options in Salvador, Nicaragua." *Washington Post*, February 19, 1982, p. A5.

Claiborne, William. "Combat Troops Quit Beirut." *Washington Post*, February 26, 1984.

Cohen, Stephen F. "The Parity Principle in U.S.–Soviet Relations," *Evolutionary Blues*, Vol. 2, 1983. pp. 60–61.

Coleman, Mary. "Nuclear Politics in the 1980's." *Journal of Psychohistory* 12, no. 1 (Summer 1984): 121–133.

"Comment." *American Psychologist* 38, no. 9 (September 1983): 1022–1029.

Cullen, Robert B. "Soviet Jewry." *Foreign Affairs* 65, no. 2 (Winter 1986–87): 252–266.

Cutler, Lloyd N. "The Right to Intervene." *Foreign Affairs* 64, no. 1 (Fall 1985): 96–112.

Davidson, William D. "Psychiatry and Foreign Affairs: A Vision and a Commitment," *Psychoanalytic Inquiry* 6, no. 2 (1986): 223–242.

Davidson, William D., and Joseph Montville. "Foreign Policy According to Freud." *Foreign Policy*, no. 45 (Winter 1981–82): 145–158.

deMause, Lloyd. "The Making of a Fearful Leader: 'Where's the Rest of Me?'" *Journal of Psychohistory* 12, no. 1 (Summer 1984): 5–21.

Denton, Herbert H., and William Claiborne. "Marines Announce Start of Pullout of Beirut Forces." *Washington Post*, February 22, 1984, p. A1.

Deutsch, Morton. "Conflict Resolution: Theory and Practice." *Political Psychology* 4, no. 3 (September 1983): 431–453.

———. "The Prevention of World War III: A Psychological Perspective." *Political Psychology* 4, no. 1 (March 1983): 3–31.

Dieckmann, Hans. "Psychological Reflections on the Nuclear Threat." *Quadrant* 18, no. 2 (Fall 1985).

DiMento, Joseph F. "Let the Nuclear Superpowers Play Pac-Man." *Christian Science Monitor*, January 19, 1983, p. 23.

Doder, Dusko. "Euromissile May Spur New Soviet Retaliatory Plan." *Washington Post*, November 30, 1982.

Erikson, Erik H. "Pseudospeciation in the Nuclear Age." *Political Psychology* 6, no. 2 (June 1985): 213–217.

———. "Reflections on Ethos and War." *Yale Review* 73, no. 4 (July 1984).

Etheredge, Lloyd S. "President Reagan's Counseling." *Political Psychology* 5, no. 4 (December 1984): 737–740.

Fascell, Dante B. "Congress and Arms Control." *Foreign Affairs* 65, no. 4 (Spring 1987): 730–749.

Fine, Reuben. "The Protestant Ethic and the Analytical Ideal." *Political Psychology* 4, no. 2 (June 1983): 245–264.

Fischman, Joshua. "The Security of Uncertainty." *Psychology Today* 22, no. 6 (June 1988): 28–33.

Fisher, Roger. "Dealing with Conflict among Individuals and Nations: Are There Common Principles?" *Psycholanalytic Inquiry* 6, no. 2 (1986): 143–153.

Fitzgerald, Ross. "Human Needs and Politics: The Ideas of Christian Bay and Herbert Marcuse," *Political Psychology* 6, no. 1 (March 1985): 87–108.

Foreign Broadcast Information Service. *Daily Report, Soviet Union* 3, no. 055 (March 21, 1985).

Frank, Jerome D., and John C. Rivard. "Antinuclear Admirals: An Interview Study." *Political Psychology* 7, no. 1 (March 1986): 23–52.

Friedland, Nehemia, and Ariel Merari. "The Psychological Impact of Terrorism: A Double-Edged Sword." *Political Psychology* 6, no. 4 (December 1985): 591–604.

Gallagher, Winifred. "Sex and Hormones," *Atlantic Monthly* 261, no. 3 (March 1988): 77–82.

Gati, Charles. "Gorbachev and Eastern Europe." *Foreign Affairs* 65, no. 5 (Summer 1987): 958–975.

Gayler, Adm. Noel (USN-Ret.). "How to Break the Momentum of the Nuclear Arms Race." *East-West Outlook* 5, no. 4 (June-July 1982): 2–4.

———. "The Way Out: A General Nuclear Settlement." *Yale Law and Policy Review* 5, no. 1 (Fall/Winter 1986): 134–156.

Gelb, Leslie H., and Anthony Lake. "Four More Years: Diplomacy Restored?" *Foreign Affairs* 63, no. 3 (1985): 465–489.

Glad, Betty. "Black and White Thinking: Ronald Reagan's Approach to Foreign Policy." *Political Psychology* 4, no. 1 (March 1983): 33–76.

Goldberg, Andrew, et al. "Leaders and Crises: The CSIS Crisis Simulations." *Significant Issues Series,* The Center for Strategic and International Studies, 1987.

Goodman, Lisa A., John E. Mack, William R. Beardslee, and Roberta M. Snow. "The Threat of Nuclear War and the Nuclear Arms Race: Adolescent Experience and Perceptions." *Political Psychology* 4, no. 3 (September 1983): 501–530.

Gorbachev, Mikhail. "An Interview with Gorbachev." *Time,* September 9, 1985.

Gould, Stephen Jay. "A Biological Comment on Erikson's Notion of Pseudospeciation." *Yale Review,* 73, no. 4 (July 1984).

Grunwald, Henry. "Foreign Policy under Reagan II." *Foreign Affairs* 63, no. 2 (1984): 219–239.

Hareven, Alouph. "Victimization: Some Comments by an Israeli." *Political Psychology* 4, no. 1 (March 1983): 145–155.

The Harvard Nuclear Study Group. "The Realities of Arms Control." *Atlantic Monthly* 251, no. 6 (June 1983): 39–49.

Herrmann, Richard K. "American Perceptions of Soviet Foreign Policy: Reconsidering Three Competing Perspectives." *Political Psychology* 6, no. 3 (September 1985): 375–411.

———. "High-Ranking Soviet Calls Reagan Administration 'Dangerous.'" *Washington Post,* October 30, 1982.

Hillis, Raymond E. "Psyche and Annihilation." *Psychological Perspectives* 16, no. 1 (1985): 51–73.

Hoffman, David. "Defense on Iran Reiterated." *Washington Post,* March 20, 1987, p. A1.

———. "Reagan Denies 'Ransom' Was Paid for Hostages." *Washington Post,* November 14, 1986, p. A.

Hoffman, Stanley. "On the Political Psychology of Peace and War: A Critique and Agenda." *Political Psychology* 7, no. 1 (March 1986): 1–21.

Holt, David. "Jung and Marx." *Spring* (1973).

Holt, Robert S. "Can Psychology Meet Einstein's Challenge?" *Political Psychology* 5, no. 2 (June 1984): 199–225.

Horelick, Arnold. "U.S.-Soviet Relations: The Return of Arms Control." *Foreign Affairs* 63, no. 3 (1985): 511–537.

Hough, Jerry F. "Gorbachev's Strategy." *Foreign Affairs* 64, no. 1 (Fall 1985): 33–55.

Javits, Jacob K. "War Powers Reconsidered," *Foreign Affairs* 64, no. 1 (Fall 1985): 130–140.

Joyce, J. M. Science Advisor to U.S. Embassy, Moscow. "The Assumption of Hostility in U.S.-Soviet Relations." U.S. Embassy, Moscow, June 4, 1980.

Kaiser, Robert G. "The Soviet Pretense," *Foreign Affairs* 65, no. 2 (Winter 1986–87): 232–251.

Kalsched, Donald E. "Fire from the Gods: How Will Prometheus Be Bound?" *Quadrant* 18, no. 2 (Fall 1985).

Kapper, Francis B. "Wargaming I." *Defense 81*, May 1981, pp. 16–21.

———. "Wargaming II." *Defense 81*, May 1981, pp. 22–26.

Kaufman, Michael T. "1,900 U.S. Troops, with Caribbean Allies, Invade Grenada and Fight Leftist Units; Moscow Protests; British Are Critical." *New York Times*, October 26, 1983, p. A1.

Kendler, Howard H. "Scientific Conclusion or Political Advocacy?" *American Psychologist* 38, no. 10 (October 1983): 1122.

Kennan, George F. "Containment Then and Now." *Foreign Affairs* 65, no. 4 (Spring 1987): 885–890.

———. "Morality and Foreign Policy." *Foreign Affairs* 64, no. 2 (Winter 1985–86): 205–218.

———. "Reflections: Two Letters." *New Yorker*, September 24, 1984.

———. "What About the Russians?" *Evolutionary Blues*. 2 (1983): 48–56.

Kern, Montague. "The Press, the Presidency, and International Conflict: Lessons from Two Administrations." *Political Psychology* 5, no. 1 (March 1984): 53–68.

Klineberg, Otto. "Public Opinion and Nuclear War." *American Psychologist* (November 1984), pp. 1245–1253.

Klugman. "Hawks and Doves." *Political Psychology* 6, no. 4 (December 1985): 573–589.

Kohn, Alfie. "Make Love, Not War." *Psychology Today* 22, no. 6 (June 1988): 34–38.

Kull, Steven. "Nuclear Arms and the Desire for World Destruction." *Political Psychology* 4, no. 3 (September 1983): 563–591.

LaBier, Douglas. "Bureaucracy and Psychopathology." *Political Psychology* 4, no. 2 (June 1983): 223–243.

Lawrence, Lieut. General Richard D. "Playing the Game." *Defense 86*, January-February 1986, pp. 22–29.

Lebow, Richard Ned. "The Deterrence Deadlock: Is There a Way Out?" *Political Psychology* 4, no. 2 (June 1983): 333–354.

Lescaze, Lee. "President Makes Three Misstatements on Vietnam." *Washington Post*, February 19, 1982, p. A5.

Lifton, Robert Jay. "Bringing the Bomb Home." *Nuclear Times*, October 1982, pp. 26–27.

———. "The Psychic Toll of the Nuclear Age." *New York Times Magazine*, September 26, 1982, pp. 52–64.

Mack, John E. "Epilogue." *Psychoanalytic Inquiry* 6, no. 2 (1986): 313–314.

———. "Prologue." *Psychoanalytic Inquiry* 6, no. 2 (1986): 135–142.

———. "Some Thoughts on the Nuclear Age and the Psychological Roots of Anti-Sovietism." *Psychoanalytic Inquiry* 6, no. 2 (1986): 267–285.

———. "Staying Ignorant about Nuclear War." *Political Psychology* 6, no. 3 (September 1985): 371–374.

———. "Toward a Collective Psychopathology of the Nuclear Arms Competition." *Political Psychology* 6, no. 2 (June 1985): 291–321.

Mandel, Robert. "The Desirability of Irrationality in Foreign Policy Making: A Preliminary Theoretical Analysis." *Political Psychology* 5, no. 4 (December 1984): 643–660.

Mandelbaum, Michael, and Strobe Talbott. "Reykjavik and Beyond." *Foreign Affairs* 65, no. 2 (Winter 1986–87): 215–235.

Mansdorf, Irwin J. "On Kelman's 'Conversations with Arafat.'" *American Psychologist* 38, no. 10 (October 1983): 1122–1123.

Mansfield, Sue (interviewed by Sam Keen). "War As the Ultimate Therapy." *Psychology Today* 16, no. 6 (June 1982): 56–66.

Massell, Sylvia Perera. "The Scapegoat Complex." *Quadrant* 12, no. 2 (Winter 1979).

Misiunas, Romuald J. "Political Consciousness and Political Change: The Soviet Example." *Political Psychology* 4, no. 1 (March 1983): 157–165.

Montville, Joseph V. "A Diplomat among Psychoanalysts." *Psychoanalytic Inquiry* 6, no. 2 (1986): 247–250.

———. "Editorial." *Political Psychology* 4, no. 3 (September 1983): 427–429.

———. "Issue Editor's Introduction." *Political Psychology* 6, no. 2 (June 1985): 207–212.

Moses, Rafael. "Empathy and Dis-Empathy in Political Conflict." *Political Psychology* 6, no. 1 (March 1985): 135–139.

Moyer, Robert S. "The Enemy Within." *Psychology Today* 19, no. 1 (January 1985): 30–37.

National Peace Academy Campaign. "Legislation Moves in 98th Congress." *Campaign Update* 6, issue 1 (Winter 1983).

Neumann, Erich. "On the Psychological Meaning of Ritual." *Quadrant* 9, no. 2 (Winter 1976): 5–34.

Nitze, Paul H. "Living with the Soviets." *Foreign Affairs* 63, no. 2 (1984): 360–374.

Nixon, Richard. "Superpower Summitry." *Foreign Affairs* 64, no. 1 (Fall 1985): 1–11.

Oberdorfer, Don, and Fred Hiatt. "Reagan Says Troops to Relocate Offshore." *Washington Post*, February 8, 1984, p. A1.

Office of Research, USICA. "What about the Americans?" *Evolutionary Blues* 2 (1983): 57–59.

Perlman, Mike. "Phaethon and the Thermonuclear Chariot." *Spring,* 1983.

Pinderhughes, Charles A. "Differential Bonding from Infancy to International Conflict." *Psychoanalytic Inquiry* 6, no. 2 (1986): 155–173.

Plous, Scott. "Psychological and Strategic Barriers in Present Attempts at Nuclear Disarmament: A New Proposal." *Political Psychology* 6, no. 1 (March 1985): 109–133.

Podhoretz, Norman. "The Reagan Road to Détente." *Foreign Affairs* 63, no. 3 (1985): 441–446.

Powers, Thomas. "Nuclear Winter and Nuclear Strategy." *Atlantic Monthly* 254, no. 5 (November 1984): 53–64.

———. "What Is It About?" *Atlantic Monthly,* January 1984, pp. 35–55.

Psychologists for Social Responsibility Newsletter 6, no. 2 (Spring 1988).

Radin, Jerome. "The Phantasy of Nuclear 'Survivability.'" *Psychological Perspectives* 16, no. 1 (1985): 40–50.

Schmookler, Andrew Bard. "U.S.-U.S.S.R.: Are We Angling toward a Shoot-Out at the OK Corral?" *Political Psychology* 6, no. 2 (June 1985): 275–290.

Scott, Walter. "Personality Parade." *Parade Magazine*, July 10, 1988, p. 2.

Sheldrake, Rupert. "Mind, Memory, and Archetype." *Psychological Perspectives* 18, no. 1 (Spring 1987): 9–25.

———. "Society, Spirit, and Ritual." *Psychological Perspectives* 18, no. 2 (Fall 1987): 320–331.

Sivard, Ruth Leger. *World Military and Social Expenditures 1985.* Washington, D.C.: World Priorities, 1985.

Smith, M. Brewster, Diane Thomas, Willis Harmon, David McFadden, and James MacGregor Burns. "Five Articles Submitted under the Title: Bridging for Peace: Theory and Action for the 1980's." *Political Psychology* 5, no. 3 (September 1984): 465–504.

Smoke, Richard. "The 'Peace' Deterrence and the 'Peace' of the Antinuclear War Movement." *Political Psychology* 5, no. 4 (December 1984): 741–748.

"The Sources of Soviet Conduct." *Foreign Affairs* 65, no. 4 (Spring 1987): 852–868.

Stein, Howard F. "Psychological Complementarity in Soviet-American Relations." *Political Psychology* 6, no. 2 (June 1985): 249–261.

Taylor, Benjamin. "Reagan's New Central American Initiative." *Boston Globe*, July 24, 1983, p. A22.

Taylor, Charles H. "Apocalyptic Power and Human Care." *Yale Review* 73, no. 4 (July 1984).

———. "Imagining Apocalypse: Godlike Power and Human Care." *Quadrant* 18, no. 2 (Fall 1985).

Thomas, Dan B., Lee Sigelman, and Larry R. Baas. "Public Evaluations of the President: Policy, Partisan and 'Personal' Determinants." *Political Psychology* 5, no. 4 (December 1984): 531–542.

"The Threat of Nuclear Theft and Sabotage." *Congressional Record*, April 30, 1974, pp. 12353–12362.

Treverton, Gregory F. "Covert Action and Open Society." *Foreign Affairs* 65, no. 5 (Summer 1987): 995–1014.

Ulman, Richard Barrett, and D. Wilfred Abse. "The Group Psychology of Mass Madness: Jonestown." *Political Psychology* 4, no. 4 (December 1983): 637–661.

"Voices from the Hearing Room and Beyond." *Life Magazine: The Year in Pictures*, January 1988, p. 37.

Volkan, Vamik D. "The Narcissism of Minor Differences in the Psychological Gap between Opposing Nations." *Psychoanalytic Inquiry* 6, no. 2 (1986): 175–191.

———. "The Need to Have Enemies and Allies: A Developmental Approach." *Political Psychology* 6, no. 2 (June 1985): 219–247.

Wallerstein, Robert S. "The Transformation of Thought That Nuclear Age Requires: Can We Achieve It?" *Psychoanalytic Inquiry* 6, no. 2 (1986): 303–312.

Wangh, Martin. "The Nuclear Threat: Its Impact on Psychoanalytic Conceptualizations." *Psychoanalytic Inquiry* 6, no. 2 (1986): 251–266.

Warnke, Paul C. "The Domestic Rationale for Foreign Enemies." *Psychoanalytic Inquiry* 6, no. 2 (1986): 243–246.

Watkins, Mary M. "Moral Imagination and Peace Activism: Discerning the Inner Voices." *Psychological Perspectives* 16, no. 1 (1985): 77–93.

Weinberger, Caspar W. "We Need This Missile." *Washington Post*, November 29, 1982.

White, Ralph K. "Empathizing with the Rulers of the USSR." *Political Psychology* 4, no. 1 (March 1983): 121–137.

Whitmont, Edward. "Individual Transformation and Personal Responsibility." *Quadrant* 18, no. 2 (Fall 1985).

"Who Has the Bomb." *Time* 125, no. 22 (June 3, 1985): 36–52.

Wiles, Peter. "Irreversibility: Theory and Practice." *Washington Quarterly*, Winter 1985, pp. 29–40.

Woolger, Roger, and Jennifer Woolger. "Athena Today: Paradoxes of Power and Vulnerability." *Quadrant* 20, no. 1 (1987): 23.

Yoffe, Emily. "The Chosen Few." *Washington Post Magazine*, November 4, 1984, p. 8.

Unpublished Material

Bernstein, Jerome S. "The Decline of Rights of Passage: The Impact on Masculine Individuation."

Deutsch, Morton. "The Prevention of World War III: A Psychological Perspective." Presidential address to International Society for Political Psychology, June 26, 1982.

Hildreth, Steven A. "Nuclear Risk Reduction Centers." Paper from the Foreign Affairs and National Defense Division of the Congressional Research Service. Updated May 19, 1987.

Jenkins, Brian M. "Will Terrorists Go Nuclear?" Paper prepared for the Conference on International Terrorism: The Nuclear Dimension, sponsored by the Nuclear Control Institute and the State University of New York Institute for Studies in International Terrorism. Washington, D.C., June 24–25, 1985.

Malicky, Mike. "Issues Surrounding 'Nuclear Terrorism'." Unpublished manuscript, December 3, 1982.

Moriarty, James Robert. "Ritual Combat. A Comparison of the Aztec 'War of Flowers' and the Medieval 'Melée'. Paper presented at a meeting of the Southwestern Monuments Association, Fall 1968.

Schneider, Claudine (U.S. Rep. from the 2d District, R.I.). "A Congressbridge to Understanding." Article submitted to the Government Information Bulletin, 1987.

Stevens, Anthony. "The Analytical Psychology of War and Peace." Series of lectures given in New York City and Washington, D.C., in 1985 and soon to be published in book form.

Other Sources

ABC Television Network. *Capitol to Capitol*. A Viewer's Guide to An Unprecedented Series of Live Satellite Dialogues Linking Members of the Congress of the United States and Deputies of the Supreme Soviet of the USSR. Fall 1987.

American Committee on East-West Accord. *"The State of U.S.-Soviet Relations."* Address by the Honorable George F. Kennan Luncheon. *Meeting of the American Committee on East-West Accord*. Washington, D.C., May 17, 1983.

Arms Control Association. Telephone interviews (staff). October 1982.

Board of Scientific Affairs, American Psychological Association. *Draft Minutes*. May 2–4, 1987.

Center for Defense Information (Washington, D.C.). *The Defense Monitor*.
Vol. 10, no. 5 (1981)
Vol. 12, nos. 1 and 8 (1983)
Vol. 13, nos. 2, 3, and 6 (1984)

Vol. 14, nos. 1, 2, 3, and 6 (1985)

Vol. 15, nos. 3 and 7 (1986)

Vol. 16, nos. 1, 3, and 4 (1987)

Vol. 17, no. 2 (1988)

Cohen, William S. (U.S. Sen. from Maine). Letter to Robert A. J. Monks. June 16, 1987.

International Physicians for Prevention of Nuclear War. Telephone interviews (staff). October 1982.

Kennan, George F. *On Russian Diplomacy in the Nineteenth Century and the Origins of World War I: A Special Report*. Kennan Institute for Advanced Russian Studies, 1986.

Kennan Institute for Advanced Russian Studies. *Meeting Report*. May 1985.

National Peace Academy Campaign. *Legislative Update*. November 1982.

Psychologists for Social Responsibility. *Press Conference, American Psychological Association Convention*. New York, August 31, 1987.

Wiarda, Howard J. *Soviet Policy in the Caribbean and Central America: Opportunities and Restraints*. A Kennan Institute for Advanced Russian Studies Occasional Paper. March 2, 1984.

Index

ABM, Anti-Ballistic Missile (Treaty), 29, 68, 177, 179
Afghanistan, 2, 21, 42, 90, 98, 101, 102, 166, 173, 174, 188
Aggression, xiv, 8, 64–73, 76–78, 82, 84, 90, 91, 104–107, 126, 127, 131, 142, 167, 168, 170, 171, 174, 180. *See also* warfare, and instinct to aggression
  instinct to aggression, 64–66, 68–72, 104–106, 167, 168, 170, 180
Aitmatov, Chingiz, 11, 30, 90
Allende, 20, 101, 173
American psyche, 51, 55, 56
American Psychological Association (APA), 73, 74, 75
American Revolution, 149
Archetype, ix, 4–14, 19, 20, 30, 33, 34, 44, 48, 52, 55–57, 62, 71, 72, 79, 80, 85, 87, 88, 91, 109, 111, 130, 167, 168, 169, 171, 175, 176, 193
  archetype of peace, 88, 169. *See also* peace
  archetype of war, 6, 48, 67, 69, 71–73, 76, 77, 78, 81, 88, 104, 105, 107, 110, 111, 165, 168, 169, 170, 175, 179, 182, 194, 203. *See also* war
  Mars-Athena archetype 49, 169, 170, 179
Ares, 48, 169. *See also* Mars
Arms Control and Disarmament Agency, xxii, 179, 198
Athena, 48, 49, 52, 169, 170, 179

Bhagavad Gita, 58, 206

Bonding, in psychological groups 120, 126–129
Breakdancing, ritual, 86, 87
Brezhnev, Leonid, 27, 28, 40, 41
Bush, George, 57, 143, 147

Carter, Jimmy, 27, 31, 39, 46, 50–54, 141, 193
CBM's, confidence-and-security building measures, 98
Center for Strategic and International Studies (CSIS), 116, 120, 121
Chauvinism, 141.
Chernobyl, 154, 155, 185
Chile, 14, 20, 101, 141, 173
China, People's Republic of, 28, 30–33, 35, 46, 48, 52, 55, 96, 108, 110, 131, 135, 144, 159, 174
CIA, 20, 22, 33, 41, 135, 143, 149
Civil defense, 28
Clausewitz, Carl von, 1, 2
Cold war, 56, 90, 131, 147, 168
Conflict resolution, 5, 34, 98, 104, 160, 169–171, 174–176, 179, 184, 194, 195, 197, 198, 200
Cooperation, x, xxi, 18, 23, 33, 35, 37, 54, 63–67, 77, 78, 87, 92–94, 96–98, 101, 103, 104, 106, 111–113, 116, 123, 124, 131, 151, 165, 167, 168, 170, 175, 179–184, 186–189, 191–196, 202. *See also* primary cooperation
  intergroup cooperation 64, 65, 78, 96, 131
Coup counting, coup sticks; 80, 86. *See also* ritual and ritual warfare
Cuban missile crisis, 80, 103
Czechoslovakia, 11, 12, 20, 136, 173

Davie, Maurice, 62, 63, 69, 71, 75, 84
Defense Department, U.S. 115, 157, 163, 172–174, 177, 188
Détente, 34, 97, 172, 179, 180
Deterrence, 1–3, 58, 60, 94, 96, 100, 103–106, 163–165, 172, 174, 178, 179
Dreams, 5, 50, 83

Eliade, Mircea, 8
Energy, xxi, xxiii, 7, 9, 10, 13, 16, 19, 33, 45, 51, 52, 55, 58, 59, 62, 66, 67, 70–72, 79–83, 85–88, 90, 91, 104, 105, 106, 128, 149, 165–170, 187
  psychic energy, 13, 19, 59, 80, 82, 85, 87, 105, 165, 166
Erikson, Erik, 125, 126
"Evil empire," xviii, 27, 31, 35, 46, 52, 57, 100, 196
Extinction, 71, 79, 96, 186
First strike, 28, 41, 46, 74, 181

Ford, Gerald R., 39
Freud, Sigmund, 5, 6, 127
Functionalism, 180, 181, 187

Gayler, Jeanne Vaughn Mattison, 183
Glasnost, 3, 21, 30–33, 35, 36, 141, 144, 147, 148, 154, 190
Global concerns, xviii, 21, 56, 57, 118, 174, 185, 186, 189–191
Globalistika, 185, 188
Goodby, James E., 123
Gorbachev, Mikhail, xvii, 8, 11, 12, 19, 21, 26, 29–33, 35–37, 46, 47, 52, 53, 55, 56, 87, 97, 102, 106, 114, 115, 120, 133, 135–137, 141, 144–148, 150, 152, 154, 156, 157, 162, 165, 182, 183, 185, 188, 191, 196
  Gorbachev administration, 26, 30–32, 36, 52, 87, 115, 185
Greenhouse effect, 186, 190
Grenada, 11, 22, 23, 51, 53, 90, 101, 143

Helsinki Accords, Final Act, 98, 99
Hero, ix, 6, 8, 9, 14, 16, 26, 30, 44– 53, 55, 56, 61, 67, 87, 88, 169
  adolescent hero, 44, 45, 49
  archetype, 44, 45, 49
  mature hero, 45, 48, 52, 55, 56
  warrior hero, 45, 46, 49–51, 87, 88
Hitler, Adolf, 5, 7–9, 125, 128, 144
Hook, as in shadow projection, 30, 127, 147, 155–157
Hoover, J. Edgar, 16

Indians, Plains, 80. See also ritual; rit- ual warfare
INF treaty of (1987), 3, 28, 29, 41, 46, 47, 87, 102, 103, 106, 111, 156, 157, 182–184, 193
Inspections, CBM's, 99, 100, 139, 156, 157, 193
Instinct to aggression, in primitive groups and tribes, 71
Instinctual aggression, 65, 68, 76, 82, 107
International Physicians for Preven- tion of Nuclear War, 201
Iran, 20, 22, 23–25, 30, 49, 51, 62, 69, 92, 98, 111, 112, 127, 136, 143, 149, 166, 167, 183, 187, 188
Iran-Contra Affair, 20, 21, 24–25, 30, 92, 127, 143
Iraq, 62, 69, 92, 98, 112, 166, 183, 187, 188

Jamgotsch, Nish Jr., 180, 182, 187, 193
Japan, 33, 79, 108, 134, 136, 176, 177, 186
Johnson, Lyndon Baines, 53, 159
Joint military or paramilitary strike force (JSF), 122
Jung, ix, x, xxi, xxii, 3, 5–7, 9, 17, 33, 37–39, 58, 61, 63, 67, 71, 78, 91, 93, 152, 158

Kennan, George, xxii, 33, 147
Kennedy, John F., 52, 159, 177
Khrushchev, Nikita S., 35, 138, 144
Kissinger, Henry, 39, 102
Kull, Stephen, 75, 76, 78, 82, 168, 181
Kuwait, 49, 50, 111, 112, 187

Latin America, 143, 149
Lebanon, 18, 19, 24, 49
Libya, 109–111, 117, 149, 167, 170, 183
Lincoln, Abraham, 56
LRTNF, 28

Mars, 48–51, 106, 169, 170, 179. *See also* Ares
Meissner, W. W., 131, 134, 135, 138, 141, 161
Middle East, 46, 54, 94, 98, 108, 166, 170, 176, 188, 189
Military-industrial complex, 176–178, 197
Mongol, 133, 134
Moral consciousness, 18, 46, 56, 78, 87, 94, 96, 169, 170, 184, 192, 196, 202
My Lai massacre, 88, 89

National Security Council of the President (NSC), 117, 118, 121, 172
NATO, 81, 98, 100, 102, 107
Neumann, Erich, 86, 87, 168
Newport Institute, xxii, 33
Nicaragua, 2, 20, 21, 23–25, 90, 98, 101, 117, 118, 143, 149, 173, 188
Nitze, Paul, 41, 182
North, Oliver, 30, 45, 143
Nuclear bomb, 79, 114. *See also* war; nuclear war
Nuclear Risk Reduction Centers, 115, 118
Nuclear war, winnable, xvi, xvii, 54, 74, 181

Observations, CBM's, 32, 40, 100, 130, 147
Office of Peace Technology (OPT), 179
Olympic games, 86, 90
Oppenheimer, J. Robert, 58
Opposites, tension of, 33, 34, 39, 42, 58, 78, 93, 94, 158
Ozone, 186, 190

Pakistan, 102
Parable of the Tribes, 60, 65. *See also* Schmookler, Andrew Bard

Paradoxical realism, 184
Paranoia, ix, 11, 17, 32, 37, 47, 85, 104, 115, 125, 126, 129–139, 141–145, 147, 149–155, 157, 158, 159, 160, 173
  American paranoia, 131, 139, 144, 152, 157, 158
  paranoid defense, 17, 18, 135, 136, 138, 140, 142, 143, 156, 159, 173
  paranoid position, 57, 138, 146, 156, 158
  paranoid position, 57, 138, 146, 156, 158
  paranoid process, 120, 126, 130, 131, 135, 136, 139, 142, 144, 145–147, 153–155, 157–159, 175, 182, 208
  paranoid projection, 27, 33, 34, 68, 84, 118, 120, 146, 155, 157, 160, 161
  Soviet paranoia, 133, 135, 137, 139, 144, 149, 151, 154, 158
Patriotism, 141
Peace, x, xiii, 1, 2, 19, 35, 48, 56, 57, 62, 65, 67, 70, 72, 73, 80, 88, 91, 94, 96, 98, 101, 103–106, 112, 114, 123, 131, 162–165, 168–172, 174–179, 181, 182, 184, 187, 192–201, 203
  peace as power, 192–195
  peace technology, xiii, 1, 2, 98, 101, 105, 106, 112, 123, 164, 170, 171, 172, 174–179, 182, 184, 193–195
Peace Academy, 197, 198
Perestroika, 3, 12, 30–33, 35, 36, 133, 141, 147, 148, 152, 154, 190
Pershing missile, 28, 171
Persian Gulf, 92, 111, 112, 187, 188
Persona, 57
Power, ix, x, xvii, 1, 9, 12–14, 17, 19, 21–25, 31, 42, 44–54, 56–61, 63, 67, 68, 71, 74, 77, 78, 82, 85, 87, 88, 90, 91, 97, 101, 102, 106, 107, 111, 119, 128, 132, 137–147, 149, 157–159, 168–171, 174–176, 178, 190, 192–196, 202
Primary cooperation, xxi, 18, 33, 35, 37, 54, 66, 77, 78, 87, 92, 93, 94,

Primary cooperation (*continued*)
97, 101, 112, 116, 165, 167, 168,
170, 175, 179–184, 187, 189, 191–
196, 202
Proxy wars, 90, 91, 101, 165, 166
Pseudospeciation, 104–106, 125, 126,
130, 165–167
Psyche, xix, 3, 35, 69–71, 76, 87, 104,
167, 196
    Russian psyche, xxi, 128, 134, 139,
140
Psychological types, 37, 38, 43, 136,
153, 175
    extravert, 38
    feeling type, 38, 39, 41
    inferior function, 41
    introvert, 38, 39
    intuitive type, 38
    sensation type, 38
    thinking type, 38, 39, 41
Psychology, ix, xv, xix, xxii, 3, 5, 7,
10, 12, 59, 63, 64, 66, 71, 75, 76,
94, 101, 125, 131, 164, 171, 175,
206
    collective psychology, 63, 94

Qaddafi, Muammar, 109

Reagan, Ronald, xvi, xviii, 11, 13, 18–
20, 22, 24, 25, 27–29, 31, 32, 34,
35, 37, 39, 41, 46–57, 60, 74, 87,
100, 102, 103, 109, 110, 114, 115,
120, 127, 141, 143, 146, 147, 152,
156, 157, 163, 166, 172, 173,
177, 179, 181, 182, 183, 188, 196,
198–200
    Reagan administration, xvi, 13, 18,
19, 22, 24, 28, 31, 32, 35, 46, 49,
51, 53, 54, 60, 74, 87, 103, 109,
110, 115, 141, 143, 147, 156, 157,
163, 166, 172, 177, 179, 181, 198
Religion, x, 2, 13, 30, 59, 64, 69, 70,
76, 78, 129
Reykjavik, Iceland, 102, 104, 160, 183
Ritual, xv, 11, 70, 71, 73, 79–89, 91,
106, 107, 109–112, 165, 166, 167,
168, 170, 175

ritualism, 86–88, 91
ritualized, 63, 70, 71, 80, 87, 90,
91, 105–107, 166, 170
Ritual war games, 166, 170
Ritual warfare, 79, 80, 91, 106, 107,
109–111, 170, 175
Russia, x, xxi, 8, 30, 34, 55, 78, 92,
128, 133–138, 142, 144, 145, 146

Sadat, Anwar, 45, 47, 52, 53, 55
SALT Treaty, 21, 27–29, 41, 68, 87,
114, 177, 179
Scapegoat, 10, 11, 13, 19, 37, 89, 90
Schmookler, Andrew Bard, 60, 61, 65,
68, 70, 71, 75. *See also* Parable of
the Tribes
Seville Statement on Violence, 73–77
Shadow archetype, ix, x, 9, 12, 15–30,
32–38, 42, 43, 47, 54, 83, 96, 98,
100, 101, 127, 132, 136, 153, 155,
157, 174, 175, 182, 191, 194,
195, 203
Shadow integration, 12, 18, 35, 100,
101, 175
Shadow projection, 16, 19, 20, 24, 26,
27, 29, 30, 32, 33, 34–36, 47,
100, 132, 174, 175, 191, 195
Solidarity (Poland), 30, 131, 159
Soviet-American Institute for War-
Peace Research, 192, 194–196,
201
Soviet Union. *See* Russia
Splitting, as a psychological defense,
47, 54, 120, 146, 161, 195, 203
Standing Consultative Commission
(SCC), 114, 115, 119
Stockholm Agreement, 100, 103
Stockholm Conference, 99–101
Strategic Defense Initiative, Star Wars
Defense (SDI), 29, 46, 103, 164,
176, 177
Sun Tzu, 15, 168
Superpower, xvii, xix, 4, 12, 22, 46,
50, 55, 97, 98, 100, 111, 112, 118–
120, 122, 136, 137, 154, 155, 157,
158, 166, 180, 181, 183, 184,
190, 193–195, 203, 204

Talbot, Strobe, 28, 41
Targets of opportunity, 107, 112
Technology
    deterrence technology, 1, 103, 104, 172, 178
    peace technology, xiii, 1, 2, 98, 101, 105, 106, 112, 123, 164, 170, 171, 172, 174–179, 182, 184, 193–195
    war technology, 60, 171, 176, 177, 179, 188, 194
Terrorism, 2, 112–117, 120–123, 143, 167
    nuclear terrorism, 2, 112–117, 120, 122, 123, 167
Thermonuclear age, 1–3, 13, 17, 46–48, 58, 73, 79, 80, 161, 172, 174
Tonkin, Gulf of, Resolution, 21
Transcendent function, tension between the opposites, 93, 94

Unconscious
    collective, xv, xviii, 3, 5–7, 65, 66, 82, 85, 86, 88, 93, 105, 111, 180, 181
    personal, 5, 6
United States Institute of Peace (USIP), 178, 197, 198, 199

Vietnam War, 22, 23, 49, 53, 54, 83, 84, 86–88, 134, 173, 174
Volkan, Vamik, 91, 125, 130, 153

War, xvi, xvii, xviii, xx, 1, 2, 6, 9, 15, 17, 19, 20, 24–27, 29, 33, 43, 45, 46, 48, 49, 51, 54, 56, 60, 61, 62–92, 94–98, 100–108, 110–112, 115, 118, 120, 121, 122, 123, 125–128, 130, 131, 133, 134, 137, 142, 144, 147, 151, 162–177, 179, 181–184, 187–189, 192, 194, 195, 196, 201, 203. See also warfare
    Iran-Iraq War, 62, 69, 92, 98, 112, 166, 183, 187, 188
    nuclear war, xvi, xvii, 54, 74, 88, 108, 115, 151, 164, 181, 184, 187, 201
War Department, 172, 173
War games, 81, 82, 91, 105–108, 111, 112, 118, 121, 123, 165–167, 170
War and peace, 169, 179, 192, 194, 195, 201, 203
War Powers Act, 25
Warfare, x, xi, 34, 41, 62–76, 78–81, 84–86, 88, 90, 91, 104, 106, 107, 109–111, 130, 135, 165, 166, 168–170, 173, 175, 179, 183, 184, 189
    definition, 64, 65
    ritual warfare, 71
    transformation of instinct to aggression to modern warfare, 68
Warner, Edward L., 27, 115
Warrior, 45–52, 54–56, 82–84, 87, 88, 170
    hero, 45, 47, 52, 53, 55
Warsaw Pact, 27, 81, 98, 100, 107, 136, 163
Weinberger, Caspar, 46, 49, 103, 115, 157, 163
Whitmont, Edward C., 169
World War II, 24, 33, 79, 80, 85, 97, 103, 128, 130, 133, 142, 144, 196
Wotan, 5, 9

Xenophobia, 129, 130. See paranoia; pseudospeciation
Yom Kippur War, 45